What They Say About Gary MacEoin

"He knows more about Latin America than I do."

Paulo Freire

"It fascinates me to find that MacEoin, starting from on-the-spot observation and analysis, has reached the same conclusions (about the systemic causes of Latin America's distorted development) as I have reached by my studies as an economist and social scientist."

Gunnar Myrdal

"In spite of his prodigious output, he never turns out anything that is not well thought-out and meaningful. I don't know how he does it."

Harvey Cox

"Once again I want to express to you my deep appreciation for your great continuing contribution to our collective sanity."

Philip Scharper

"No one else who has written in this area for the *Washington Post* has come close to the excellence of your provocative ideas and insights and the felicity of your expression."

David M. Rosenfeld

"You communicated your thoughts incisively and succinctly. . . . Thank you, again, for joining us on 'Good Morning, America.' "

David Hartman

"I have never learned so much in two weeks as on Oxfam's Nicaragua/Honduras study tour. I think (I hope) I will never be quite the same. I can't say enough good things about Gary. What patience and energy!"

Jim McCauley

"For me the most important experiences of the Oxfam tour were having the first opportunity to go to Cuba; and meeting Gary MacEoin."

Lee Cranberg, M.D.

"Thanks for opening up Central America to me. Many of us regard you as the father of a new school of Latin American interpretative journalists."

Ann Nelson

"The autobiography is learned, passionate and compelling—one leaves it with regret and returns eagerly. A wide circle of MacEoin admirers, friends, and 'students' will receive the publication with excitement and gratitude!"

B. Davie Napier
President Emeritus
Pacific School of Religion

"To read this book twice is almost a given duty—first to get a canvaswide feeling for the breadth of this man's pilgrim-way, and second to concentrate on the many golden nuggets that stand out and demand attention and review."

Joe Reed, Esq.
Tucson, Arizona

"*Memoirs & Memories* is a study in the growth and experience of a wise man, and it should teach the rest of us that it is possible, in spite of governments and ideologies, to define the confusion we live in."

Nan Eisner
Librarian
University of Arizona

"Admittedly, fate has much to do with where we are and how we act at any given moment, but I feel that there has been an amazing continuity to your vision and to your dedication. The manuscript is for me a visit to an old and cherished friend whose written record reminds me of the axiom, 'Those who do not read history will be condemned to repeat it.' "

Richard Senier
Vatican II Correspondent
Newsweek

Gary MacEoin

MEMOIRS & MEMORIES

Para Edie

¡En la lucha!

Gary

Feb. de 1990

TWENTY-THIRD PUBLICATIONS
Mystic, Connecticut

Twenty-Third Publications
P.O. Box 180
Mystic, CT 06355
(203) 536-2611

ISBN 0-89622-317-5
Library of Congress Catalog Card Number 86-50892

Foreword

On a warm, sunny October afternoon in 1963, I sat with Gary MacEoin on a concrete bench outside the USO on the Via della Conciliazione in Rome. We had just met for the first time at one of the daily press conferences held for English-speaking journalists covering the Second Vatican Council. In the course of an hour's conversation I learned how difficult it would be to classify Gary MacEoin. He was no ordinary journalist, but rather philosopher, theologian, economist, lawyer, linguist, litterateur, racconteur, and biographer. Despite these encumbrances he was a Gaelic humorist.

"We must pray for the canonization of Martin during this Council," he remarked. Noting the presence of some 240 African bishops, ten percent of the hierarchy at this momentous assembly, I replied, "Martin De Porres?" referring to the recently beatified black American. Gary laughed at the suggestion. "Not a-tall," he answered, with that charming Irish accent which he still retains, "Martin Luther, of course." This simple statement was, I would learn, typical of the man. The Council could be, if let be, the return of the church to the people, the end of the Imperial Papacy, the completion of the Reformation. Gary MacEoin helped me to look beyond the façade of the Vatican Council and the Roman Curia and to separate fact from fantasy and managed news.

Ten years before I had read his autobiography, *Nothing Is Quite Enough*, and now, meeting the author, I felt the same outrage I had felt then, outrage at the injustice handed Gary MacEoin by the church. I was at a loss to understand why this mild-mannered man did not, himself, feel outraged. He had studied for the priesthood for eleven years as a member of the Redemptorists only to be denied holy orders at the last moment. He was never given the slightest reason for the action of his superiors. His legitimate appeals to ecclesiastical authority by virtue of his perpetual vows were dismissed out of hand. Nor, as the present memoirs remind us, would his superiors let him return to the lay state without additional treachery. The order, the hierarchy, the church owed him nothing, not even the dignity of an answer. Half of his life had been stolen from him.

"I never said that I didn't receive justice," MacEoin cautioned me, "only that it was never made known to me." This precision of thinking and economy of language have characterized all of his 26 books and innumerable articles. And don't let that soft voice and lack of aggression fool you. You don't often win an argument with Gary MacEoin.

I had mistakenly thought that the title of his autobiography referred to the rebuffs he had received in his search for justice. Getting no answers. Nothing. But I have discovered I was wrong. It referred to religious poverty. He was explaining its essence. "I owned nothing. But nothing was quite enough."

After leaving religious life, Gary MacEoin earned a bachelor's, master's and doctorate degrees "all without attending a single class." In addition, he became a member of the bar. He has written on Latin America, Northern Ireland, and, most recently, on the Sanctuary Movement, of which he is one of the principal articulators.

"The Second Vatican Council changed my life," he told me last year and I suppose that many journalists would admit to that, despite the return to "business as usual," with the coming of Pope John Paul II and his episcopal appointees. I can't think of any American who came to Rome equipped as well as MacEoin. Not that the rest of us lacked distinction. Robert Kaiser of *Time* magazine wrote without restraint of curial intrigue. Michael Novak set the Catholic world on its ear with countless articles and several books filled with insight and hope. Whenever the shy, gentle John Cogley, (former editor of *Commonweal*, considered the premier

American Catholic layman) spoke, everyone else listened in awe. (Cogley died in the late seventies on the eve of his priestly ordination in the Episcopal church.)

The four sessions of Vatican II were indeed a special time. After an initial nervousness, cardinals and bishops, clergy and laity, journalists and editors, became friends. All this was made easier by the warmth and generosity of the Italian people who were not overly impressed by any of us. Most of all, it was a special time because we had Pope John XXIII, whose love and humility helped all of us to remember who we were and how short life is.

Being away from home for such a long time, we tended to rely on each other for emotional support, supplying football and hockey scores, discovering a chef who could make a real hamburger or apple pie, congratulating each other on a piece well written. And when John F. Kennedy was assassinated we cried together, watching the first television transmissions from home in awful grief. Everywhere we found ourselves stopped by sobbing Romans, who, recognizing us as Americans, embraced us, consoled us. They just had to talk to someone. Like all Americans, we would never forget where we were when we heard "the news." It was to our good fortune that my wife and I were with Gary and Jo MacEoin when we heard of the President's death.

Many of us had assembled for Pope John's death watch in June and the conclave which chose Paul VI. We hoped against hope that Paul would be another John when we knew that he never could be John.

In his introduction to "What Happened at Rome," John Cogley wrote, "I suppose every journalist who covered Vatican II was tempted at some time to write a book. . . . I am glad I said no. For Gary MacEoin has written the book I wish I could have written." MacEoin has repeatedly written that type of book, unusually prophetic, usually hopeful but, with the passing of the years, increasingly despondent about the justice of our American and Catholic institutions.

He has pleaded to deaf ears in *Latin America: The Eleventh Hour*, and *Northern Ireland: Captive of History*. Thirteen years ago he and I were about to collaborate on a television series that included, among other subjects, the institutionalization of torture. I remember being shocked at the suggestion that our government would be involved in the training of terrorists and torturers. But, of course, Gary knew what he was talking about. He had been there.

The series had to be cancelled because of Jo's serious illness. For the next twelve years Gary's journalistic activities, although enough to strain the energies of many a younger person, had to come second. He moved from New Jersey to Tucson, Arizona, with Jo, better to care for her. And through the long loneliness which he suffered when Jo's condition deteriorated and she had to be removed to a nursing home, he visited her every day, cared for her personal needs unceasingly, while watching his life's meager savings deplete. Yet, whenever he was asked if he needed anything, the answer was always the same. "Nothing, I have everything I need."

But, of course, he changed Tucson, too, promoting ecumenically-based programs for the poor and disenfranchised, formulating the rationale for challenging our immigration laws and illegal practices of the Immigration and Naturalization Service, insisting that we obey our own laws, be true to our best selves.

Gary has reported from Medellín, Colombia, from Recife, Brazil, from Haiti, Dar-es-Salaam, Baghdad, Belfast, and Saigon. In addition to *Time* and *Life*, he has written for *Christianity and Crisis, The Progressive, The National Catholic Reporter, America, Cross Currents, Informations Catholiques, Le Monde, Herder Correspondenz*, to name just a few. He has brought study groups to the Dominican Republic and to Havana, Cuba, never taking anyone else's brand of truth for granted, but preferring to have a look himself. Wherever the rights of individuals are in jeopardy, you can be sure that Gary MacEoin has known about the problem before anyone else. He continues to prick the consciences of the powerful. Whether commenting on the Contras in Nicaragua, CIA sponsored assassinations in Chile and Argentina or liberation theology, Gary MacEoin has continued to prophesy against injustice, still without raising his voice. He is still skeptical of managed news whether governmental or ecclesiastical. It is no irony, I think, that he has never been proposed for a peace prize, that he has never been awarded an honorary degree.

Every now and then, riding in a car or while helping to clear away the dinner dishes, he will gently correct the Latin quotation you have dared to utter, challenge your views on everything from the coffee cartel to Mary Daly's latest book. Suddenly, moved by heaven knows what distraction, Gary MacEoin will recall a line from Yeats, or a verse from "The Queen of Connemara." For this native of County Sligo is, after all, an exile.

The journey of the present memoirs is less poetically described than that of *Nothing Is Quite Enough*. It is as if the Gary MacEoin who has seen so much and suffered so much, knows that each sentence or paragraph must be full of the substance of things. Recently, after a couple of years without seeing him, I picked him up at Logan Airport, Boston. I was struck by the slight, almost fragile figure that approached me with open arms. He carried a small overnight bag over his shoulder, nothing more. "Do you have any luggage on board?" I asked. He laughed with the same amusement I had encountered so long ago on the Via della Conciliazione. "No, nothing. I have everything I need."

Nothing is quite enough.

Richard M. Senier
Newsweek Correspondent
at Second Vatican Council

Contents

One Must Ask the Right Questions

"You run well but off the track," Saint Augustine of Hippo quipped back in the fourth century. How often that criticism is applicable! Activities pursued in the honest belief that they benefit not only ourselves but the common good can destroy rather than construct. Some two decades ago, already past middle age, I found myself facing such traumatic self-analysis.

My main activity in the 1950s, as editor of technical magazines in Spanish and Portuguese, was the export to Latin America of U.S. technology in agriculture and allied industries. I was proud to contribute to better ways of growing and processing vegetable and animal products in tropical Latin America. Results were visible and tangible. A strain of rice yielding well on unirrigated uplands and harvested before the red-winged blackbird arrived in Venezuela from the United States for his annual gorging represented a scientific advance that promised more people a better life. So did the introduction of hybrid wheat and corn, of high-yield dairy cattle and pasteurization of milk.

I quickly formed ties of friendship with and respect for the small group of North Americans who serviced the communications industry of Latin America, peddling news, features, comic strips, paper, ink, radio and television transmitters and programs. We met at newspaper conventions in

Havana, Caracas, or Bogota, at equipment manufacturers and chemical association conventions in Miami Beach. We made a good living, and none of us seriously questioned the assumption that, by spreading the know-how and mores of the United States in Latin America, we were contributing to the betterment of the hemisphere. If we benefited, so did the people who bought our wares. And what more should one ask in a business deal?

Knowing such people, I was never impressed by the simplistic anti-American propaganda portraying United States business people as bloodsucking vampires. We were running well, but I gradually began to question the direction. Unlike my colleagues, I did not confine myself to the luxury hotel and country club circuit. Having built up freelance connections, I spent considerable time in city and rural slums in search of stories, developing significant friendships with people sunk deep in the debris of the progress of which they were the victims.

Clichés collapse in such contexts, whether those of the salesperson or those of the moralist. When you come to realize that the parents are hungrier than the grandparents were, and that the children are hungrier than their parents and have less opportunity to drag themselves up to a human level, you look below the surface. And what you see is that the system is not working, that it is not opening opportunity for more people, that the gap between rich and poor is widening, not narrowing, that the end result of the input of capital and know-how is greater poverty and vastly greater frustration. When you know a woman who has for six months been waiting in line at the clinic for an operation without which she cannot work, her children meanwhile hungry and in rags, you begin to share her anger. The fact that her work is prostitution loses relevance.

Equally eye-opening for me was the insensitivity of the wealthy Latin Americans to the conditions of the poor who produced the wealth they flaunted. For these oligarchs the class system was an immutable fact of life. I know luxurious clubs in London and New York, but none to equal that in Pereira in the Colombian Andes, a club built and operated on coffee produced by workers living in destitution, their sons driven to join the guerrillas for lack of alternatives. Dom Helder Camara of Recife, Brazil, has popularized the epithet of Herodian to describe such oligarchs. Toynbee, in *A Study of History*, had already used the word to describe a class who—like Herod's henchmen in Palestine at the time of Christ—exploit their fellow countrymen for the benefit of foreign overlords. If anyone deserves the Ugly American title, it is the Latin American Herodians.

By the early 1960s it had become clear to me that the capitalist system was not working, or rather that it was working for the few at the expense of the many. I was not yet convinced, however, that it could not work. During the entire previous history of the human race, our control of our environment was so limited as to prevent the creation of truly human levels of living for more than a small minority. But in the twentieth century an explosion of knowledge leading to the harnessing of the atom and the introduction of the cybernetic era radically altered the equation. For the first time a world society in which every individual could enjoy adequate food, clothing, shelter, education, and health, within a framework of liberty and dignity, had become possible.

I was accordingly enthused when President Kennedy in March 1961 announced the Alliance for Progress, a program formalized in the Charter of Punta del Este five months later. The Charter was a treaty binding the United States and the Latin American republics to commit their resources to a common effort to develop the entire continent for the benefit of all its inhabitants. It started out with enormous enthusiasm, dazzling plans, overwhelming rhetoric. But the honeymoon was short. The United States, the principal source of capital for the joint venture, soon forgot the social objectives and allowed the global corporations and the Latin American oligarchs to siphon off the profits, leaving the rich richer and the poor poorer.

While I struggled with this dilemma, another and even more traumatic one presented itself. I had grown up in a traditional Roman Catholic milieu. A childhood in the West of Ireland was followed by nearly twelve years of isolation in the junior and senior seminaries of a religious order. I emerged with a clear concept of the meaning of life. We lived in a world of completed and fixed essences. God had made the decisions and determined for each what to do and not to do. We were called to acceptance, conformity, resignation, and fulfillment of duty. Good and evil, right and wrong, were carefully departmentalized and ticketed.

Specifically, a series of papal statements since the mid-nineteenth century had defined for Catholics how they should think about social problems. These statements presented the capitalist system as fixed for all time by God's inscrutable decrees, the divine purpose placing a few rich and powerful over the many poor and powerless to ensure the necessary testing before entry into eternal bliss. Pope Pius IX in 1849 had warned that "it is not given to men to establish new societies and communities opposed to the natural state of human affairs." Pope Pius XI had echoed him as recently as 1939: "God has determined that there should be rich people and poor people in the world so that virtues may be exercised and merits proven." The only way the popes recognized for dealing with the obvious injustices in the world was to persuade the rich and powerful to be more Christian in their treatment of the poor and powerless. My experience, however, was challenging that approach. The failure of the Alliance for Progress was once again confirming the lesson of all history: power yields only to counter-power.

By the early 1960s I was beginning to suspect something today universally recognized—that poverty in all parts of what has come to be known as the Third World results from the same causes. If I was going to understand Latin America better, I felt, I should see for myself what things were like in Africa and Asia. Then, as I had firmed up plans for what became a fourteen-month voyage of discovery, I secured several assignments for coverage of the Vatican Council then underway in Rome. It was a logical first stop on my way to Africa.

The Council proved catalytic for me. It brought together, in addition to some two thousand bishops, many of the world's finest minds: theologians, philosophers, historians, biblical scholars (Catholic, Protestant, Orthodox, and even Jewish). Here also were several hundred of the world's most informed journalists and writers drawn from diverse cultural and religious contexts, all struggling to make sense of this labyrinthine crossword puzzle. Interaction was unending at all levels, at sidewalk coffee tables, at lectures, at late-night trattorias, and especially at the daily press conferences in which panels of experts explained the underlying issues at that day's session of the council. It was a unique graduate course in religion and in human relations.

Only then did I become aware of the extent to which we Catholics had become trapped in a legalistic system that determined our thinking and our actions. Although the Holy Office lacked the physical force available to the Inquisition to which it was the successor, its anathemas and social pressures effectively stifled dissent and limited discussion within the church to the field of its choice, the code of canon law presented as the ultimate rule of faith and action.

What was refreshing and life-renewing was to hear prestigious theologians insist that not only was the code of canon law something totally distinct from the rule of faith, but that the survival of the church as a meaningful and credible reality involved the replacement of legalism by the freedom Jesus had proclaimed as the birthright of his followers. To discover, too, that this was no new madness, but the slow development of reflection by many individuals in many places, previously suppressed by the Roman authorities, but now daringly proclaimed in their presence, and striking an echo in all who listened.

Openness did not come easily. Even after St. Peter's Basilica had reverberated to the applause of bishops when Cardinal Frings of Cologne raised the taboo issue at a Council meeting and denounced the Holy Office as a scandal, some remained cautious and hedged their bets. But two theologians struck me as ready in all circumstances to say what they thought: U.S. Jesuit Gustave Weigel, and German Redemptorist Bernard Häring. Their courage was contagious. Soon we had Dan O'Hanlon rejecting indulgences more forc-

ibly than Martin Luther had ever done. Edward Schillebeeckx was rescuing the history of the eucharistic presence from the no longer tenable theories about the nature of
material elements into which the Scholastics and the Council
of Trent had squeezed it. Hans Küng was chipping away
happily with the tempered chisels of his low-key words at
the pyramidal structure of church authority.

In this company I came to appreciate the radical significance of Teilhard de Chardin. I was able to purge my mind
of assumptions with which I had never felt comfortable but
with which I had previously felt obliged to live. I could finally reject the notion of fixed essences, of creation as completed by the evening of the sixth day, of humans having no
purpose in life other than to procreate, to learn how to jump
through theological hoops, and to respond like Pavlov's dog
to arbitrary stimuli. Teilhard showed me a design that de-
meaned neither God nor his creation, a design clearly em-
bedded in Genesis, even if not previously recognized. To
pursue the magnificent metaphors of the Genesis story, God
molded the original chaos into ever more perfect forms of
being until he reached a stage where he need no longer intervene. To borrow a phrase dear to economists in the third
quarter of the twentieth century (though now properly consigned to oblivion in the context in which they bandied it
about), he had achieved the point of take-off, making further
pump-priming unnecessary. But the perfection of which the
created condition is capable was still far from achieved. It is
for us to pick up the challenge, as each previous generation
in fact picked it up in diverse ways, some affirmative, some
negative, using our abilities to make the world, the universe, struggle toward heights as yet unseen and only dimly
divined in the dreams of poets and prophets.

This is nothing less than an apocalyptic vocation. In direct
challenge to the pseudoproverbial saying that we mustn't
play God, that is precisely what it commissions us to do. We
are very finite and ignorant gods indeed, liable to make mistakes that could be earth-destroying and race-destroying.
Yet we have no choice but to try, and no rules but the rules
of our own collective wisdom and judgment.

For the believer this understanding of the human engagement has profound implications. It eliminates all arbitrary and aprioristic limitations from our moral decision making. We can no longer take refuge in any assumption that some actions are natural and others unnatural, that there is any limit to our right and duty other than the limit imposed by the community evaluation of what will promote the perfecting of the species. It creates dilemmas that are frightening to many, from abortion to euthanasia, from homosexuality to infidelity in marriage. Yet I believe we must face these dilemmas. It is easier to live a slave than free. But unless we have the courage to see that we are free and use that freedom to build a better world, we deny our vocation.

Such insights were enormously liberating. I could now see the church as a community dedicated to working with others, subordinating its institutional interests to the overarching task of creation, seeking to heal the wounds of conflict with Orthodox and Protestants, even to recognize the deep injustices Christians had committed against their Jewish parents and the continuing role of anti-Jewish prejudice.

Conversion, nevertheless, was far from universal. For many the conditioning was too deep, or the challenge to privilege too unbearable, and the Council played politics to accommodate the unaccommodable. But the monolith had been shattered. Catholics who so wished could live as citizens of the twentieth and twenty-first century, no longer schizophrenic in a culture in which change had become the only constant.

Even greater than the impact of the theologians at the Council was that of the prophets. The first so recognized was Paul Gauthier, a French priest living as a laborer among the Arabs of Nazareth whose poverty he shared. Like a modern John the Baptist, he descended on Rome to upbraid the Council Fathers. "You do not even have the issue of poverty on your agenda," he challenged. "How quickly you have forgotten Pope John's prophetic words that the church is for all people, but especially for the poor." A coalition identifying itself as the church of the poor gradually formed around him. It influenced the Council

statement on the church in today's world and started the
most radical church changes since the Protestant Reformation, the movement—particularly strong in Latin America—
to identify with the oppressed against oppressor regimes.

With a renewed sense of purpose and urgency I resumed
my journey when the Council recessed. I visited every country on the European, Asian, and African shores of the Mediterranean, meeting—among many others—Greek Orthodox
leaders in Athens, Patriarch Athenagoras in Istanbul, the
feuding Christian spokespeople in Jerusalem, and the Coptic
leaders in Cairo. I went up the Nile to Khartoum, Juba, and
Kampala, then through Kenya, Zambia, and Rhodesia (now
Zimbabwe) to Johannesburg and its adjoining black shanty-
towns, east to Durban, then west and north to the Congo,
Nigeria, and Ghana. Then east again to Pakistan, India,
Singapore, Vietnam, Hong Kong, Taiwan, Korea, and
Japan.

Dominating this kaleidoscopic melange of race, scenery,
and climate in my memory is a nightmarish pastiche of
human degradation, grotesquely misshapen figures, leprous
limbs, emaciated frames, elephantiasic legs, rotting human
flesh, an impression fortified by the suqs of Baghdad, the
ruins of Samarra, the manure-littered roads of Karachi's
slums, the fly-infested eyes of the children of Cochin, the
rickshaws of Saigon patronized by the American-assembled
prostitutes, the floating hulks crowding Hong Kong's bays,
the hordes of uprooted Koreans begging at the gates of the
U.S. officers' club in Pusan.

From there back to Latin America, to naked Indian tribes
deep in Surinam, to the mudflats of Belem at the mouth of
the Amazon where humans fight each other and the river for
space to build a shack on stilts; to Manaus a thousand miles
up the river, ghost town of the world's first rubber boom
whose massive opera house once reverberated to Caruso's
voice; to the Putamayo jungles two thousand miles west on
the border of Ecuador with Colombia and still in the steaming Amazon basin; south to the model city of Brazilia, designed to be forever slum-free yet ringed with slums before
half finished; north to the promised "Pittsburgh" of Venezu-

ela where the Caroni cascades down the precipitous Guayana mountains into the sluggish Orinoco; finally to Delano in central California, where America's stoop labor had begun its unequal and still unfinished struggle to rise to its knees; pausing on the way to draw breath and observe one more aspect of oppression among the Indians of Guatemala's highlands.

How to make an intellectual synthesis from these emotion-laden experiences? That process still engages me. But before going further, I need to sort out the positive from the negative elements in the past that perforce stays with me as I struggle toward the future.

2

Everyone Starts From Somewhere

When I married in July 1937, my wife—under the quaint laws and conventions imposed on Ireland's civil society by the Catholic church—had to resign her job. Woman's place was in the home, and a working woman might be tempted to interfere with the natural law which made procreation the primary end of marriage. But I had what was then a good salary, six guineas a week (about $31 in 1937) as an editorial writer on Ireland's biggest daily. Ten dollars a week for rent, six for food, and another six toward the hire purchase of our miniature car, still left enough for a weekly movie and the gradual accumulation of basic furniture and kitchenware.

Pictures to decorate the living room were in a different category, however. We both wanted pictures, but they should be good. For the moment, we had to be content with passe-partout framed views of Dun Laoghaire Harbour and Kilkenny Castle which I had photographed the previous year when flying with an air circus.

Great was our excitement, accordingly, when a friend asked us to care for a Kernoff original for the several months she planned to be away. Harry Kernoff was a Lithuanian Jew who had won a deserved reputation in Dublin as an impressionist. For reasons that will become gradually clear, my taste in paintings was limited basically to Renais-

sance and baroque. When Kernoff's work arrived, all I saw
was a mess of meaningless blobs and lines. "Turn it to the
wall," I urged my wife. "It gives me nausea." Instead, Jo
made it the focus of the living room, forcing me reluctantly to
penetrate its mysteries, to identify not only the outlines but
the meanings of buildings, the mystery of proportions, the
sense of wonder and perception and love that the artist had
wanted to share with me. When our friend reclaimed her
possession six months later, I was desolate.

Still I knew I had been enriched. I often think of Harry,
whom later I got to know rather well. I recall in particular
one evening I stopped to offer him a lift. I was returning
from work. It must have been late 1939 or early 1940, after
World War II had started but before the fall of France, because I was still in the privileged category of a ten-gallon a
month gasoline ration that ended when the Germans
reached the Atlantic and unleashed the U-boats. Harry had
been visiting Myles-na-gCapaillin, a nom-de-plumed civil
servant equally famed for his devastating satire in English
and Irish in the *Irish Times*, and for his bibulosity. Harry
declined my offer with a level of courtesy that indicated several hours of Myles's hospitality, assuring me there would
be a tram along any minute. The spot where Harry was sitting on the footpath was half a mile from the nearest tram
line, and besides, public transport, which was rationed like
everything else, had stopped for the night an hour earlier.

This incident, typical for me of Harry's unstructured yet
fruitful life, has its own symbolism. My main reason for in-
troducing him, however, is because the way contemplation
and reflection revealed for me the depth of meaning in his
painting seems to parallel my discovery of the meaning of
my own life as I relive it. Each part has followed what preceded with little sense of order or purpose. It was usually
enjoyable to ride high on the waves that swirled me rudder-
lessly from place to place and from activity to activity. But
at any given moment, I could see little more than blotches
and scratches. Years spent in one kind of preparation
seemed wasted as events involved me in totally disparate
activities. And yet today, as the portrait nears completion, it

also approaches meaning. When I seek a purpose and a direction in my life, I cannot think in terms of the classical painter—or the classical philosopher or theologian—who can present with firm strokes the day-to-day creation of a design by an all-wise and all-determining God. I must rather see myself in impressionist terms, each element reflecting the uncertainty of the human actor, ambiguously open to many interpretations—even to the existentialist's interpretation of meaninglessness—yet all finally coalescing in an artifact, something useful made by an intelligent being. The totality undergirds my faith and supports my hope that an ultimate designer meant it—me—to be something more than a foam fleck on a breaking wave.

My early education established the pattern or lack thereof. We lived on the edge of a village of twenty houses in a clearing in the peat bogs that dominate the West of Ireland and much of the Midlands. The school was the biggest and most impressive edifice in the village, and—everything being a matter of scale—I long considered it the apex of human architectural achievement since the ill-fated Tower of Babel. It actually consisted of two rooms, with separate entrances for boys and girls. Each room had desks grouped in three areas, each dominated by a cane-wielding teacher. Attendance was voluntary, the British government, which then directly administered the whole of Ireland, having never introduced compulsory education. Rather, it had long penalized instruction of the mere natives, and it was a proud memory of my family that a maternal great-grandfather had taught an illegal "hedge school," gathering his students under the shade of a tree in a secluded mountainous area; and that a paternal grandfather had with his own money and efforts built one of the first legal schools in the district. The peasants of Connaught are in large part the descendants of the aristocrats and middle classes of medieval Ireland driven across the Shannon by Cromwellian and other English invaders. Though utterly impoverished, they never lost their cultural heritage and folk memory, and education remained always the mark of social standing. It was common for teenage boys and girls to continue at school until the money arrived from an uncle or elder brother to pay the passage to the United States. Many bigger boys spent part of the year making hay in the English Midlands or picking potatoes in Scotland, followed by a month or two in the Lancashire coal pits, then returned to school until the potatoes were planted at Easter and they emigrated once more. Formally, these schools taught only the primary level, but the teachers in each offered whatever they happened to know. One of my brothers went to such a school that included Latin and French in the curriculum.

Our school served not only the village but the surrounding countryside. Attendance of even the pre-teenagers was irregular, depending on seasonal demands of the tiny farms worked almost exclusively with hand implements. Small children helped to plant, mold, spray and pick the potatoes, to weed the oats and barley, to de-maggot the sheep, to spread and stack the turf and later load it into creels balanced astride tiny donkeys whose hooves were allowed to grow to nearly a foot in length to keep them from sinking under the loads in the peat bog.

In consequence, notwithstanding the prestige of learning, the teachers had to struggle constantly to maintain the average attendance of seventy-two without which the Department of Education would re-classify us as a two-teacher school. Because of such a crisis, I set off bravely one morning in the month of April 1912, two months before my third birthday, to be enrolled as a full-time student. Custom ruled every detail of life, and custom dictated that children went barefoot from Easter till All Saints (November 1). In passing, that was no hardship. One of the happiest of my youthful memories was the annual shedding of shoes and clogs, worn during summer only to Mass on Sundays. In my school bag was a double slice of buttered homemade bread, my sustenance until my return home at 3:30 or 4:00 in the afternoon.

The education I pursued in this one-room school for the following ten years was narrow in scope but intensive in a few key areas. The British colonial system carefully sanitized the curriculum. Geography consisted of memorizing the counties and chief cities of England, Scotland, Wales and Ireland. We also memorized the principal manufactures of English cities, but as Irish cities produced only children for export, they caused less trouble. History was a laundry list of wars and dynasties, and the ruling dates of English kings and queens. Religious instruction, one half-hour daily, involved learning by rote the answers to such questions as who made the world and what is the state of grace. We envied the three or four Protestant kids who were allowed out to play while we struggled with words that scarcely had meaning for us.

English, however, was a wide-open subject. Presumably, the authorities were convinced that sufficient exposure to the great minds who had formed their language and values would finally convert the wild Irishie into happy English children. Memory was stressed over meaning, and Shakespeare took precedence almost to the exclusion of all else, except for an occasional foray into such esoteric nonsense as Macaulay's History of India and the duller novels of Dickens and Scott. Starting approximately at the age of nine, I learned by rote an entire play of Shakespeare each year, ten lines being assigned daily to be repeated word perfect the next day. The Merchant of Venice came first, followed by The Tempest, Macbeth, Julius Caesar, As You Like It, and King Lear. No attempt was made to elucidate the ideological underpinnings, the anti-Semitism of The Merchant of Venice, or the meaning of words outside our language and experience, such as the rebel's whore to whom the fortune of the merciless Macdonwald is compared in Macbeth. We learned each line, repeating the unknown words the way they were spelled, then moved on. That continued into high school, until 1923, the year after the Irish Free State came into existence. As first Minister of Education for the new state, Eoin MacNeill—an expert in early Irish Laws and history and one-time commander in chief of the Irish Volunteers (later known as the Irish Republican Army)—attempted to downgrade memory and elevate the status of meaning. His success, however, was shortlived and never more than partial. Leaders of both church and state had, like me, learned their Julius Caesar. As politicians they appreciated the wisdom of Caesar's comment to Marcus Antonius: "Yond Cassius has a lean and hungry look; he thinks too much: such men are dangerous." So passive memorization of the wisdom of the ancients again replaced the adventure of education.

It was a hard way to do it, but in retrospect those years of living with Shakespeare provided a unique foundation on which to build a career as a writer. The Irish have often been admired for their poetic and imaginative expression in the English language. I am convinced that this concentration on Shakespeare in the village schools over many generations is a significant factor.

But schooling was a mere fraction of the formative process. Isolation from the outside world was such that at age thirteen I had never visited the county town twenty-five miles away. Yet the quality of life was extraordinary. When my friend Rubem Alves, one of Latin America's most important theologians, excoriates the destruction of imagination by the consumer society in its innate thrust to commercialize all human activity, I think back automatically to that village society. Imagination flourished. Our material resources were minimal but our self-confidence was boundless. We saw ourselves as active participants in a struggle to free ourselves from a foreign domination that had persisted through many centuries and which encompassed the entire island of Ireland. We believed we had achieved the goal when in 1921 the enemy agreed to withdraw the armies of occupation from most of the country and recognize our right to choose our own government. Of course, the reality was more complex, as the development of neo-colonial institutions and relations progressed over the following half century. But for us at the time, the effect was dramatic. Life was on our side.

The direct intervention of my parents in my upbringing was so low-keyed that today they would be called permissive. I was the sixth of nine children, and most of the routine of caring for the younger ones fell to those who were older. In addition, the homogeneity of the community effectively excluded issues of conformity and non-conformity. In their own way, nevertheless, my parents played a decisive part. In retrospect, the most important thing my father did for me was to treat me as a person. He made his living as clerk of the local court, a one-man operation except for the monthly visit of a judge to deal with such crimes as making poteen (moonshine), poaching salmon, or having one's name inscribed in Irish—when the law demanded English—on the donkey cart, the normal mode of local transport of goods and people.

The rest of the month, his office hours were devoted principally to reading books that ranged from Oscar Wilde and Oliver Wendell Holmes to the Modern Encyclopedia. My mother ensured an unending supply. She would take off for Dublin at least once a year to visit her countless friends. She knew many leaders of the nationalist revival, people like William Butler Yeats, George (AE) Russell, and Countess Constance Markiewicz, as well as Sinéad De Valera whose husband was making history just then by escaping from Lincoln Jail and smuggling himself out of England and into the United States disguised as a stoker on a tramp steamer. My mother was an active proponent of the cooperative movement, and a frequent visitor to our home was the pioneer of farming cooperatives and former Wyoming rancher, Sir Horace Plunkett.

On her trips to Dublin, my mother would attend book auctions in the secondhand book stores along the Liffey quays, returning with grab bags of literature. My father read everything piecemeal, and I followed along. There was nothing scientific about the process, but it did encourage eclectic tastes that have stayed with me. In deference to my mother's concern, he would make token efforts to hide from me books considered inappropriate for eight- to ten-year-olds. I recall specifically in this category *The Three Musketeers* by Dumas, and Henry de Vere Stackpoole's *The Blue Lagoon*. But they were always hidden where I had no difficulty in finding them, a fact which I am sure did not escape him.

One of his idiosyncracies was a passion for algebra. Solving complicated problems gave him the pleasure that many get from crosswords. This fitted in well with my primary school courses, because mathematics—presumably judged value-free—held a place of honor second only to that of English. We were solidly grounded in arithmetic in the first grade, then moved on to algebra, and about the age of ten I crossed the Asses' Bridge and was introduced to the mysteries of geometry as formulated by the Greek pioneer, Euclid. The teachers took pride in their mathematical knowledge and used the rod liberally to ensure its transfer to their pupils. Thanks to my father's help, I generally escaped the rod, at least in the mathematics classes. By the age of thirteen, when I left home for boarding school, I had a substantial understanding of quadratic equations and the theory of probabilities.

By that time, I was also familiar with techniques for raising queen bees and dividing colonies of bees without waiting for the natural process of swarming. My father had been trained as an agronomist at the Albert College, Dublin, back in the 1870s when that profession was still in its infancy, and he was justly proud of his apiary, his fruit trees, vegetables, flowers and ornamental shrubs. He was in constant demand all round the countryside to capture swarms of bees, to prune apple trees, and generally to advise on all sorts of farm problems. He was equally in demand to draw up wills, resolve family disputes, and prepare affidavits for old-age pensions. He welcomed my company on these expeditions, and he taught me a great deal by treating me as an associate of equal standing. I took this for granted, which was obviously what he intended, but it was only much later I came to appreciate its significance. One becomes responsible by being treated as responsible. One learns how to keep bees by keeping them, and how to raise vegetables by raising them. I did in fact learn more than I realized about the processes of farming, an area of knowledge that later proved valuable when I became editor in New York of two magazines of scientific agriculture which circulated internationally, one in Spanish and the other in Portuguese.

My parents, devout church-goers, were without a trace of bigotry. Although there were only five or six Protestant families among the six hundred in our parish, our relations with them were always respectful and generally cordial. One of these families we ranked among our closest friends, a relationship infrequent in that society between people not connected by blood ties. And when the Protestant clergyman from a neighboring town came to visit his scattered flock, he never neglected to stop into our home for a chat and a cup of tea.

Of course, our own clergy were also regularly involved with us, both professionally and socially. They did have considerable influence in community affairs, but the attitude of my parents was far from the servile submission to their whims that one finds portrayed in the literature of the Irish in America, and which is usually assumed to have been imported from Ireland. The reality seems to me more nuanced. The Irish who emigrated after the Great Famine of the 1840s were the dispossessed, representing the lowest strata of the population in economic standing and education. They were powerless and leaderless, completely dependent on their priests to speak for them and build a society in which they could function.

Those who remained in Ireland had some land and other possessions, with the accompanying education and the sense of community characteristic of rural living. The priest was respected, but he was not the exclusive leader or spokesperson. In fact, from the development of the Home Rule movement in the late nineteenth century and of the separatist *Sinn Fein* ("ourselves") early in the twentieth, the clergy saw their interest as seriously divergent from the aspirations of the people. They feared the thrust for independence would bring to power new leaders with whom they would have more trouble than they had with the London government.

My parents were aware of this, as were our neighbors. They lived on good terms with the priests, but they did not let them overstep their function. Even as children, we sensed the ambiguities. The relationship was dialectic, an element in the anti-authority syndrome characteristic of the Irish, a syndrome understandable in the light of an experience of law as a tool used by enemies to deny justice. My subsequent experience as a member of a religious order worked in the opposite direction, for there I was brainwashed into a reverent and unquestioning submission to the divinely-guided decisions of those placed in authority over me. In the long run, the original conditioning was more powerful.

When I recall my mother, I recognize without hesitation that the greatest value she taught me was that there is nobody above me or below me. She had an amazing sense of the innate quality of people, rejecting all claims to honor or privilege not based on one's individual worth. That attitude was seriously challenged during my subsequent training as a seminarian, the principle of hierarchy being sacrosanct for the priests who were its beneficiaries. But my original training survived, in spite of the problems it created for me. I treasure it.

My mother, through her interests, activities and acquaintances, played a big part in our knowledge of and identification with the revival of national consciousness. Yeats, Synge, Russell, and Lady Gregory had founded the Abbey Theatre just a few years before I was born, and this was quickly followed by the establishment of Sinn Fein by Arthur Griffith as a political party committed to reaffirmation of Ireland as an independent nation. It was the modest beginning of the great anticolonialist movement that influenced the thinking and tactics of the young Gandhi and would in the third quarter of the century knell the death of empires on which the sun never set. I was seven when a handful of poets, professionals and dreamers seized the main post office and other public buildings in Dublin, proclaimed the Republic, and held out for a week against the might of Britain. The incident might not have had more resonance than many similar ones in the long conflict between the two neighboring islands, were it not for the foolish overreaction of the British authorities who court-martialed and shot the principal leaders, even bringing the veteran socialist labor organizer James Connolly, mortally wounded in the fighting, before the firing squad in a wheelchair for the coup de grace.

The response was instantaneous. The descendants of sev-

enteenth-century colonists in Belfast and its hinterland, still
regarded as usurpers and land-grabbers, feared the loss of
their privileged status protected by British bayonets. Apart
from them, the entire country, including the dispossessed
minority in northeast Ulster, united behind Sinn Fein. Net-
works of economic, social and cultural activities were created to provide a legal facade for the military organizations
being formed in every town and village. Figures of international reputation, like Sir Horace Plunkett and George Russell, came and went as promoters of the cooperative
movement designed to break the British strangle hold on the
economy. I remember Russell in particular, a talented
painter and mystic poet, well known on both sides of the At
lantic for his writings under the pseudonym AE. A gentle
man, he could cut to the bone when angered, as when he delivered the definitive judgment of Rudyard Kipling for pros-
tituting his great literary talents in defense of his imperial
paymasters: "ever quick to defend the strong against the
weak." And Countess Constance Markiewicz, cousin of
Yeats, made an indelible impression when she came to the
village to review the Youth Section of the IRA—a group of
boy scouts for the public record—wearing the same uniform
in which she had fought rifle in hand in the College of Sur-
geons during the Easter Rising.

Our overview as school children of these events was understandably limited, as was indeed that of our parents, especially as the conflict escalated. British troops were en-
camped in every city and town. The police were placed
under military control and issued rifles. Their ranks were
augmented by the Black and Tans, many of them thugs enlisted from British jails. After them came the Auxiliaries,
the demobilized commandos of World War I, trained in techniques of terrorism and brutality. The Irish responded with
guerrilla warfare and with a weapon that is an essential concomitant, massive civil disobedience. A parallel under-
ground government was set up, to which alone taxes were to
be paid. Sinn Fein courts dispensed justice, often in Solo-
monic terms, as when the elder of two brothers feuding over
the family farm was told to make the division and give the

other first choice. Railroad tracks were lifted and road bridges destroyed to prevent troop movements. Cut off from the outside world, people had to live as best they could from local agricultural resources. We had not yet entered the radio age and only occasionally did a week-old and heavily censored newspaper from Dublin find its blackmarketed way into the village, there passed from house to house. But morale was high, and it grew as the British withdrew their military outposts to central fortresses and closed down the police barracks in the villages and smaller towns. As they left, each hated symbol of foreign occupation went up in triumphant bonfires to mark an Irish victory.

Today I am well aware of the broader factors, especially the importance for Britain of American opinion during World War I and the subsequent peace negotiations and division of spoils, that played a part in the resolution of the Anglo-Irish conflict. But I have tried to recreate what I saw and understood at the time, a barefooted David facing and defeating a jackbooted Goliath. The enormous growth of guerrilla warfare in Latin America and elsewhere in the present neocolonialist and neofascist era is often dismissed as wanton barbarity incapable of achieving the results sought by the kidnappers and execution squads. My early experience continues to remind me that desperate people will do desperate things; and that, besides, the factors can so fall together as to make their quixotic gestures fruitful. Nor do barefoot kids with hand grenades and automatic weapons in the jungles of Southeast Asia or the mountains of Central America surprise me. That is the age when learning is easiest and reflexes fastest.

Such is for me a continuing effect. To return to that period, there were immediate responses which played their mysterious part in directing me on the paths I have traveled. Like all around me, I was caught up in all phases of the Gaelic revival, and I set out to acquire a proficiency in the long-proscribed Irish language equal to that in the dominant English. I lived in an area in which most of the older people had greater or less ability to converse, though few could read. The traditional role of *seanchai* ("storyteller")

survived and was held in honor. A seanchai able to narrate
ancient sagas in prose and verse for a week without a repetition could always count on an appreciative audience around
the blazing turf fire on long winter nights. Irish was still forbidden during school hours, but teachers and pupils could
and did stay voluntarily after class for Irish lessons. Volunteer teachers gave lessons at other times, and we gladly
pledged to use only Irish in all circumstances in which it
would serve our purpose. Meanwhile I read avidly in Irish
history and folklore, discovering a world of heroes, myths
and faerie twilight unknown to Dickens and little known to
Scott.

Of all the local seanchai, the one who most fascinated me
was an old shoemaker. I would spend hours in his little
workshop after school, instead of going home to eat. He enjoyed a listener to break the monotony of his lonely activity,
particularly someone as obviously appreciative as I was of
his infinite knowledge. It was always a delight to watch the
skill with which he formed a shoe on a wooden last, holding
the leather pieces in place with short sharp wooden tacks
while weaving fine white threads into a cord of the proper
thickness and strength and rubbing the cord in cobbler's
wax until it came out shining black and ready to sew. Meanwhile, he discoursed incessantly. In addition to the conventional folk tales, such as the Valley of the Black Pig and the
part it would play in the final defeat of the English invaders,
he had by his own efforts acquired a profound knowledge of
the career of Napoleon and particularly of his military adventures and misadventures. Although his formal education
did not go beyond primary schooling, he had a sensitivity to
the geomilitary strategies and the ability to deal with people
that were Napoleon's key weapons. His detailed descrip-
tions of terrain, disposition of opposing armies, infantry and
cavalry charges, and the strokes of genius which wrested
victory from the arms of defeat were such that I was long
convinced that he had been an eyewitness and participant.
For a child, the age and memories of an old man cover the
entire past. Regrettably, he had died long before historians
decided that neither Blucher nor Wellington played the de-

ciding part in Waterloo but a miserable attack of hemorrhoids which prevented Napoleon from sitting all day in the saddle. He had never doubted that the Corsican was more than match for the German and Englishman together.

A language both makes and expresses a mentality, and our study of Irish language and literature certainly contributed to our self-identification. But revolution requires, to use the word now popular, a praxis. Deeds had to measure up to commitment. In the summer of 1920, accordingly, a little before my eleventh birthday, I was inducted into the Irish Republican Army as an *Oglach*, a junior warrior.

The ceremonies were less than spectacular. We assembled in the long late June twilight which Ireland shares with Newfoundland, Alaska, and other regions in the same northern latitudes. We chose a high point to avoid surprise enemy attack, the overpass on the one-track railroad on which service had long been interrupted by the Black and Tan war.

The four or five inductees were taken singly behind a fence to meet the company's officers, whose ranks and functions had hitherto been an official—if universally known—secret. Squatted conspiratorially on the ground, they evaluated our potential as cannon fodder, then received our commitment not to yield voluntary support to any usurping government, but to acknowledge and defend the Irish Republic.

Integration into the full company of twenty "men" followed, with some close drill and a route march, the military snappiness of which was not enhanced by the fact that all of us, including the 16-year-old "captain," were barefoot. Subsequent familiarization with firearms was conducted mostly with wooden guns, but samples of the real thing were occasionally available. I soon acquired proficiency in assembling, serving and operating such disparate weapons as a Mauser, a Lee-Enfield, a parabellum and a 5-shot Colt revolver, a muzzle-loading 45.

My induction ceremony was slightly marred by an ideological issue which has agitated the IRA throughout its long history, leading to the split in 1969 into Provisionals and Officials, a split which so complicated the already confused role of the IRA in both the Republic of Ireland and Northern Ireland as to lead most people to despair of ever sorting things out.

Today's Provisionals are the physical-force men who detonate explosive charges in hijacked cars on Belfast streets and pick off the British soldier or bush-jacketed Orange extremist who carelessly exposes himself to their telescopic-sighted snipers. Their single and simple objective is a united Ireland free of every British presence and survival, an idyllic backwater in which all live harmoniously a lifestyle dictated by a fundamentalist and unreformed version of Roman Catholicism.

The Officials, on the other hand, recognize that the average person in the Republic of Ireland is worse off after sixty years of nominal independence than his or her counterpart still under Britain's direct domination in the six counties of northeast Ulster known as Northern Ireland. Like many fellow Catholics in Latin America and elsewhere, they have since the second Vatican Council in the 1960s turned to Karl Marx for socioeconomic enlightenment and grown to identify the Dublin government no less than that of Belfast as neocolonial and oppressive. They have taken to the sidelines in what they regard as an irrelevant struggle, but they have not turned in their arms. Instead, they reserve them for 'defense,'' while concentrating their efforts on building an alliance of the dispossessed on both sides of the existing divide to sweep away all privilege one day in an all-Ireland people's republic.

At the village level in the West of Ireland in 1920, the teenage social analysis was less formal, but the basic understanding of the lived reality was present. We farmed more than fifty acres in a village in which most families were raised on ten or fewer acres of reclaimed bogland, the meager income augmented by the annual migration of fathers and older sons for fall harvesting and winter coal mining in England and Scotland, and by the remittances of sons and daughters who had taken what was then the journey without return across the Atlantic. Only a few shopkeepers (and teachers who like my father had a salary to supplement farming income) could afford to send their children to a distant town for the secondary education unobtainable locally.

Class consciousness and class conflict were not highly developed, nor were differences in living standards pronounced. Josué de Castro, raised in a family of modest means in Brazil's hungry Northeast and later head of FAO and author of the classic *The Geography of Hunger*, describes this aspect of his childhood in terms that closely parallel mine. Most of his companions suffered from malnutrition in a way he did not, but he shared their sense of hunger as life's dominant emotion, a terrible fear that not enough food existed in all the world to fill a belly that never knew what it was to be sated. "I discovered the hunger of an entire population enslaved by the anguish of looking for something to eat. . . .I also saw men seated on the railing of the old quay murmuring monosyllables, a stalk of grass between their lips from which they drew its green juice, while from the corner of their mouth ran a greenish saliva that seemed to me. . .the dribble of hunger." De Castro describes how he and his companions would roam around the countryside in search of food, stealing mangoes and other fruit from the trees, chewing and sucking the sugarcane stalks. Similarly, my companions and I on our way from school would break into a field to rip some turnips or succulent mangolds out of the ground, smash them apart with a sharp stone and eat them raw under a fence. For us it was not stealing. We were hungry.

De Castro and I equally realized that such camaraderie and shared experience gave us insights vouchsafed to few. But it did not change our basic class difference. I was angry but not really surprised, accordingly, when one of the "officers" wondered aloud in the course of my induction ceremony whether bourgeois elements in the society were to be fully trusted. It was a salutary experience for me, as no doubt similar experiences were for De Castro. Unless he is aware of the objective differences between his experiences and theirs, the outsider can—with all the good will and expertise in the world—do little to promote the true interests of people of different class, culture or race. The concrete issue was bridged over by a compromise suggested by the "captain." A formal swearing-in would be postponed but I would become a de facto member of the company. Apparently the issue was then forgotten, for I participated fully in training and courier activities until I departed two years later to a boarding school a hundred miles away.

That journey, which took two days in the troubled conditions of the country, marked the effective end of my military career. I literally moved into a new world with a different time scale and different life values. Previously, my forays from my home village were on horseback or a borrowed bicycle on dirt roads to a neighboring market town. My furthest trip ever was a distance of twenty-five miles to the seashore on Killala Bay, the first time in a Bianconi car, a stagecoach drawn by four horses introduced to Ireland by an enterprising Italian; later, in a 12-seater internal-combustion charabanc, product of the fertile mind of an American descendant of a nineteenth-century Corkman. The rhythm of life was determined by the seasons, the price of cattle, and the price of tea. Tradition governed the great events of life, birth, marriage, and especially death. Everyone belonged, each with a place and proud of a defined function. The dominant events were the annual fair held each Ascension Thursday, the annual village sports, the football and handball tournaments with teams competing from various villages, the paramilitary marches led by the village fife and drum band eternally repeating the only tune it ever half-mastered, Clare's Dragoons, and other obscure but ultimately significant contributions to civil disobedience which wore down British endurance and obstinacy.

In this culture, the notion of individual liberty—while not explicitly rejected—had slight impact on one's life. The process of socialization was the more effective for being unreflective, the home, school, and church acting in unison to prepare the individual emotionally and technically to perform one of the various functions supportive of society. A significant difference in benefits, material and emotional (prestige), distinguished the functions, encouraging pressures to channel the most talented into those judged more valuable to the society, a selection process operated through a network of social relationships that left the individual minimal career choice.

Service to the church outranked all other, a logical consequence of the theological assumption that the sole purpose of life was to save our souls, a purpose achieved by performing faithfully the duties of our state of life, avoiding evil and doing good within the extremely narrow and specialized definition given these terms. To avoid evil was in fact the effective sum total of the obligation of those not chosen for an active part in the church's ministry, the means established by God to outwit the ever active devil and save souls from damnation and hell-fire.

Educational level and potential were key elements, especially for boys, in determining who were called to this special service. A girl's situation was somewhat different, since convents needed considerable numbers of so-called lay sisters whose chief requirement was the physical strength and amenability to cook, clean, and keep house for the "choir" sisters who performed as nurses, teachers, and administrators. Boys could move in several directions in the service of the church, the decision being made at about the age of twelve, by which time it was assumed that the primary education to which all were exposed could reasonably establish the potential of the "candidate."

The most obvious, and generally most sought after, was acceptance by the local bishop to train for ordination as a priest in his diocese. That involved five years of internship in a school controlled by him and operated educationally and administratively by his priests, a process which took the student through the high school course and from which he emerged with a high school diploma. The training in the "minor seminary" served as an introduction to the subsequent major seminary program. It was a strictly controlled and usually Spartan lifestyle with academic courses leaning heavily toward the classics. Exposure to contemporary thinking was minimal. The social sciences were ignored, and the philosophy of education frowned on questioning by the student and stressed passive ingestion of everything offered by teachers and textbooks.

The same lifestyle and philosophy of education continued

at an intensified tempo for six or seven years in the major
seminary, and the successful candidate emerged sealed by
the church as endowed with the knowledge and grace required as assistant to a pastor in his task of resolving all
problems in every order of his parishioners, and pro-
grammed to move up himself in due course to the seat of
wisdom. The prestige of the office carried with it a lifestyle
and financial rewards that placed the diocesan priest at the
top of the economic scale in the typical rural parish and close
to the top among the most successful merchants in the
larger towns. In addition, his money and influence combined
to improve significantly the prospects of those closely related by blood or marriage.

The attractiveness of such a career for ambitious families
is obvious. But there were problems. While some schol-
arships were available, most candidates had to carry the expense—high in relation to the financial condition of the typical rural family—of twelve years of boarding school. In spite
of this, the competition was extreme, so that only those with
the highest academic records and most influence were accepted. Others settled for membership in a society which
sent its priests to do mission work in China or Africa, or
found a priest-short bishop in England or the United States
willing to pay the cost of training in return for a commitment to join his diocese. The prestige rewards for the family
of these candidates was still high, even if material benefits
were slight or nonexistent.

Substantial leakage occurred at all points in the system.
No significant moral stigma attached to the reject, whether
by his own choice or otherwise, during or at the end of the
high school training. The education in the diocesan school
differed little from that of other secondary schools. The influence of the church on society was such that the traditional
classical training considered the ideal preparation for the
seminary was also regarded as normal for those planning
further education in business, law, administration, or all but
the most specialized of society's needs. The distortive impact of this education on civil society was increased by the
many who left the seminary. In spite of the techniques used

to discourage such withdrawal, they numbered at least half of the total entrants.

One discouraging technique was the absence of accreditation for civil purposes of the courses given in the major seminaries. Although most of the subjects studied would have qualified for credit if taken at the same level in the university, and although the standards were usually as high as those demanded by the university, the seminarian who left after four, five, or six years had at most the equivalent of a high school diploma to offer the prospective employer. The principal exceptions were those who had been training for the diocesan clergy and paying the cost of their education. They normally emerged with a B.A. or an equivalent primary degree that opened the way for them into desirable jobs in government service and business. The most obvious reason why the others were denied an equal benefit for their equal education was that the church authorities feared that too many youths would flock into the free or cut-price seminaries simply to take advantage of the upward mobility provided and leave when they had acquired the qualifications that would ensure them good jobs. While in principle, the reason for staying—as for entering—was a divine call to this kind of life, the value of supporting structures was recognized in practice.

Another important category was that of religious orders whose members lived in monasteries scattered all over the country. Many monasteries had a secondary school attached in which its members taught. They catered mostly to the children of the well-to-do, the most prestigious being boarding schools with a few day pupils. James Joyce provided a definitive description of these schools in *A Portrait of the Artist as a Young Man*. Other monasteries were primarily contemplative, the members spending their time in prayer and study, some also working in the fields protected by high walls that enclosed the massive buildings. Yet others combined the contemplative life with more or less frequent sorties to give parish missions or preach retreats for the many convents of nuns. While membership of a religious order did not normally ensure to the family of the member the financial rewards that could be expected though a son in the diocesan clergy, its prestige value was extremely high. These were the ones who had sacrificed everything and responded in the most total manner to the divine call to perfection. Even the canon law of the church was specific on that point, describing their manner of living as the state of perfection. Their freedom to devote their lives to prayer and study ensured the availability of a detached and informed elite whose books and other devotional writings and preaching gave a tone and quality to the whole of society.

To leave any of these groups after having completed the course of studies and been ordained to the priesthood was a violation of a social taboo so radical as to force the individual to adopt a new life and a new identity in another country. To leave before the decisive event of ordination to the priesthood was already a major loss of face for both the individual and his family, survivable but long remembered. Reintegration into society was for the individual a tough process. To go back to his family and village was an unattractive possibility. Yesterday, he was the chosen one, now the reject. His studies and seminary life had isolated him emotionally from family and friends. Work appropriate to his self-identification and practical qualifications was effectively nonexistent. One who chose that alternative usually ended up as an unproductive and often unwanted member of his family group, wandering through life without aim or ambition. Society, however, was unconcerned. It was so sure of the rightness of its objectives that the enormous waste of talent and destruction of human beings was judged a reasonable and unavoidable price to attain its purposes and perpetuate its values.

3

"And Heard Great Argument"

From my earliest childhood it was taken for granted that I would study for the priesthood. No doubt my rapid progress in primary school and insatiable appetite for reading contributed. It was further assumed that I would follow two cousins in the religious order of the Congregation of the Most Holy Redeemer, or less formally, the Redemptorists. Accordingly, I was sent, aged thirteen, to a Redemptorist secondary school more than a hundred miles away. Alfonso di Liguori, a lawyer from Naples, founded the order to minister to the goatherds of the Abruzzi. Shocked by what he saw on a visit to this impoverished part of south-central Italy in what was then the Kingdom of Naples, Liguori gave up his law practice, became a priest and committed himself and his followers to preach to these "most abandoned souls." The group has grown over the years to a membership of some seven thousand spread around the world. Well into the twentieth century their main activity was the preaching of revivalist-style missions with plenty of hell and thunder in the sermons, preferably to people resembling the Abruzzi goatherds in their lack of formal education.

Such specialization of function undoubtedly helped to develop a concept of religion that saw God primarily as a marine sergeant dealing with a bunch of hopeless recruits. All human enthusiasms were suspect. Love was a beautiful word that Jesus frequently used, but the day-to-day driving force to keep depraved natures under control and herd us forward on the path of virtue was fear, fear in particular of the hell-fire that followed inescapably if one had the misfortune to be called to account while in the state of mortal sin. As to what constituted mortal sin, the list was endless, catalogued and cross-indexed in manuals of casuistry that were represented as reflecting the true teaching of Liguori handed down in his spiritual family by an unbroken tradition; in fact, an anti-intellectual parody of the theological principles formulated by the astute and liberal Neapolitan lawyer.

The school to which I went was to all intents and purposes a junior seminary. All students were interns, and we were cut off totally from the outside world except for eight weeks in summer and two at Christmas with our families. During term, we had no newspapers, no radio, nothing to distract from the purpose for which we were all there—all forty-five to fifty of us—to become Redemptorists. Recruitment was largely a matter of chance, coupled with the ability of parents to pay the modest fees. I really played no active part in the decision. The notion of a vocation, a call from God to lead this particular kind of life, was much bandied about but never analyzed. Questioning was absent from our preparation. From the moment we entered the secondary school, we were assured by venerable men in long robes, whose right to speak in the name of God neither they nor we challenged, that we could be absolutely certain we had a vocation binding us until death. We could lose that vocation only by our own fault. To lose it placed our soul in eternal jeopardy.

The regime was a Spartan one, up at 6:20 and lights out at 10:30. We worked a seven-day week, at least twenty hours of class, and thirty of study under supervision in a big room in which each had a desk. We ate three adequate meals daily. An hour of recreation followed midday and evening meals; a shorter recreation after breakfast and between classes. Silence was demanded and enforced outside recreation. On Tuesday and Thursday afternoons we had two hours to walk in the country or play games, but then it was back to the study hall until bedtime. Each day started with compulsory Mass, and shorter periods of prayer broke up the day. Classes on Sunday dealt with the Scriptures and other religious subjects, losing entirely the social gains achieved when the law of Moses ordained the Sabbath as a day of rest to break the monotony and burden of six days of work. Thanks to this experience, I have never regained the human meaning of Sunday that was part of the peasant tradition in which my life had begun. I think my loss has been great, as is that of today's world where the official work week is five days but the emotional impact of the consumer society has converted life into a seven-day-a-week rat race.

The school enjoyed substantial economic subsidization by following the programs of the state Department of Education. Since nearly all Irish secondary schools were owned and operated by priests and nuns, they in turn exercised considerable influence over the content prescribed by the state. For them, preparation for life as priests or nuns in Ireland or on a foreign mission was the primary value of education, and they slanted the courses in the appropriate directions. Science and the arts were held in slight esteem. Latin and Greek characterized the educated man. Mathematics were needed to pass the state examinations to which the subsidies were related, but they were a necessary evil. Anyone with a superior knowledge of the subject, such as I had absorbed in grade school, was some kind of freak.

High school in Ireland was normally a five-year course, and a pass with honors in the final examination, the Leaving Certificate, placed the student at the academic level of a diploma from an American two-year college. The content of one's knowledge was, nevertheless, significantly different. The creation of the Irish Free State in 1922 had transferred Irish from its previous disapproved status to one of privilege. By the time I graduated in 1927, I was fully bilingual in English and Irish and had read widely in the classics of both languages and more extensively in modern Irish than in modern English literature. The limitation on reading con-

temporary English literature was deliberate. The world outlook of such as John Galsworthy, Arnold Bennet, H.G.
Wells and Mark Twain, not to mention D.H. Lawrence or
James Joyce, could play no constructive part in the molding
of a future priest. Little did my censors suspect that, thanks
to my father's catholic reading tastes, my mind was not
quite the tabula rasa they thought they were preserving.

In high school I also acquired a comparable familiarity
with classical Latin and its literature, and a level not much
lower in classical Greek. Latin, the language of the principal
philosophy and théology texts that would dominate the subsequent seminary studies, was particularly stressed. Starting with Caesar's Gallic Wars, I worked my way through
most of Cicero and a fair sampling of Livy, Sallust, Tacitus,
and the elder Pliny, while concentrating in poetry on Ovid,
Vergil and Horace. Catullus was highly admired, but the explicitly amorous content of most of his work limited our
study to selected samples. Greek began with Xenophon,
then moved on to Homer, Thucydides and Plato. In those
years I further acquired a fair speaking and excellent reading knowledge of French. Here the content of my reading
was even more narrowly controlled than in the classics.
Apart from very dull plays of Moliere and his school, I was
limited almost exclusively to polemical works of Bossuet
and members of the ultramontane school that continued to
the late nineteenth century to fight the Enlightenment and
the French Revolution, nostalgic for the imagined glories of
an earlier Christendom. The only exception I can recall was
Daudet's *Lettres de Mon Moulin*, slipped surreptitiously to
me one day by a professor in a rare moment of enthusiasm.
But as my father's bookshelves had generous selections of
Victor Hugo, Georges Sand, Balzac, Zola and similar popular novelists of those days, I already knew that modern
Frenchmen's concerns were not limited to papal politics.

Other than languages and a smattering of mathematics,
the curriculum focused narrowly on religious studies and
history and geography. Religion consisted of polemical texts
that marshalled endless arguments, to be learned by rote
and fed back word-perfect to the teacher, proving the truth

of everything presented by the Catholic church for our belief and the falsity of all opinions that contradicted or even deviated from the official line. The notion of social studies had not yet come into fashion, so history and geography were treated as separate subjects. Geography was largely a memorizing of countries, cities, rivers, mountains, seas, populations and products. History, although broadened in area and scope from its grade school form, remained primarily political, the comings and goings of armies, the strategies of generals and intrigues of prime ministers and princes. There was no sense of growth or development, still less of continuity. As the concept of *dialectic* did not exist for us, neither did the word. We dug deep into the glories of ancient Greece and Rome, then jumped to the prosaic squabbles of European dynasties in the nineteenth and twentieth centuries.

The seeming illogic of this misunderstanding of history perhaps affords a clue to the radically wrong underpinnings of an education that in itself had much to commend it. It was posited on a theology, a philosophy, and a cosmology of fixed essences and circular movement. Knowledge was a fixed amount, or at least everything worth knowing had already been determined, though unfortunately mixed with much error against which the students had to be ever on guard and ever protected. Far from setting out on a voyage of discovery, we were simply being escorted on a well-charted course by expert pilots. Once we learned how to read the maps and the blueprints through a long apprenticeship, we would in due course graduate to the pilot class and devote our lives to guiding others along the predetermined ways. We insiders were lucky. Possessing the truth, we had no need to grope in the dark.

It was a grossly elitist world view, supportive of a rigid class structure with a place for everyone and everyone in place. As such, it had no choice but to favor the status quo and condemn any effort to alter a distribution of wealth and power inexorably established as part of an eternal divine plan. It was not until much later that I had occasion to explore that aspect and the part it played in the formulation of Catholic teaching on the social order from the early nine-

teenth century onward. But it expressed itself clearly after
the creation of the Irish Free State in 1922. The clergy
closed ranks immediately against the social reformers who
wanted to build on the political victory and modify the economic structures so that the have-nots would obtain the benefits they had been promised would automatically follow the
transfer of decision-making from the powerful in London to
the powerful in Dublin.

The church had long professed to lead the fight for independence. In reality, it was so wedded to the status quo that
it always feared its bargaining power would be less with a
native government than what it had built up by astute political double-dealing with London. It was determined that if a
change came, the most conservative groups in Irish politics
would take charge.

Statements of Pope Pius IX and Pope Leo XIII on the
right of individuals to ownership of property were consequently invoked to brand as a violation of the natural law
every attempt to redistribute wealth, no matter how
nuanced. Perhaps the height of this absurdity was a massive
and successful campaign to have the state recompense the
shareholders when it took over the bankrupt railroad system. The reasoning was simple. It had long been the established policy of convents to invest in railroad shares the
dowry each nun brought on entry, the equivalent of the
dowry she would have brought her husband if she had married. Held intact while she lived, it passed on her death to
the order. A Christian state, it was argued, could not allow
the innocent nuns to be pauperized because of the lack of
foresight of their financial managers.

Behind the high walls of our schools and recreation
grounds, we had no continuing knowledge of what went on
outside, but items like the above filtered through in sermons
in church and in occasional comments from professors, always naturally colored to match the monolithic view which
the priests' training had provided and which we were in the
process of absorbing. We were in every sense people apart,
not knowing or understanding the problems and concerns of
the many on the other side of the wall. Even when home on

vacation, we were regarded and regarded ourselves as different, already committed to a way of life that needed protection from common hazards and temptations. The trivia which made up the lives of others we were taught to regard as such, namely, trivia of no real significance. When our time came to function as their spiritual guides and mentors, our professors and the weighty books that helped them transmit to us the wisdom of the ages would have taught us all the principles we would need to solve any possible problem that might confront us.

Isolation from the contamination of the world and of mundane affairs applied most rigidly to association with girls. The vocation to which we were not only aspiring but already committed involved celibacy as a basic element. Sex in consequence had no part to play in our lives, and the stirrings and turmoils normal to adolescence were represented as temptations of the devil and challenges to our virtue. We had no instruction in the purpose of sex and its place in the economy of life. For me as a country boy, this was not so serious. Having been raised among animals and having delivered my first calf unaided at the age of eleven, I had a fair understanding of the mechanics of copulation, pregnancy, and birth. But the city kids were left to blunder through with what they had picked up on street corners. I remember being approached very shamefacedly by a twenty-one year old from Belfast, brought up strictly at home and moved at twelve to the junior seminary, where he and I were classmates. He was in his second year of philosophy, and the particular treatise we were studying required some understanding of heterosexual relations. He couldn't work out the day's assignment because he had no idea where babies came from.

This atmosphere of cultivated ignorance made some adolescent masturbation and homosexuality inevitable. Life was organized to minimize them. For example, two students were forbidden to converse under any circumstances, even in an open public place, without a third being present and participating in the conversation. Infractions, especially if there were indications of sex play, no matter how innocent, were punished by immediate expulsion. But the basic strategy was to fill our lives with activity, combining plenty of strenuous exercise with an ascetic regime. This, according to the unquestioned philosophy and assumptions, would achieve the necessary sublimation and transform the sex drive into a dedication to higher things. And in fact the endless round of study and other activities reduced the issue of sex and of projected lifelong celibacy to the status of a marginal issue for me, and I think for most of my companions. It was not until much later, and as a result of observing the problems of various friends, that I began to question the law imposing celibacy on all priests engaged in the active ministry in the Latin rite of the Roman Catholic church.

High school was followed in 1927 by the year of intense testing known as the novitate or noviceship. I have described the events of this year, and of the following years of study as a seminarian, in a book published in 1953. I feel no need to revise that account. Written after twenty years of reflection on the events, it remains valid more than thirty years later in spite of kaleidoscopic changes both in the world and in the Catholic church. Today I'd express some judgments more harshly but would not want to change the perspective. Accordingly, I limit myself here to summarizing those experiences to the extent that they contributed to making me the person I now am.

We led a busy life in the novitiate, a function assigned to every moment from the clanging of the great bell at 5:25 in the morning until it tolled twice seventeen hours later to announce lights out. The Master of Novices, a thin, gray ascetic man of sixty who kept his impulses inhumanly in hand, lectured us every day. We read spiritual books at stated times morning and afternoon. Even during meals each novice in turn read aloud a chapter from the life of a saint or some similar work of devotion. The day's first exercise was a half hour of formal meditation kneeling in the chapel, with a similar period in midafternoon, and a third before the evening meal. Unobtrusively, unconsciously, this steady rhythm of activity reflected itself not only in external demeanor but in our self-image and worldview.

Indoctrination of the novices concentrated on the emotions and the will. Seminary courses would later provide intellectual justification of their faith and the mechanics of prayer. But as novices we took all this for granted, just as the recruit preparing for battle takes for granted the justice of his cause. We accepted without question the new scale of values which made the denials and rigors of this life seem unimportant when weighed against its benefits. The Master of Novices, nevertheless, provided a minimum of theory to accompany and support the practice. In daily conferences he explained that separation from the world and self-abnegation were not ends in themselves but means to bring us closer to God. Our task was both negative and positive. The vows of poverty, chastity, and obedience which every member of a religious order had to profess were designed mainly to insure the negative. Devotional exercises were directed to effect the positive. They occupied more than nine hours each day, the principal ones being meditation, Mass, recital of the divine office in common, reading of spiritual books, and such traditional devotions as the rosary, way of the cross, visits to the Blessed Sacrament, and examination of conscience.

My lifework has brought me into close connection with various bureaucracies (and to work in some), including that enduring and self-regulating bureaucracy, the Roman Curia, and I identify certain elements as characteristic. Imaginative and innovative people create a bureaucracy and endow it with complicated mechanisms and techniques of functioning. It is then staffed with mediocre and unimaginative people who lack the brains and incentive to understand how the machine functions. Happy at their dull tasks of fueling and oiling, they are never tempted to tamper or innovate. If the bureaucrats are further persuaded that the system is divinely sanctioned so that all they do is blessed on earth and ensures eternal rewards, the bureaucracy is impregnable. In retrospect I recognize that the religious order into which I was being integrated had the qualities of an enduring bureaucracy. Mediocrity was a virtue. Any indication of excellence or a desire to pursue studies or concerns distinct from the established way was an indication of pride and a temptation of the devil.

Molding into this system was furthered by a process of isolation which reduced the individual to total dependence on a superior, to whom alone he was encouraged to express his concerns and who alone had the divine mandate to tell him what he must and must not think and do. As novices, we were isolated from the professed members of the community. They included about a dozen priests whose principal activities were to go about the country preaching missions and retreats, and while at home to conduct the services of the public church attached to the monastery. We joined them physically for various religious exercises each day, and we ate in the same dining room at a separate table; but we spoke only to the Master of Novices and his assistant. Even the superior of the house, who was authorized to speak to us, left us severely alone. On very important feasts, we joined the priests for a half-hour of recreation; but even then convention forbade them to inform us about issues currently in the news or discuss any subject calculated to distract our thoughts from the pursuit of interior recollection.

An average community also included five to ten lay brothers who maintained the buildings and garden, prepared meals and served in the kitchen and dining room. One was a tailor, another a carpenter, another a gardener, another a cook. The community had no servants. Each looked after his own room, made his bed, swept, dusted and polished. We novices also swept, dusted, scrubbed and polished the public rooms and corridors in our section, a chore performed by the lay brothers in the rest of the monastery and in the public church. A lay brother normally elected that status because he lacked the education or inclination to study philosophy and theology. He was discouraged from theoretical studies that might develop tastes or attitudes distinct from those of his companions. If he wanted an outlet for his energies, he could find it in a trade or craft. Lay brothers formed a sub-community of their own. They ate at a table apart and stayed by themselves at recreation times. Lay novices constituted yet another group, cut off as completely as we were from all contacts other than their Master of Novices and his assistant.

Meanwhile, we were isolated from each other by almost continuous silence and by a formalism of relationships that prevented a truly human meeting of the minds. With the Master of Novices present at the hour of common recreation after lunch and after dinner (except Friday when the silence was total for the entire day), the novices had no opportunity to develop an independent group life of their own. The first half of each recreation period was spent walking in the garden, two leading with the Master of Novices, the others following in threes. For the second part, we all sat around a table in the common room and joined in general conversation led by the Master of Novices. With at least one witness to every dialogue, no confidences were exchanged.

What not to discuss was well established. The taboos extended to almost the entire range of our previous lives, our families, our former friends. All those things lay behind. The quicker forgotten, the better. We were left with little more than the weather, the progress of vegetative and flower life in the garden (on which subject we were well informed because we dug, weeded and planted in silence for a half-hour each morning), the saint's life which one of us read aloud while the others ate, plans for the celebration of an upcoming religious festival, a sermon we had recently heard. The two hours of recreation became the dullest part of the day. It is impossible, with all the good will in the world, to talk about nothing to a stranger. And that is what we were becoming, even those who had been classmates for the previous three to five years.

One thing I must say for the system is that it worked. By the end of the year of noviceship, we had been so molded as to see the life style of the order as normal and desirable. We had been transformed from schoolboys into members of an elite, identifying our goals and values with those of the order, and grateful to it for having chosen us for the honor of membership. We had achieved a high level of independence of material things. We were content in our bare cells. We ate with moderation, kept strict control of eyes, ears, and tongue, slept only enough to maintain health and strength, endured heat and cold with patience, practiced penitential exercises. And we were convinced that we understood our motivations for wanting to continue this way of life, that we were not rejecting the bad in favor of the good, but the good in favor of the better.

Ambiguities nevertheless remained. Our life, we were assured, was one of unbroken joy in the Lord. In fact, what dominated it was not joy but duty. The problem was one for which Catholic theology did not then have, and did not until many years later discover, a solution. In an over-literal interpretation of the first chapters of Genesis, as filtered through Greek and medieval thinkers, it saw human life on earth as a time of testing, without intrinsic purpose, to provide an eternity of happiness or of suffering according to the way the particular tests assigned by God were accepted and performed. But a person's actions really achieved nothing, since God had already endowed the world with all the perfection proper to it.

Yet it is a basic fact of observation, confirmed by the findings of the life sciences, that what gives one a sense of self-identification, a radical joy, is the ability to achieve, to create, to build. And this by definition we were denied. In spite of all the professions of a community of love and sharing, we were in fact being immured in individual isolation cells. Our only valid relationship was with a God up there on high, outside and apart from the world, who transmitted inscrutable decisions to us through a superior whose every whim and prejudice carried with it the stamp of divine approval. The underlying assumptions were not of a struggle toward liberation but of a permanent relationship of domination and subservience. The services which we would in turn later perform for the laity were to be conceived within the same framework. We would by ordination receive mysterious powers to enable us to perform divine rites of which they had to partake in order to come successfully through their period of testing. Our role would be to dominate and domesticate others.

Such ambiguities remained deep down. They were not discussed by the Novice Master nor were we encouraged to analyze them for ourselves. Instead, we were urged to accept with simple and unquestioning faith the way God had mapped out for us, to be grateful that we had been chosen for special service that would earn commensurate reward in the life to come. And although the further point of reward in this life was not spelled out, it was an underlying reality we had known from earliest childhood. To be a member of the clergy was to enjoy prestige and social privileges, a status which the canon law of the church insisted was necessary to enable the clergy to perform their duties without outside interference.

As I look back now, I see solid reasons why a youth of nineteen, with so little experience of life, might and should hesitate to commit himself irrevocably (as it seemed) to poverty, celibacy, and obedience. But in the actual circumstances, the decision made itself. There were no effective choices. And besides, after a whole year of absence from classes and study, I was looking forward to the following six years of exploration of the wisdom of the ages within a framework that would still be restrictive but far freer than the ascetic rigidity of the novitiate.

Isolation from the outside world was almost as total during the six years of seminary training as in the novitiate. The seminary consisted of a group of battered buildings haphazardly constructed over the years—without benefit of architect—deep in the countryside of East Galway, flat, barren, and waterlogged. A small electric plant chug-chugged noisily from early morning to bedtime three days a week to charge batteries that lighted dim bulbs over our study desks. Our life required few mechanical complications. There was not even a telephone. It was judged essential to the contemplation of knowledge on which we were to concentrate that every outside distraction be ruthlessly barred. Neither newspaper nor radio would disturb our solitude.

This regime made possible the acquisition of enormous amounts of knowledge. Unfortunately, the process was marred by the same radical defect that underlay the teaching process in our high school. Education was understood as the transfer from professor and textbook of truths long since immutably established. God had spoken in the Bible, and had commissioned the church to transmit and interpret truth for all time. Subsidiary to this overarching control and guidance, we had the wisdom of the ages going back to a primitive revelation of God put into formal and irreducible shape by the Greek philosophers, especially Aristotle. Saint Thomas Aquinas and other great churchmen of the Middle Ages had reformulated Greek thought under the guidance of the church to purify it of errors introduced through human frailty, thus producing the *philosophia perennis* of the Scholastics, a system of thought that provides all the answers anyone ever needs, and consequently endures for all time.

Later thinkers swollen with their own pride, especially after the Protestant Reformation of the sixteenth century, had formulated other philosophies and deceived many by their brilliant sophistries. Foremost among them were Voltaire and the Encyclopedists, Descartes, Spinoza, Leibnitz, and Kant. Because of their continuing pernicious influence, it was important to understand their characteristic errors and know how to demonstrate the falsity of their conclusions. This our textbooks did for us briefly and decisively, building up straw men to be sliced into chaff with razor-edged syllogisms. We did not read the actual works of these philosophers. That, our professors assured us, would be a waste of time. But I was able during the two years of philosophy to go far beyond the dry-as-dust textbook which sufficed to pass the examinations. I read much of Aristotle and Plato in the original Greek, Saint Augustine, Saint Bernard, Saint Thomas Aquinas and others in Latin, and Cardinal Mercier's Neo-Scholasticism in French.

A professor who proved too liberal for the system and survived only a single year did me a great favor by lending me Bertrand Russell's *Introduction to Philosophy*. It immediately made sense to me by bringing the apriorisms of the Scholastics face to face with the reality we know and experience. What becomes of a table when you cover it with a tablecloth? What color is red in total darkness? How sweet does the rose smell when nobody's smelling it? What must you stand on to find out where you're standing? It was not till much later that I realized clearly that the radical difference between Russell and my textbook was his choice of our existential experience as starting point in the search for truth instead of a theoretical set of first principles to be taken from a storehouse in which objective and unchanging truth is already safely deposited. But he did open up for me the excitement of a search for understanding which I pursued with all the means at my disposal.

Four years of theology followed philosophy. The first two concentrated on dogma, an exposition of the truths of the Catholic faith as revealed by God in the Bible and in the tradition of the church. It involved significant exposure to the beliefs of other religions, Christian, Jewish, Islamic, and Oriental. Here again, the stress was polemical. We were still more than thirty years from the Second Vatican Council's laudably objective examination of the spiritual values enshrined in all the world's great religions and particularly the common Christian values retained and flourishing in the churches issued from the Protestant Reformation. Our concern was simply to formulate the ways in which we were right and they were wrong.

The parallel study of the Bible was more fruitful. The approach to interpretation tended to be narrowly literal and fundamentalist, conditioned by the decisions of the Biblical Commission created in 1902 by Pope Leo XIII "for the promotion of biblical studies and their protection from error." Nevertheless, major exposure to great literature that has dominated Western thinking for thousands of years was inherently exciting and stimulating, especially since we were encouraged to study the books in their original languages, adding to our previous knowledge of Greek and Latin two years of classical Hebrew.

For the final two years the major concentration was on moral theology and canon law. In the Jansenistic and casuistic spirit of the Catholicism of that time, moral theology was a cataloguing of all the possible sins a person could possibly commit, an evaluation of the gravity of each, and an analysis of the circumstances that might increase or lessen the guilt of the sinner. The need to classify, cross-reference, and index all the ways in which Catholics might imperil their salvation resulted from the distorted emphasis long placed on the obligation to confess one's sins to a priest and receive his absolution for them. It effectively released lay Catholics from making moral decisions. They simply abdicated that function to a priest who disposed of one complicated situation after another in as routine a manner and with as little regard for the total circumstances as does the typical police-court judge in dealing with charges of drunken brawling or accosting.

Canon law appealed to me from the first moment. The laws governing the functioning of the church as a social structure, the relationships of the parts, the identification, distribution, and application of power, and all of the thousands of elements that ensure a highly centralized control of a body of many millions of people scattered across the globe, go back to the Roman Empire. Roman law, as developed and codified from the third to the sixth century, gave the Christian church official status and allocated to it a wide diversity of social, cultural, and educational activities. Later, as the church itself acquired temporal power and expanded its jurisdiction to determine such things as the right of Christian kings to dispossess infidels of their lands and other possessions and of Christian merchants to carry black Africans across the sea into perpetual slavery, canon law developed and changed to meet the needs of each period. The loss of the Papal States in the nineteenth century and the tightening of centralized control to match the fortress mentality with which the papacy faced the threats of the twentieth century led to the codification promulgated in 1917 that constituted our basic study document.

My earlier mathematical training and bent may have played a part in my admiration for this small book, strictly logical, finely honed, determined with the precision and verbal economy that reflected thousands of years of marriage of Latin and lawyers every possible issue that had arisen or might arise in the life of the church. In addition, of course, it spelled out an order of priorities that by now I had come to accept as not only normal but divinely dictated. It caused no surprise to find the church structured to ensure the total control of Rome over all its parts, of the pope over the bishops, of the bishops over the priests, of the priests over laymen, with women—including nuns—reduced to a level of perpetual tutelage. Nor was it until much later, and as a result of experience still to be described, that I realized that it represented the triumph of law over love, a parody of the message of Christ. At that time I simply studied it with uncritical enthusiasm and developed a respect for law which later led me to study the common law and become a lawyer.

That respect I still retain in spite of the shocking abuses committed by lawyers both in the churches and in society. I regard their profession as one of the noblest and potentially most helpful to the powerless of the earth in their efforts to assert their basic human rights against the greed of the powerful. Law and its practice remind me of a comment Cervantes made more than once in his writing about medical doctors, presumably reflecting on the ways of his own father who in the fashion of that time combined the roles of barber and surgeon. The science of medicine is noble, he said, in spite of the inability of many practitioners to measure up to its requirements. So it is with law.

It was the custom to have the professor single out a student each year to present and defend a thesis in Latin before a general assembly of students, professors, and the ten or twelve other priests who lived in the same house and went out periodically to preach missions in neighboring parishes or retreats to convents of nuns. I was picked for the job in my second year of philosophy and again in my third year of theology. Each experience produced for me unanticipated and disconcerting results.

The inspiring professor of my first year of philosophy had been replaced by a young man, serious, devout, and devoid of imagination. He didn't think I was as interested as I should be in my classwork. Perhaps the fault lay in the dry bones of the treatise on logic which opened the year, but I found equally little to inspire or even hold attention in the

long commentaries he read mournfully from authors as unin-
spiring as himself. In any case, he decided to make me do
some serious homework, the assignment being to prove that
a world exists outside and independent of the thinking mind.
Our ontology textbook dealt with this issue as it did with
other basic problems of philosophy. A few sweeping generalizations gave the reader the impression that the philosophers who had taken the problem seriously were little better
than imbeciles, then disposed of it once for all with a couple
of sidestepping syllogisms.

I started without real enthusiasm on what was to prove a
critical life experience, my first serious questioning of something that previously had seemed too obvious to investigate.
I reread the pertinent section in the class textbook, then
looked at the treatment of the issue in several other similar
textbooks available in the library and in other "safe"
sources such as Cardinal Mercier and a contemporary Irish
professor of philosophy named Coffey who had contributed
two enormous volumes to the subject. For all of them there
seemed to be no problem that a syllogism could not resolve.
But by chance I also found in the library the major writings
of the eighteenth-century Irish philosopher, George Berkeley, the father of subjective idealism. His analysis was convincing. As I read and reread him, one conclusion gradually
formed and clarified itself in my mind. There did not seem to
be any proof that realities outside and other than the thinking mind existed. Either one took it for granted that they
did or refused to take it for granted. In either case, there was
no sense in trying to convince people by reasoning that they
were wrong.

The conclusion ran counter to everything I had been
taught. It undercut the entire structure of universal truth
clearly knowable by human reason built by the Scholastics
on Aristotelian foundations. I couldn't believe it. I spent
another week checking and rechecking before I ventured to
present my dilemma to the professor, analyzing for him the
various syllogisms by which the Scholastic and Neo-Scho-
lastic authors attempted to defend their stand, then bringing out the unacceptable assumption each argument seemed
to me to contain.

"That's perfectly true," he agreed offhandedly, as though the matter scarcely merited concern, "there's really no way to prove it." Then, noting my shocked astonishment, he added with a dry smile: "Now we just have to go ahead and prove it."

I left his room in a daze. The whole thing was for him a pure formality, a piece of play-acting. And I was being instructed to become a party to a sham, a negation of the intellectual process to which we were purportedly committed. But I had been well conditioned. I did what I had been told to do, stringing together the required number of words in the proper form, assembling the dissident opinions, Kant, Descartes, Hume, Berkeley, Russell, Santayana, and the rest, and pulverizing to my own satisfaction—or at least to that of the orthodox—both them and their authors. The students assigned to propose objections assembled four or five strawmen. A friend passed them to me in advance, so that I could have the orthodox answer at my finger tips when the final act of the farce was played out.

The thesis assigned me in the third year of moral theology was a defence of the position on recidivism of the founder of the Redemptorists. In recognition of his holy life and his works for the church, he was proclaimed a saint and his name was added to the very select group—some thirty in all—who have been given the official title of Doctor (teacher) of the Church because of the importance and orthodoxy of their writings. He is acknowledged as one of the most important moral casuists in his impact on confessional practice. In criminology recidivism refers to repeated and habitual relapse into a pattern of crime, and in psychiatry to the chronic tendency toward the repetition of criminal or antisocial behavior patterns. In moral theology, it concerns the propriety of a confessor giving absolution to a penitent who habitually relapses into sins for which he has previously expressed repentance and been given sacramental absolution.

Among the Redemptorists there was an absolutely firm tradition that their founder had taken an extremely hard line on this issue, calling for the withholding of absolution unless the penitent could produce real evidence that he was

breaking his bad habit, and that it was their duty to continue to preach and practice this hard line in an age when a
more benign approach sponsored by Jesuit theologians was
generally accepted by the clergy. I naturally started out
with this assumption, only to discover from my reading of
Liguori's own extensive theological treatises and my study
of the historical context in which he wrote, that the Redemptorist tradition was arbitrary and probably contrary to the
facts.

The Jansenism which had developed in France in the seventeenth century had quickly spread to Italy and other
countries. In spite of various papal condemnations, its
teachings of a very strict moral code and a Calvinistic insistence on the total corruption of human nature by sin was
accepted in a more or less modified form by most theologians for at least two centuries and continued to influence
the attitudes of confessors in some countries, notably Ireland and the United States, into the twentieth century. Only
the Jesuits held out consistently against it from the beginning, and in the period of Liguori the pro-Jansenist feeling
was so strong that the Jesuits were regarded as unaccep-
tably lax and calculated to demoralize the confessional with
their new casuistry. From my study of the sources it seemed
clear to me that Liguori agreed with the Jesuits while ap-
pearing for political reasons to oppose them, always able to
find some indication of more than average sorrow in the
recidivus who approached him and hence able legalistically
to reverse the presumption of insincerity.

When I mentioned my suspicions to my professor, I was
quickly made to understand that such radical revisionism of
a stand consistently adopted by Redemptorists for some
two centuries would be poorly received from a mere student.
And once again I followed the counsel of prudence, which by
now had become ingrained habit, ignoring what I subsequently came to regard as the finest line in Liguori's volumi-
nous works: "I have the utmost respect for the opinions of
the Fathers of the Church and of learned theologians, but I
regard even more highly the truth as I see it." In any case, I
wrote and defended my thesis in terms that rocked no boats

and made no waves. If my conscience needed any assuaging for my prevarication, I easily stilled it by reminding myself that the goal of ordination to the priesthood was just round the corner. After I had finished my seminary studies and was assigned to an active ministry as a priest, I would be in a freer position to pursue my interests and voice my conclusions with some authority.

Things were not to work out like that. Exactly three weeks before the date fixed for the ordination to the priesthood of myself and my seven or eight classmates, I was summoned by the Father Provincial who had come to the seminary especially for this purpose and notified verbally that I was not being recommended to the bishop for ordination. It was a bolt from the blue. Absolutely no hint or suggestion to prepare me had preceded it. When I found myself able to speak, I said I was prepared to wait for whatever additional period of trial or testing might be judged necessary, if there was a doubt as to my readiness. The Provincial quickly disillusioned me. He was not talking about a delay. The decision was final, permanent and irrevocable. It meant I would have to leave the order.

4

From Theology to Journalism

I asked for time to think and to consult with my spiritual advisers. There were two of them, both elderly Redemptorists, the one living in the seminary, the other—my Master of Novices five years earlier—living in another house but able to come within a few days. The first of these, with whom I had been in the habit of reviewing the state of my mind and conscience regularly over several years, was as shocked as I had been. He advised me to appeal to a higher level what was obviously a mistake or misunderstanding. The Master of Novices, whom I had not seen for a considerable time, was a man totally dedicated to the system and fixed in his conviction that whatever the superiors had decided had to be fair, just and correct. He had a sharp and penetrating mind and subjected me for several hours to harsh cross-examination, taking me through every moment and event of my seminary life for clues as to what had gone wrong. I emerged from that ordeal exhausted but triumphant. He had reversed all his assumptions and committed himself to use all his substantial influence for me.

The first thing was to find out the reasons for the decision. That seemed no problem until I approached the Provincial and was blandly informed that the decision had been made in conformity with Canon 970 of the Code of Canon Law. This one-sentence canon, wedged in the middle of a long section of the Code dealing with the procedures involved in preparing for and receiving ordination to the priesthood, cut the ground effectively from under the applicant's feet. It authorized the Provincial to deny access to ordination without stating his reasons and without any legal hearing. The seminarian was left with two appeals, one to the Superior General of the Order, and a second to the Holy See; but in both cases, a blind appeal, since the appellant has no idea what reasons underlay the original decision.

I was still officially a seminarian in good standing, although within a matter of days it had to become publicly known that I was not being ordained with the others. But the course of studies was so arranged that a further year followed ordination, and I continued to attend classes for several months while I prepared and dispatched my first appeal. In it I covered substantially the same ground as in my earlier interview with my former Master of Novices. The answer came quickly and was brusquely unhelpful. The Superior General concurred with the decision of the Provincial.

From the initial meeting in which he had informed me of his decision, the Provincial had insisted that the only course open to me was to ask for a dispensation from the vows that bound me to life-long membership of the order and say good-bye with a minimum of noise and disturbance. This immediately brought into focus a curious oversight in the Code of Canon Law. The procedures involved in getting rid of a professed religious were set out in detail in Canons 654 through 668. They required convincing proof that the individual had violated a serious rule at least three times, and was warned after each of the first two violations that a third would bring expulsion. No such warnings had ever been given me, since no such situations had ever arisen. And while under Canon 970, the superiors could deny me ordination to the priesthood without giving reasons, under Canons 654–668 they could not exclude me from membership. From the viewpoint of the Code, we had a stand-off.

As the weeks went by, and as I showed that it was my intention to pursue every possible channel of recourse, the pressures to force me out mounted. The strain was affecting my health, and the Provincial decided to transfer me from the seminary to another house, purportedly to get better medical attention. The concrete effect was to isolate me from my fellow students and leave me in an anomalous situation, with nothing to do, in a community of thirty or forty priests, most of whom were twenty to forty years older than I and all of whom by now knew through the grapevine that procedures had been initiated to get rid of me. I had my meals with them and joined twice a day in common recreation. But I was effectively shunned or ignored by all except two, one of whom was a known dissenter whose friendship was the kiss of death, and the other of whom was my cousin.

Turning the wheel a little tighter, the Superior General about this time wrote me a grim letter in which he said he would be forced, if I persisted in my refusal to ask for a dispensation, to obtain a special decree from the Holy See dismissing me from the order whether I liked it or not. I didn't believe him then. Much later, I learned more of the functioning of the Roman Curia. It utilizes the Code when that is to its bureaucratic advantage. Otherwise, it finds ways to circumvent and negate its most specific provisions for the benefit of friends and the convenience of the system. I then realized he had not been bluffing. But my immediate response was to seek the final remedy provided by Canon 970, an appeal to the Holy See.

As in my earlier appeal to the Superior General, I was still running blind, lacking even an adviser familiar with procedures. I had, however, spent my days in the library reading not only the Code but as many commentaries and related works as I could lay hands on. The new document was longer, more organized, and expressed in what I considered elegant Latin, but basically it was the same as before. I was fighting blindfold. In due course, it went off to the proper official, the Prefect of the Congregation of Religious, and I watched anxiously for the arrival of the mail day after day and week after week.

Knowing what I now do about the delaying tactics of the Roman Curia, I might have resigned myself to years of waiting. But when some two months had passed without even an

acknowledgment, I decided on another tack. I sent a copy
of the appeal with a covering letter to the papal nuncio in
Dublin. I did not then know but was to learn later that this
was no run-of-the-mill papal nuncio steeped in the conventions and diplomacies of Roman ecclesiastical training. He
was Archbishop Paschal Robinson, an American of Irish
descent who had been for years an editor in a New York
publishing house before becoming a priest and had counted
Mark Twain among his authors. He obviously read his mail
and acted on it. He also had a low opinion of the state of the
church in Ireland and particularly of the level of its leadership. He immediately filed a cable to Rome and got an answer by return which did nothing to help me substantively
but at least ended the suspended animation. The curial answer to my many pages of eloquence was a three-word sentence worthy of the Delphic Oracle: *parendum superioribus
suis* (let him obey his superiors). No issue of obedience had
ever arisen. I had never been ordered to do anything I had
not happily done. The one thing my superiors wanted me to
do, to leave quietly, they could not order me to do. On that
point, at least, canon law was clear—although, of course,
there was always the possibility, as the Superior General
had threatened, that some official in the Roman Curia could
sign a document overriding the clear prescriptions of the
Code and have me unceremoniously ejected. It would have
been interesting, potentially rewarding in the financial
sense, and highly embarrassing for many people, if I had
forced them to take that road and followed up with a lawsuit
in the civil courts. But I, of course, had no legal advice. The
thought did not even enter my head, and the likelihood of
any good lawyer accepting such a case would have been
slight in the existing socio-religious atmosphere in Ireland.

When I had digested for some days in the silence of my
cell the import of the Curia's sibylline response, I came to
realize instinctively what many years later I have learned to
formulate scientifically: the powerful will use all means at
their disposal to repel a challenge to their power, and the
only way to overcome their power is to mount superior
power. I had still no hint of the reasons which impelled the

original decisions—nor do I have today—but practically
speaking they had become immaterial. Once the decision
was made, the entire club would rally to repel any challenge
to the authority of the member who had made it. I knew I
could drag the charade out probably for several additional
acts, but I also recognized that each extension would increase my bitterness and emotional exhaustion without
achieving any corresponding benefit. So I determined to use
the slight bargaining power I derived from the desire of the
superior to present our parting as amicable and by mutual
agreement.

After all my years in isolation, ever since childhood, I had
practically no idea of what life would be like outside the
monastery, or what would be involved in making a living. A
significant part of the process of incorporating young people
into the life of a religious order consisted of persuading them
of the dangers and wickedness of the world from which they
were being saved. The ascetic literature, at least from the
fourteenth-century *Imitation of Christ* usually ascribed to
Thomas à Kempis, has hammered on this theme. And long
before, Saint Augustine had done his share of vivid painting
of the ways of men and women in his *Confessions*. With the
supports abruptly pulled from under me, how would I survive such lures?

At the practical level of making a living I was equally
uninformed. I had heard about millionaires who had lost
fortunes overnight and jumped to death from Wall Street
skyscrapers. But we were now in 1933, and that was years
earlier. I had no idea whatever of the continuing impact of
the Depression, a word I had never seen written with a
capital nor even heard spoken as in earlier times people
spoke in whispers about the Plague or the Great Hunger.
But I had grown up in Ireland, a country with a perennial
excess of intellectual workers and an old-world inelasticity in
its job-filling mores. I was too old at twenty-five for the kind
of job one might with luck and influence get on emerging at
nineteen with a high-school certificate, the only paper qualification I held. The civil service, in particular, was consequently closed to me. At my age, entrance would require a

university degree or a law qualification. My father, with the youngest three of his nine children still in college, was already retired. There was no question of turning to him to subsidize me for several further years. I was already committed in my own mind to get the university qualifications to which I felt in equity entitled to match my years of study. But that could only come when I could afford to pay from my own earnings.

So I proceeded to negotiate with the Father Provincial for enough money to support me until I could find a job. On that principle, he was adamant. He would undertake no continuing obligation. The best I could settle for was a lump sum and a promise. The lump sum consisted of twenty-five pounds to buy street clothes, and twice that amount as working capital, a total of $300 at the exchange rates then prevailing. The promise, which he refused to commit to writing, was that he would pay part of the cost of law school if and when I could raise the balance. Later, it was cynically repudiated.

The launch into the unknown, however, was not what most concerned me. Neither was the problem of getting a job, for I had no idea how difficult that was going to be. Besides, I had a brother and sister who shared an apartment in Dublin, he an assistant in a pharmacy and she a civil servant, and they had offered to let me live with them until I could get on my own feet. A short quotation from my earlier book describes what really hurt. "I was not bitter at the decision that had been made so much as at the way it had been implemented, at the discovery that so many who had professed themselves brothers had, when I needed the understanding and backing and comradeship of a brother, thought only of their own reputation or convenience or vested interest. I was most bitter at the senseless social atmosphere traditional in Ireland both within the Congregation and in the entire community which branded as rejects if not as reprobates all who, in such ways as I, had experienced such things as I. The philosopher endures his neighbor's toothache patiently, but each knows where his own shoe pinches. A few months ago the universal social attitude had been my attitude. Now I saw it for the first time consciously, and looking at it, saw it as cruel and cruelly unjust."

The bitterness at having found duplicity and callousness where I had been guaranteed justice and brotherhood was compounded by shame. Given all the automatic presumptions in favor of those who had decided on behalf of the order that I should be eliminated, I had to conclude that everyone who knew me—my own family included—must believe I had been guilty of heinous behavior to merit such punishment. It took years to purge myself of that emotional handicap.

These were harsh lessons, and I believe unmerited. In retrospect, nevertheless, I know they benefited me. They started a reflection that still continues on the impact of structures and institutions on all we think and do. In ecclesiastical and civil affairs alike, power not only corrupts but blinds. Trickery and deceit become legitimate means to protect the system. People who live good and honorable personal lives distort their judgment with syllogisms, theological casuistries, or legal quibbles to such an extent that they can justify to themselves the destruction of innocent individuals for the sake of a common good which they believe God in his wisdom entrusted to their protection.

One conclusion I soon reached was that nobody is free while enslaved to an institution—a church, an employer, a political party, or whatever. I, accordingly, set myself the goal of achieving economic independence in order to be free to think what I believed I should think, and to say what I thought when I thought it should be said. That, needless to say, is a very complicated process, and—as a wider experience of the world later taught me—attainable only by a tiny minority of exceptionally privileged persons under the capitalist system, and apparently by none under the state capitalism to which the Marxian dream has degenerated in Soviet Russia and its satellites. Most human beings are trapped by their economic, social, cultural, and political circumstances, incapable of breaking out of a routine of poverty and monotony, taking advantage of whatever opium happens to be available, be it liquor or religion. I was a fortunate exception. My education and accompanying social status as authenticated by the pieces of academic paper I was gradually to acquire, made me a potential member of this privileged group. But even with these advantages, the process is complicated and few have the vision or will to pursue so difficult a goal. It calls for resources of income that cannot be arbitrarily cut off by institutional fiat, combined with access to media of communications, similarly untouchable, through which to express one's opinions. To achieve this situation, I had to sacrifice many desirable things. But I believe the end was worth the cost.

I cannot claim to have started with any lofty, world-saving objective in mind. My goals were modest enough and personal. I had been victimized once, and if I could help it, that wouldn't happen again. Besides, my sense of my potential contribution to the community was strictly limited by the world view I had internalized. If life was simply a testing time, and if all things worth knowing were already known, what room was left for discovery or adventure? To tamper with a perfect creation was to fly in the face of heaven.

More concrete concerns, moreover, took precedence over philosophies of life. Aged twenty-five, my head full of unsalable knowledge and empty of the mechanics of living, the need to survive came first. Of course, I was not the only one in that situation. Approximately half of the thousand or more youths who entered Irish seminaries each year left either voluntarily or involuntarily before completing the course. If they could have been organized into a mutual-aid society, as were priests in the United States and elsewhere when they began leaving the clerical structures in considerable numbers in the late 1960s after the opening provided by Pope John and the Second Vatican Council, they could quickly have become a power bloc. But in the social atmosphere, what they sought was anonymity, and an alibi to account for the years missing from their lives. A few with wealthy parents went through college or medical school, then to the civil service or a job—most likely in England. Many returned to their native villages to live the life of a recluse, of benefit neither to themselves nor to others. It was relatively easy to be lost in Dublin with a population approaching half a million, but openings were few except as a barman in a saloon or a clerk in the off-course betting shops. Many, after an unsuccessful search in Dublin, crossed the channel to a job in a saloon in London or to join the British Army, where enlistment became easier as the Nazi threat swelled ominously in Germany.

The year that followed, I can see in retrospect, was probably the most decisive in my life. I answered all kinds of advertisements, went the rounds of the employment agencies steadily, followed up the leads unearthed by friends, and nevertheless an entire year passed before I got my first steady job. The nearest thing before that was a few hours a day at starvation wages teaching a class of students who needed make-up work to graduate from high school. Their problem was social maladjustment more than intellectual inadequacy, and I was let go after three weeks because I had no idea how to keep them in line. Hardly surprising, in view of my background.

One thing, nevertheless, remained clear. I was determined not to go the way of the saloon hand or the mercenary soldier. So in addition to my futile job-hunting, I committed myself to freelance writing, establishing a routine of a thousand words a day seven days a week, and making up the next day if short of target the day before. I had no guidance and slight idea of what is involved in writing for profit. All I knew was that people did send articles to newspapers and magazines, and books to publishers, and were paid when their work was accepted. I was further handicapped by an obstacle which I identified only much later. Isolated from the issues and concerns of potential readers, I had no clue of what to write about.

Ignorance didn't stop me trying. I rehashed articles from all kinds of sources, encyclopedias, reference books, travel books, old magazines, everything I unearthed in the public library. I wrote short stories of sorts and several chapters of a pulp novel, a spy adventure set in Poland during World War I. I kept at it, even though it gave me no pleasure, no sense of accomplishment. Every line was written in blood. I was obsessed with the notion, hammered into me by teachers of composition at school, that a writer must have style. It didn't flow, didn't hide the absence of thought. I would take a book and search page after page until I found a sentence I could plagiarize or bowdlerize, and thus build up my day's quota of a thousand words, using as few as possible of my own.

It was certainly the hard way. Rejection slips mounted up at the rate of three or four a week. But finally one morning, as I went through the newspapers in the reading room of the local library, a title across three columns on the editorial page jumped out at me. It dealt with a religious event that was coming up shortly, and my first reaction was that another had beaten me to the punch. Closer inspection established my name as that of the author. I was in. The material was mostly taken more or less verbatim from an encyclopedia, but at least the subject was one I knew something about, so the editor's selection made more sense than I yet realized.

Months passed before lightning struck again, but I now knew there was no going back. A friend introduced me to the man who was in the process of setting up the Irish Folklore Commission. He liked my command of Irish and my familiarity with the western seaboard, still largely Irish-speaking and the repository of folk traditions going back thousands of years. He started to train me as a folklore collector, the job to begin as soon as the formalities for setting up the Commission were completed. We traveled together in the depth of winter through Galway, Mayo, Sligo, and Donegal, meeting famous story tellers and recording on Edison cylinders—no tape-recorders then—as we went. But he knew my commitment was to writing, and he helped me put together a series of articles on traditional practices and customs which I sold for what was then a fancy fee to a prestigious Sunday newspaper in London. It was a turning point. Before the series had ended, I had a staff job as a junior reporter on a Dublin daily.

My objectives were still narrowly personal. In one sense,

this was inevitable. The struggle to survive was all-absorbing, and one must eat before one philosophizes. But there was a more basic reason. The religion I had known, for all its high-sounding rhetoric, had absorbed the values of the capitalist society in which it had functioned for several centuries. I would later come to realize that this was true not only of Ireland but generally, and that religion had not only absorbed the values but become a valuable ally and bulwark of a system that defended the strong from the weak and that glorified greed as connatural to man and the prime mover of human progress. In any case, I was not fired by any mission to change the world. My concern was to get the share to which I felt entitled and the corresponding benefits.

A preliminary step, as I still saw it, was to acquire the bits of academic paper to which I felt my education entitled me. That wasn't going to be easy. A reporter in Dublin in those days worked six days a week, and his ten-hour day could be spread out to suit the needs of the office from ten in the morning to midnight. Attendance at college lectures was consequently out of the question. The University of London, however, had what it called an extern degree. This dispensed with lectures but prescribed a detailed study course with tests to ensure that it had been fully covered. The requirements were so high that few attempted it without substantial private tutoring, a tradition in the English university system. What was more common was to do part of the course as an extern student, then enroll as an intern for the final year, take lectures, and escape with a much less demanding final examination.

Neither alternative was open to me. Unable to afford tutoring or a year fulltime in class, I had to do it the hard way. I even had to start with the entrance examination for British universities. The so-called Economic War, on which Britain embarked against the Irish Free State during the 1930s rather than submit economic issues under dispute to the International Court of Justice, embittered all relations between the two countries, and British universities refused to accept the Irish university entrance examination which I had earlier passed. But that was more a nuisance than an

obstacle. British illogic allowed one to choose any five subjects from an enormous list. I picked five which for me required no preparation at all, Irish, English, French, Latin,
and Spanish. I was in.

The final, several years later, was something else. My
major was Spanish language and literature, with a French
minor. The minor was easy, six hours of written examination and a 15-minute oral. But the major called for seven written examinations of three hours each, followed by a sixty-
minute oral. The course covered philology, phonetics, an
essay in Spanish, translation into and from Spanish, and the
entire range of literature from the *Poema de Mio Cid* in the
twelfth century and the *Siete Partidas* of Alfonso the Wise
in the thirteenth all the way to Miguel de Unamuno in the
twentieth. On my first try, the oral examiner was English,
and he couldn't see how an Irishman isolated from all the
paraphernalia of scholarship could meet the requirements,
so he failed me. A year later, I was lucky to meet a Spaniard
who was able to judge my achievement on its merits.

After that ordeal, all was smooth sailing. With an honors
B.A. from London, I was able to register for a Master's at University College, Dublin. I again chose Spanish, judging correctly that I'd be the only candidate for Master's in that subject, and that instead of formal lectures, I'd merely have to
report informally from time to time to the professor assigned to supervise my work and satisfy him that I was
doing the research for the dissertation that was the principal requirement for the degree. After the M.A., the same
technique worked to get a Ph.D.

All this, nevertheless, took a considerable number of
years, and my fortunes had fluctuated significantly in the
meantime. After about a year at reporting the trivia that
constitute the life of a junior reporter, the police courts, a
pony show in Connemara, a livestock show in Sligo, in-
quests, fashionable weddings, sermons by controversial
clergymen, meetings of benevolent associations and charity
balls, I decided I was ready for bigger things. I joined with
another reporter to start a news agency to service both
Irish and British newspapers. We figured we could intro-

duce to Dublin a system common in many multiple-newspaper cities, under which routine events were handled by an agency, leaving the newspaper reporters available to dig into issues of special interest to each. The police courts, for example, were normally covered by four men, one from each of Dublin's four publishing groups. In fact, only one man took notes of the drunk-and-disorderly and similar cases that formed the daily docket, while the other three played cards or drank in a neighboring saloon, to be filled in later by the one whose turn it was to work. But the newsmen's union, of which I was a member, took a rigid stand against any rationalization, fearing an ultimate loss of jobs, and that part of our project never got off the ground. Our stringing for cross-channel newspapers went better, if somewhat erratically, until my partner and myself split on an issue of journalistic ethics, and with the help of a lawyer divided up our contacts. I was again a freelance, but now with some established assignments, some proof of ability to write, and some knowledge of the world in which I lived.

The experience which stands out most clearly from this period was a six-week adventure with an air circus. Sir Alan Cobham, a British air ace of World War I who would later make a major contribution to the development of aviation by his pioneer work in refueling in flight, had in the depth of the Depression assembled a group of unemployed airmen, acquired a half-dozen war-surplus planes, and made a business of barnstorming. Having covered Great Britain from Land's End to John o' Groat's, they decided to try their luck in Ireland. The advance man arranged a tie-in promotion with a Dublin daily, a deal that involved sending a photographer on the tour. It was a motley collection of moth-eaten craft, single-seaters and two-seaters with open fuselages, most of them biplanes. There was one bigger plane with closed fuselage that carried four to six passengers and produced revenue by selling ten-minute trips. Most of the planes could attain speeds of ninety to one hundred miles an hour, but there was one pusher (propeller behind wings) which was all-out at sixty. That was approximately the limit of the autogiro also. This precursor of the helicopter had a conventional front propellor but was sustained in the air by three blades which revolved horizontally above the fuselage and allowed the machine to hover and land vertically. It needed a runway, however, to get off the ground. A clutch engaged the lifting blades and spun them. The clutch was then disengaged, letting the lifter blades spin freely. Meanwhile the propellor was revved up to start the machine forward on the ground, from which the pilot by application of the parallelogram of forces slowly lifted it after a run of about a hundred yards. The pilot in leather jacket and helmet sat in an open cockpit, and a second cockpit immediately behind could be used by a co-pilot or passenger, similarly attired.

The program called for forty one-day stands, starting in Dublin, and visiting every city and town of any appreciable size in the entire country. In a few towns, a race course was available, but usually the show was based on a big field, preferably without surrounding trees or high hedges. The photographer's job was to occupy the rear seat of the autogiro, taking pictures as it flew from one town to the next, then hovering over the main square of the new town at noon and photographing the town. Each day's paper provided a coupon on which the height at which the autogiro hovered could be filled in. The actual height was announced at the show which ran through the afternoon, and the winner got a free flight.

The newspaper had three staff photographers, but all three absolutely refused to undertake the assignment. They had good reason for their stand. As I learned later, not a single member of the air troupe would take a ride in the autogiro, the pilot of which they regarded as crazy. The problem was basically that the metals then available were unequal to the stresses imposed on the rotating blades. One of them could snap at any moment causing the unbalanced machine to plummet to earth.

Caught in a bind, the newspaper's promotion manager recalled that I had been using a camera to illustrate my freelance work. Over a cup of coffee we made a deal, and a couple of days later I lifted unsteadily off the surface of the earth for the first time. There was a moment of total terror as we staggered past telephone wires and tree tops, to which I can liken only the subsequent experience of the solid ground trembling under my feet in an earthquake. But the emotion passed when we climbed to five hundred feet and I got busy with my Rollei as we followed the railroad from Dublin to Mullingar.

My experience with this group of daredevils and the daily and nightly meetings with people from every part of the country carried forward significantly a process which my work as a reporter had already started, the process of re-formulating my grossly unbalanced understanding of what is involved in life in society. I was gradually coming to recognize that I had little appreciation of people as people. The rigid division of mankind into we and they which had become second nature to me in the monastery was not easily dislodged. While "they" had concerned us to a significant extent, especially in our moral theology studies, it was in the same way as his specimens concern a butterfly collector. "They" were the object of our concern but not of our love. That was an emotion that had been carefully screened out of us. We had been taught to live and think as individual units, to maintain relations on the intellectual level and repress emotional reactions. It took continued exposure to a variety of people in a variety of situations to realize that they were not all intellectual automata, that the daily dealings of personal and business life are affected by complex motives and emotions, that more people enjoy helping you up than doing you down.

From my brief but eventful career with the air circus, I also carry constantly with me an experience which then seemed trivial but which in the course of time came to symbolize and concretize for me the way in which the exploiter in every age and clime deceives himself in his dealings with his victims. One of the concessions that traveled with the group was a mobile bookstore specializing in aviation literature. The concessionaire moved his wares from location to location in a van and displayed them each day in a tent set up on the side of the flying field. At night he slept in the tent, and we were only a few days on the road when he suggested to me that there was plenty room in the tent for a second cot. If I cared to buy one, he would welcome the company and I would save hotel costs.

We bunked together for the rest of the tour, taking a hotel room one night a week to scrub the week's dirt off in a bathtub. He came from a working-class family in the English Midlands, had been conscripted at eighteen to fight in the trenches in World War I, later got a job as a sales clerk in a bookstore. He liked to chat for a while after bunking down at night, and he usually regaled me with his adventures, mainly amorous, behind the lines in France and Flanders during the war. Sometimes, we discussed more serious matters, as one night when we lay under the stars on the edge of a more than normally sleepy and decayed Irish provincial town. "I can't understand, Mac," he said to me, "why you people (the Irish) can't make more of yourselves. If only you would give us a ten-year franchise, we'd turn this one-horse town into a bustling center of industry and business activity like the average town in England. You have everything that it needs, but you just don't seem to have the skills to get started."

I was too astonished to attempt a reply, pretending instead that I had dropped off to sleep. But I thought to myself as I lay silently awake that it was incomprehensible that a man who had lived for years with books, even if his formal education was limited, didn't realize that his country had been in control of this town and every town in Ireland for hundreds of years, and that this was the end result of that experience. Later I would discover that his attitude was typical, that for those who wield power and their followers, history is—in Toynbee's felicitous phrase—"something unpleasant that happens to someone else." The Irish have long memories, as have the Latin Americans, the American Indians, and the blacks of the United States. The powerful flatter themselves with the myth of their superiority and despise those whose inadequacy prevented their making it.

It was about this time I met in the home of a newspaper colleague the woman I would marry a year later. She was

Josephine ("Jo") Delaney, and she worked in the Irish
Sweepstakes which, in those days, had replaced the Calcutta
Sweepstakes as the world's most famous lottery. She was
responsible for the personnel records both of the permanent
staff and of the hundreds of temporaries hired four times a
year in the closing days before each drawing, a complicated
task in the pre-computer era. An ability to make friends
matched her technical skills. She was to prove a loving,
supportive companion over a long lifetime, a valuable aide in
cultivating contacts and in investigative leg work, as well as
an excellent typist and secretary when I needed one. Her
father, Daniel Delaney, was a musical conductor, friend of
John McCormack and Victor Herbert, an Associate of the
London Royal College of Music and guest conductor for Sir
Thomas Beecham. One of the most popular features on Irish
radio was *An Dáréag*, his group of twelve voices who sang
popular songs of all countries in Irish. Jo's mother, Mary
Byrne, came from a Wicklow family with a many-generation
record of militant Irish nationalism. She was the mother-in-
law *sans pareil*. In her eyes I could do no wrong.

A preliminary to marriage was a steady job, and after
considerable searching I landed a highly desirable one as
editorial writer and features editor of Dublin's biggest daily
paper. The job had the added attraction of starting at seven
in the evening. That meant I could finally attend lectures
and accomplish my long-standing ambition of studying law.
I completed the courses in 1943 and was admitted to practice as a barrister-at-law.

My future was now as clearly projected as anybody's future could possibly be. I was six years happily married, had
a son nearly four years old, and had bought a heavily mortgaged suburban home. It would take several years before
the law practice, which I immediately began, would provide
a living, but in the meantime I could continue my newspaper
work at night while spending the day in the Law Library
and the courts. Ahead lay wealth, influence, and prestige as
a member of the small group of intellectuals, professionals,
and politicians who then constituted—later to be joined by a
few business and industrial moguls—the high society of Dublin and Ireland.

A telephone call less than a year later started a process which put me on a radically different course. Again, the series of coincidences was little short of incredible. An old daily newspaper on the island of Trinidad in the Caribbean had fallen on bad times, been acquired by a group of local businessmen, and needed an editor to revitalize it. An Irishman in Trinidad was brother of the editor of a provincial weekly in Ireland who enquired around and was finally steered to me as the person most likely to be qualified. I wasn't really interested, but I talked the matter over with Jo. Always adventurous, she persuaded me to explore further. After several cabled exchanges, we decided to decline the offer gracefully by imposing impossible conditions. We had underestimated the sense of need of the Trinidadians. Our conditions were accepted. I spent Christmas 1944 at sea and a few days later stepped ashore on the tropical island that was to be my home until 1949.

5

Twilight of Colonialism

Trinidad provided a previously unexperienced form of social and political structure, one I was shocked to find had
survived two world wars purportedly fought to open to all
people equal access to political and economic opportunity.
As a citizen of the country that had been England's first col-
ony, a country then engaged in what has proved an abortive
effort to escape the neocolonialism that followed the technical ending of open foreign domination, I was not ignorant of
the reality of traditional imperialism. My reading had also
included considerable literature about the colonial system.
But much of this had stressed the "white man's burden,"
the process of patient civilizing of primitive peoples, a process by now substantially achieved or at least being aggres-
sively pursued at great sacrifice to civilizing powers moved
by altruistic and humanitarian motives. The Atlantic Charter promulgated by Roosevelt and Churchill in 1941 had
put the seal on this policy. The colonizing powers spurred
the colonies on to greater contribution to the war effort by
assuring them that henceforth all were partners in a common enterprise.

My first impressions seemed to confirm the validity of
these claims. Port of Spain exhibited a high level of material
development, with all the facilities of a European city. Most

of the world's races and colors were represented in the business and professional community of this crossroad of commerce. In public speeches and private conversations, those I met were loud in the praise of the "mother country," a visit to which gave them status only slightly less than the pilgrimage to Mecca gives the True Believer.

It did not take long, however, to sense a deeper reality below this happy surface. A newspaper editor has to identify the lines of power and probe the hidden mechanisms politicians use to achieve their objectives. I soon began to doubt the sincerity of the monotonous profession of commitment and of gratitude for so many benefits received, not to mention the endless expressions of loyalty to the "crown," the supreme symbol of the equality of all and of the equality of opportunity and benefit guaranteed to all under this system of law and justice.

The size of the territory—less than 2,000 square miles—and a population then only half a million made Trinidad a manageable area of study. I gradually came to recognize that I had stumbled on a microcosm of the international structures of which we who live in the materially more developed countries are the beneficiaries. As such, it merits some detailed analysis. The subsequent development of my views on world order flowed logically from conclusions I reached and decisions I made in Trinidad.

The first obvious factor was the racial distribution and its function in fixing the social, economic, and political order. More than forty percent of the population was black. The word normally used was "colored," a word descriptively more accurate, since the group ran all the way from almost unadulterated African through infinite permutations and combinations with Europeans, Asiatic Indians, Chinese, Lebanese, and even some Carib ancestors. Nearly equal in numbers and growing more rapidly than the blacks were the so-called East Indians. When slavery was abolished in the mid-nineteenth century, the blacks demanded working conditions unacceptable to the plantation owners. The British government sided with the latter and began the importation of substitute indentured workers from the Indian subconti-

nent, a process that continued until, in the first quarter of
the twentieth century, the Indians at home acquired enough
political clout to end it. In theory, the employer paid the return passage to India at the end of the specified number of
years. In practice he gave instead a miniscule plot of land on
which to plant vegetables while continuing to work in the
cane fields.

Other groups were small but influential, the Chinese in
business and to some extent in banking, the Lebanese as
small merchants and door-to-door salesmen. At a higher
level were the Creoles, a group of families who boasted British or French ancestry. Most had some Negro or other non-
European blood, an observable fact they resolutely sought
to deny, or at least to diminish by sending their children to
Europe for marriage partners. Some were merchants who
assembled the cash crops of the peasants into larger units
suitable for processing or export. Others were land-owners,
growing cocoa, coffee, and citrus. A few were still influential
in sugar, the island's main agricultural resource. With the
rationalization of the sugar industry worldwide, they had
been in large part marginalized by the big British firms that
monopolized the major import-export activities, setting the
prices at which they bought what they wanted and those at
which they sold what they felt like selling.

One characteristic of the system was the totality of the
thought control or brainwashing. To begin with, I never
came across a single person who did not identify audibly and
with all apparent sincerity with the British system of which
they all proclaimed themselves beneficiaries. The household
gods of every little shack included union jacks and pictures
of the royal family torn from the gaily colored promotion
materials generously distributed by the Information Office.
The education system included no Trinidad history but laid
substantial stress on the glories of Empire while painting a
negative picture of the neighbors whose misfortune it was to
live under less enlightened rulers. That included the independent republics of the Caribbean and the adjoining Latin
American mainland, as well as the inhabitants of the
French, Dutch and United States islands. The claim that the

British had done more for their colonies than the other imperial powers was flagrantly absurd as far as the Dutch possessions were concerned, at least, but even those few who had an opportunity to see for themselves never breathed a suspicion on their return. Even had they wanted to, they lacked any vehicle to express themselves. The press—as I quickly discovered—reflected faithfully the position of the colonial administration and of the business interests who owned it. If some business interests had views different from those of the Governor, they carefully kept them to themselves. To stay in business required open support of a system that dispensed import and export licenses, exchange permits, and a mountain of other official forms.

So successful was the thought control that most people believed they were living in a democracy. The island had a legislative council with an elected majority, and the impression that it made the decisions was sedulously cultivated. In fact, its powers were minimal. The executive was completely independent of it, both for day-to-day operation and for the career concerns of its members. The Governor and his principal associates in the administration were part of an imperial system operated by the Colonial Office in London and taking their orders from it. Trinidad paid their handsome salaries as long as they were posted there by the Colonial Office, but they could be moved at any time if one of them should create a local problem. Most of them were English and many conformed to the traditional stereotype of the younger son who was shipped off to the colonies because he was making a nuisance of himself at home.

I had a particularly amusing experience with a British civil servant, picked by the Colonial Office as an expert in factory labor law to draft an ordinance on safety in Trinidad factories. He came to my office one day and said he would appreciate a story in the paper about the benefits of a uniform safety code. It sounded worthwhile, and I asked some questions. The oil industry, he explained, was excluded from his area of jurisdiction, this being the principal industrial activity on the island. Decisions on oil policy were made in London and in secret. Trinidad had no voice in selling prices, negotiating royalties, determining rate of extraction, or whatever. So what does that leave, I asked. To my amazement, although he had been more than two years in Trinidad on this single assignment, he had made no attempt to identify the factories for which he was supposed to be drafting a safety ordinance, something I quickly figured could be done with a bicycle in a week.

He was extreme but not atypical. I knew another higher civil servant who had been on salary for eighteen months without taking a single step toward starting the job for which he had been engaged, one he was well qualified to perform, a survey of the state of agriculture. The reason was an unresolved conflict over the terms of reference under which he was to function. Survival in that type of situation calls, of course, for a special temperament. The frustration would have driven me crazy in a month of enforced idleness. It was here that I began to formulate the law which (as mentioned above) I was later to apply to the Roman Curia: the more consistent the level of mediocrity of functionaries, the more solid and longer-lasting is a bureaucracy. What is essential is the genius to create machinery that fools can operate, combined with a training system that ensures that only fools will operate it. An intelligent person will try to circumvent or short-circuit or improve, and that's the end.

The British were almost as good as the Vatican at that kind of thing. They were similarly convinced of their vocation to rule. A man apprenticed to a trade at fourteen and taught to operate a single machine would find himself forty years later in charge of a printing shop or a paint factory, operating exactly the same type of machine and teaching others to perpetuate his particular skill. It made for dreadful inefficiency, ignoring technological progress, but so long as United States, Japanese, and other competition was excluded by political control, it worked. And as long as the empire was big enough, a percentage of the inefficient output of Trinidad added to the total wealth and well-being of the mother country. The beauty of the system was that it cost nothing to operate. Whatever the metropolitan government did for Trinidad was paid for out of the Trinidad revenues.

There was, in addition, the occasional big rake-off for those well placed. Shortly after World War II, when oil prices were rising rapidly as wartime controls were eased, pressures developed to revise the agreements under which the company paid a few cents a barrel in royalties to the Trinidad exchequer. The negotiations were conducted in secret in London between the directors of the British-owned company and the British Governor of Trinidad, and he came back to announce with great fanfare that he had won for the Trinidadians an enormous improvement in terms, while refusing to divulge the basis on which agreement had been reached. The reality was that the agreement was plain highway robbery. It was in the tradition of the agreement then and for several years longer in force in Iran (then Persia), under which the British navy—the world's biggest—was entitled to refuel at all times without paying anything at all for the wealth it pumped from Iran's soil.

Nobody, however, discussed such issues in Trinidad, and few had any idea of what was really happening. Normally, people cooperated because their livelihood and upward mobility depended on conspicuous loyalty. But the system had teeth also. I was not long on the island when the head of the Information Office came to visit. He was a black Trinidadian personally well disposed toward me. More than once he went out of his way to keep me out of trouble. But this visit was official. I could be put in jail, he told me, for an item I had published in that morning's newspaper. I looked at the item, then expressed my astonishment. It was a straightforward report of a speech—a rather fiery speech—to oil industry workers by a trades union leader. The laws of democratic states as I had hitherto known them, I said, fully protected a newspaper that gave a fair account of a public speech. But not in Trinidad, as my friend quickly demonstrated. The penal code, as written and as applied by the courts, made some of the speaker's remarks subversive of public order and calculated to stir racial discord. The police wouldn't move against the speaker, a known firebrand who reached only a few people around him. By giving his words national impact, the newspaper editor placed himself in jeopardy. After that, I spent more time studying the criminal code.

The government's partisan support of business quickly surfaced in emergencies. Once, after protracted negotiations, the Port-of-Spain dock workers struck. With rapidly rising prices and the post-war shipping boom, their demands were modest. The employers, nevertheless, including United States firms that had a share of the shipping business because of United States military bases in Trinidad, simply refused to negotiate. Within a week, as shipping accumulated in the bay, the Governor declared an emergency. The British army occupied the docks and moved the cargo, although there was absolutely no food shortage or other crisis. The strike collapsed, many of the dockers losing their jobs to newcomers from the reservoir of unemployed.

That experience gave me an insight into an issue of labor organization still hotly contested all over Latin America, with U.S. business, the open and covert agencies of the U.S. government, and the AFL-CIO all on one side, and most Latin American workers on the other.

Trade unions, the argument goes, should limit themselves to getting for the worker the best possible wages and working conditions, remaining neutral in politics, or at least avoiding a primary political role. Here they offer the example of the United States, where organized labor's situation is the envy of workers all over the world because it concentrates on its own technical problems and leaves politics to politicians. Union deals with political parties are pragmatic. They support friendly candidates rather than parties en masse, and leave their members free to make their own political decision. The rationale is that government is neutral as between capital and labor and should be encouraged to stay so, thus enabling labor to make its own deals with capital as one equal with another.

Whatever merit that argument may have in the United States, where organized labor has clout, it is inapplicable to the situation I knew in Trinidad, or indeed to that in any of the countries now known as the Third World. Its basic fallacy is the assumption of a relative balance between the demand for labor and the available supply. The characteristic of the economy in Trinidad—as in similar countries—is an enormous oversupply of potential workers living in such conditions of ignorance and destitution that they will take any work offered them at any wage. Lacking all economic leverage, the union organizer does not negotiate as an equal. He must begin much further back on the difficult process of persuading the more intelligent and more daring workers to build themselves some political power as an essential preliminary to the bargaining process. Equally fallacious is the other assumption that the government is an impartial arbiter. Governments are creatures of power. A group in society that monopolizes power monopolizes the government.

Even for the United States, the argument omits many factors. It overlooks labor's bitter and violent struggle for the right to organize, a struggle in which farm workers and others are still engaged. In addition, it assumes an equality of bargaining power, with an impartial arbiter representing the general good, neither of which factors is present. Capitalist economic theory holds that labor gets its fair share when workers' wages equal their contribution to the product, the balance of the benefit going to management and capital in the proportion of the contribution of each. Marxist theory would reject this starting point, claiming that capital is wealth created by the workers and unjustly taken from them. But even on the former basis, the United States worker has never achieved his fair return since the Great Depression of 1929, while capital has always received more than its fair return. For thirty years, up to 1960, labor slowly won back a part of what it had lost, but after 1960 it ceased to improve its position further, although it was still about a third below its "fair return." Capital, on the contrary, has continued to increase its disproportionate share. Its actual return in 1960 was 51 percent above fair return, and five years later it had raised that percentage to 62. By the 1980s, labor's bargaining power was down to vanishing point in most areas of the U.S. economy.

Before I leave Trinidad, let me summarize my experience. The city that provided my first impression was indeed a modern town with paved streets in good condition, traffic lights, courteous policemen. It was well lighted at night, graced with spacious parks, a magnificent racecourse, well-stocked shops, beautiful homes, abundant running water, neat lawns, and spectacular flowering trees. It was a town of stone and steel, with heavily protected police and military barracks strategically distributed. But it was a town of ten thousand inhabitants, whereas the total urban population was a hundred thousand. The other ninety thousand lived in huts and shacks piled on top of each other in the neighboring hills. These were places of ill-fame and ill-repute, without running water or garbage collections. At three in the morning the people began their daily trek to the edge of town to stand in line for a can of water drawn from the stoup. If they delayed until the town people began to shower at six, they would have no water that day. Supply lines and pressures had been planned to serve the town, not the hillsides.

The distribution of property and benefit found in Port-of-Spain was repeated throughout the island. In the center the best land produced and exported the island's traditional wealth, sugar, on huge British-owned estates. In the oil-bearing south, tens of thousands of acres were held and fenced off by companies, then mostly British and all foreign, the land unused except for the drills and pumps, and the pipe lines leading to the ports and tankers. Apart from a few who had steady jobs as oilfield or sugarmill workers, the peasants lived on poorly paid seasonal work and grew what food they could on land unsuited to the great god, sugar.

Who, then, were the eulogists of the system who had surrounded me on my first arrival? They were the small minority needed to maintain the system and speed the flow of profits back to the metropolis. They were teachers, doctors, dentists, lawyers, policemen, small merchants and shopkeepers, truck and bus drivers, all the intermediate layers between the colonizers who controlled big business and held in their hands the reins of government and the dispossessed masses.

Self-important as this group was, an unbridgeable gulf separated it from the upper crust, the inner circle of decision makers sent out from the homeland to make the political and economic decisions and to ensure that the society would remain stable, hierarchical, submissive, and loyal. To "go up" to England to be educated gave enormous prestige to one of the Herodians, but not even a doctorate from Oxford or membership of the Inner Bar altered the ultimate reality. The system was summed up for me once by an Englishman who had spent thirty years in the colonial civil service, ending up as head of the Government Printing Office and awarded the M.B.E. for his merits. He had left school at fourteen to become apprenticed to the printing trade, and reached the top by bureaucratic attrition. "In all those years," he boasted to me in an expansive moment, "I never had one of 'them' sit on my balcony." Entertainment for cocktails on one's balcony was the most common and least formal method of social exchange. What the retired printer was telling me was that no Trinidadian could hope to achieve his social status.

In this he was typical not only of the semi-educated misfits sent by Britain to lord over its colonies but of the mentality of colonizers generally, a mentality still common among United States businessmen overseas. Frantz Fanon described it in *The Wretched of the Earth* as he had seen it in his native Martinique. The colonizer, he wrote, is psychologically forced in defense of his own reality as a person, never to go behind the façade of civilization in which he lives in his fortress town surrounded by sycophants. His contacts are only with his own and within the stockades he has built to protect himself from an undefined and unanalyzed area of irrationality out there in the slums and the countryside, of a mass which can ultimately be controlled only by force, by the force which he keeps in the background but at his arbitrary command. Meanwhile, he is careful to keep reminding this irrational mass that force adequate to crush it is never far away. It is visible in a score of stylized expressions, the Changing of the Guard at the Governor's Palace, the military pageants, the overflights of warplanes, the regular replacement of one regiment from the metropolis by another, the fleet showing the flag, the quick introduction of re-

inforcements at the first suspicion of disturbance, the proc-
lamation of emergency and use of the military to break
strikes.

The colonizer knew why his solid town and good life differed from those miserable hovels. The native was lazy, un-
reliable, untrustworthy, incapable of making his own decisions or ruling himself. It would take generations to
incorporate civilized values needed for autonomy. The colonizers seemed unaware that their structures prevented the
native from acquiring their expertise in administration and
political decision-making; the so-called legislative council a
front for the imported Governor and packed with his yes-
men, higher education limited to technical skills they could
profitably use without endangering the political control.

Attitudes remained unchanged in the years that followed
World War II. The typical colonizers were as unrepentant
as Churchill in his pathetic insistence that he would not pre-
side over the dismemberment of the British Empire. They
made no preparations for the inevitable change that swept
them away in the 1950s and the 1960s, seeking rather—like
the Belgians in the Congo—to ensure a vacuum of political
organization and power. No matter what the final outcome
of this decolonizing process, history will not absolve those
who could have facilitated it, yet failed to do so.

The churches shared the racist attitudes of the colonizers.
In principle, the churches of the Anglican community in the
British colonies of the Caribbean and the adjoining mainland
were autonomous and elected their own bishops. That, however, wasn't how it worked in practice. When the diocese of
Trinidad fell vacant, the bishops met and voted to authorize
the Archbishop of Canterbury to name a successor. Needless to say, he was English. The Roman Catholic situation
was not less curious. The French missionaries of earlier
times had been replaced by Irish, with Colonial Office approval, about the turn of the century. The Irish priests as individuals tended to be more sympathetic to the have-nots and
to encourage charitable activities and development of cooperatives for their benefit. But as an institution they benefited the foreign oppressor, just as the missionaries had

done in China, in India, in Africa, and elsewhere in politically or economically dependent parts of the world. They provided the educational substructure needed to maintain the system. They preached a gospel of submission to constituted authority. They participated in all the functions designed to legitimate the oppressive institutions. And they believed—and implemented their belief in practice—that only they had a true understanding of the message of Christianity, and that many generations must still pass before the decision-making processes could be safely entrusted to people who were still only a short step from barbarism.

As I came to understand the system of which I was an integral part, my dissatisfaction grew with the restrictions under which as editor I had to operate. They were compounded by the business practices of the enterprise, practices I could not ignore because I was a director as well as editor. I proved no match for my opponents, established members of the business community, and a protracted struggle ended with a bitter separation.

In 1948 I got a job in the information division of the Caribbean Commission and within months was division chief. The Commission had been created during the war as part of the Roosevelt-Churchill rhetoric about a common free world effort to give the colonies the skills and economic base they needed to emancipate themselves and join the world comity as equals. Its formal task was to coordinate economic and social policy for the British, French, United States, and Dutch territories in the Caribbean and on the adjoining mainland of Central and South America. The staff, including secretaries, numbered about fifty, directed by a board of the four metropolitan powers, each with an effective veto on all decisions. Conferences were held and reports prepared on all possible aspects of modernization, education, health, fisheries, transport, industrialization, inter-territorial relations, agriculture, and so on. The information section developed elaborate machinery to divulgate the results, including weekly radio broadcasts in English, French, Spanish, and Dutch blanketing the territories, and a monthly magazine in the same four languages. But in the absence of significant content from the operational departments, the divulgation effort was largely wind.

I was dealing with people who had risen to the upper ranks in the respective colonial administrations of the four imperial powers, and I soon realized they shared two major concerns. Their first allegiance was to their own career. It was protected by faithfully studying and implementing the devious instructions of the policy makers at the distant centers who determined what was good for whom and in what doses.

An enlightening experience was provided by a report on tropical agriculture prepared for us by a prestigious agricultural economist from a major French university. Selection had taken many months, because the four commissioners had to agree to allocate an equally important study to a scientist from each of the other three imperial powers. The Frenchman then spent half a year in travel and accumulation of data, finally emerging with a weighty tome that was read and approved—with the appropriate unsubstantial suggestions that in such situations are de rigueur for each person in the hierarchy. Since the end result was to be translated into each of the four official languages and published, it finally landed on my desk.

Later I learned that I should have concerned myself solely with the form. The content was much too technical to be subjected to the judgment of an itinerant journalist. But for better or worse, that had not been clarified in advance. I, accordingly, made a detailed evaluation of the content. It was a shameless defence of the colonial system in general and of the French colonial system in particular. Its conclusion was that the colonies always had been and still were a heavy burden on the metropolitan countries but one they should try to continue to carry indefinitely because it was obvious that the backward peoples of the tropics could never make a go of it on their own. All of this was buttressed by a mess of statistics so obviously rigged that even with the limited facts at my disposal, I was able to show how unscientific the entire exercise was.

My critique had two results. The report was withdrawn

for basic revision. And I made myself a bunch of enemies in high places, not just the Frenchman but all the others who had okayed his report before it reached me. Well, it had already been clear to me that my career at the Caribbean Commission was unlikely to be long or satisfying. The new developments merely gave urgency to a decision that had already been taken in principle.

Quite apart from career prospects, my wife and I were agreed that we should move from the Caribbean. Our son, now nine, was approaching the age when colonial officials and other expatriates sent their children "home" to be educated. The reason was cultural rather than educational. The local secondary schools, both government-operated and conducted by religious denominations, had high standards, the level ensured by the enormous determination of the more talented blacks and East Indians to get to the top. But the children of expatriates—particularly the boys—were inescapably drawn into the cultural attitudes of the local white community, seeing themselves as entitled by the fact of being white to the first place in church, in social clubs, in jobs, without regard for ability or effort. They inevitably became lazy, arrogant, and racist. It was not our idea of what we wanted in a son. But neither did we belong to the English tradition of packing the sons off to a boarding school at an early age and having them brought up as strangers to their parents. That left only the alternative of moving to a place where we could all live together while our son was being educated.

The possibility of returning to Ireland did exist but was not attractive. Newspaper jobs at the level I had reached seldom occurred, and the more desirable alternative of devoting myself full time to practice of the law called for substantial capital which I had not succeeded in accumulating. Actually, another change had taken place which was not as clear to me at the time as it subsequently became. Having lived for nearly five years as a member of the decision-making group in society, I would find it hard to readjust to Irish employer-employee relationships, in which the employee was expected to do what he was told and leave the thinking to others. The difference was brought home to me concretely two years later, after I had moved to New York but had not yet succeeded in establishing myself satisfactorily there. The Irish government decided to start a news agency, and I applied for the job of editor in chief, indicating the salary level I expected and formulating in considerable detail the authority and discretion I would need in order to perform to my own satisfaction the job defined in the prospectus. Within a short time, I received a cable indicating that my salary requirements would be met but ignoring absolutely what had for me been the main issues to be determined. I didn't even bother to reply.

In practice, the only alternative to returning to Ireland was to move to the United States. My attitudes were extremely ambivalent. Like every Irishman, I had many relatives living there, several first cousins and vast numbers less close but identifiable. For them it had been the land of the free and the home of opportunity. Yet the American relationship to Ireland had not been uniformly commendable. The "No Irish Need Apply" was a well-known aspect. And whenever Irish Americans appealed for support of Ireland's claim to independence from Britain, the official American attitude had favored the British side. The United States refused to use its influence at the critical moment of the Peace Talks after World War I to allow Ireland to present its case for self-determination on the same basis as Poland and Czechoslovakia. In the long subsequent conflict over partition of Ireland, the United States had accepted the British claim that it was a domestic British issue. In World War II, Roosevelt had been nastier even than Churchill in his condemnations of the neutrality of the Republic of Ireland, still swinging his cousin's big stick in 1944 when it was already clear that the matter had long ceased to be of major strategic importance. Our feelings, consequently, were mixed as we moved from the islands to the American mainland.

[6]

New York From the Underside

Jobs were scarce in New York in 1949, especially for forty-year-old immigrants. The many newspaper people I had met while in the Caribbean were sympathetic, and they moved me from newspaper office to newspaper office, from contact to contact. Interviews followed a persistent pattern. The potential employer looked at my resumé, saw the Caribbean and fluent Spanish, immediately categorized me as a Latin American expert. Now, as I soon learned, in the United States one is permitted only one specialization. It matters little what it is. Sooner or later a buyer appears for every specialization, however esoteric. But a specialization excludes its holder from other activity. So here was I a Latin American expert, although my expertise in Latin American affairs was minimal, and nobody was buying Latin Americanists in the New York news business just then. The Korean War was still a year away. Television was playing havoc with newspaper advertising. Newspapers weren't even replacing those who retired or left.

The need to survive embarked me on a course I would otherwise not have considered, a course that radically altered my life's direction. At conventions in Latin America, I had met the editor of New York's small Spanish language daily. Having nothing better to do, I dropped in one day to say hello. By pure chance, I had come at a moment of crisis. The rapid growth of New York's Spanish-speaking population had sparked a second daily. New machinery and fresh ideas were developing a product that was cutting deep into the sales and profits of a former monopoly. Increasing the pressure, the newcomer decided to start a Sunday edition, and the owners of my friend's paper realized that to survive it must follow suit. However, they were unable or unwilling to invest additional capital, and the composing room was already over-extended by the demands of six issues a week. The identified need was for a specialist to plan greater coordination and more efficient use of equipment and personnel both in the composing room and in the news room: in other words, to raise productivity by a sixth without anybody noticing it.

The job wasn't really difficult. In six months the new rhythm was self-sustaining. But by then I had learned another fact of New York life. Each segment of the subculture has its own wage scale, a scale designed to buy labor at the bottom efficient price. For the Spanish-speaking, that involves living at levels that must be seen to be believed. In our newsroom were lawyers, university professors, and other professionals forced—usually for political reasons—to leave their homelands. One had been a cabinet minister of the Republican Government of Spain which Franco had overthrown in the late 1930s. But deficient English and lack of the skills New York esteems made them effectively unemployable outside the subculture. And the distressing discovery I had made was that I was being paid some 25 percent more than they were. My salary was $115 a week, far below my own calculation of the minimum needed to live modestly in New York, where my unfurnished apartment was costing $106 a month. The emergency that had led to my hiring justified my wages while it lasted. The routines I had introduced could be maintained by someone on a much lower salary. I could, in consequence, look forward to a pink slip in my envelope any Friday.

The circulation war with our competitor was, however, still on, and we were losing. From an average daily circulation of thirteen or fourteen thousand over a number of years, we were down to ten thousand when the Sunday edition started and we lost another thousand in subsequent months. I went to management, suggested a colleague to replace me as Sunday editor, and offered to tackle the now critical problem of circulation. The salary was the same, but I had a breathing space while I searched for an alternative, a search that ended nine months later with a more secure and somewhat better paying job as editor of monthly magazines in Spanish and Portuguese. Meanwhile I learned more about New York than many do in a lifetime there.

To sell a product, you have to know who buys it, why, and where. Each major New York newspaper had its own distribution organization, but the dozens of small dailies and weeklies in Italian, Spanish, German, Yiddish, Russian, U-kranian, Greek, and other languages contracted the work to independent operators. By the time I came on the scene, one organization had established an effective monopoly for the boroughs of Manhattan, Brooklyn, and the Bronx, the areas containing most of the estimated 600,000 Spanish speakers who were our potential readers. It was located in the heart of the Jewish Lower East Side, within walking distance of my office on Canal Street, a busy center of sweat factories, outlet stores, and warehouses between Chinatown and the Little Italy that clustered around Mulberry Street. The distributing organization was one hundred percent Jewish, as were the vast majority of the newsstands they serviced. The bosses had started as newsstand workers and fought their way to the top in one of New York's toughest jungles. Probably no group in New York's chequered subcultures, not even the Irish, has been as thoroughly enshrined in literature as the East Side Jews, most of them Eastern Europeans, escapees from pogroms and humiliations to become entrapped in a whole new net of disadvantages in a strange environment, yet endowed with a resilience that broke through all obstacles.

These characters were tough, and they gave me a tough time. We were entitled to check their records to see where they distributed the newspaper each day, how many copies per stand, how many unsolds. But nobody had ever checked systematically, as I began to do. They thought I was questioning their bookkeeping, though my purpose was quite different. They were placing copies in some thirteen hundred locations in the three boroughs, and I was assembling a language map of New York to determine where to concentrate efforts and where to ignore. That involved visiting every single one of those locations, talking to the vendor, studying the flow of traffic past his stand, urging him to increase or cut the order as the situation indicated. I guess I earned their respect for sticking it out against all the obstacles they put in my way, because the attitudes gradually changed as two things became clear: one, that I was on the level; and two, that the success of my methods was confirmed by rising sales and falling returns.

Getting to know who our readers were in such areas as Spanish Harlem and some of the tough sections of Brooklyn was a still more traumatic and informative experience. In Trinidad, I had myself been an expatriate, an outsider enjoying the benefits and status accorded the white overlords. Even if I never fully accepted the propriety and inevitability of the differences between the system's beneficiaries and its victims, I was primarily an observer, the white liberal dogooder whose commitment seldom survives the test of reality and which indeed is seldom put to that test. Now I was seeing things differently in two ways. The Puerto Ricans who were crowded into these fetid slums were American citizens supposed to enjoy equal access to all the benefits of the society, equal education, equal job opportunity, equal provision of such social services as street maintenance, lighting, sanitation. In addition, I was coming to recognize—at least partially—that my own prospects were related to theirs, that my economic rewards were a function of my participation in this subculture.

There was still, of course, the ubiquitous explanation that the poor are poor because they are lazy, incompetent, lacking in ambition, or simply like the life they lead. I had enough direct experience of working with blacks and East Indians in Trinidad to know that this rationalization is nonsense. The close relationships I established with many people trapped in the Spanish-speaking subculture of New York led me to a further enlightenment, which like all generalizations is only a generalization, yet one that expresses a profound truth. The poor work harder than the rich for less reward, and the very poor must work day and night simply to survive.

Our apartment was in a racially mixed neighborhood on the west side of Central Park, a few blocks from 110th Street, the southern edge of Harlem. We lived in a parish that had been almost entirely Irish a generation earlier but in which more than half the people who would identify themselves as Catholic, if asked, were now Puerto Ricans. My awareness of the existence of this enormous Puerto Rican population around me was a by-product of the language map I had put together as a tool in my promotion work. I had learned to identify the food stores, the eating places, the clubs, and the storefront churches, the density of which gave a good idea of the proportion of Puerto Ricans in each sector of the city. It was common knowledge that the overwhelming majority of Puerto Ricans were baptized Catholics and regarded themselves as Catholics. But there was an extraordinary anomaly. One almost never saw a Puerto Rican in the parish church. It had the usual parish plant, a grade school, parish hall and substantial office and residential buildings, and it still carried on as it had done when the parish was completely Irish.

As I went my rounds, I found the same pattern in other areas with heavy concentrations of Puerto Ricans. And when I expressed surprise to some of the clergy, they had their answer. The church door is open. Everyone is welcome. They know their obligation to attend Mass. If they don't live up to it, that's their problem. Over the previous decade, some half million Puerto Ricans had settled in New York, but the archdiocese continued on its way almost as though they didn't exist. An office for the Spanish-speaking had recently been created in the Chancery, and a few churches—one on 14th Street and one or two in Harlem— provided some services in Spanish. But the parish in which I

lived was typical. It was the melting-pot philosophy at its
crudest. If they want to melt into us and accept our ways,
we won't raise any objection.

I refused to believe that no Puerto Ricans were interested
in their religion, and I decided to investigate further with
the idea of developing some features to help sell the newspaper. Through the office for the Spanish speaking at the
Chancery I established contact with a young priest who had
recently arrived from his native Europe and had already
embarked on the task of making the archdiocese conscious of
its obligations to the latest wave of migrants, the Puerto Ricans, a task that would occupy him for a decade and lead to a
broader involvement of and challenge to the church in the
United States in its missionary approaches and perspectives. He was Ivan Illich, and it was his good fortune or genius to make a profound impression on Cardinal Spellman. He
had already begun to develop the radical criticism of church
structures and practices which in later years had a worldwide resonance. I still possess the copy he gave me of what
must have been one of his first formulations of his theories,
written in a complicated, closely-reasoned style that demanded a high level of concentration and cooperation from
the reader. It was called "Missionary Poverty" and it re-
minded me in its basic thrust—though not in its style—of one
of the most moving and important documents ever penned
by a missionary, St. Patrick's Letter to Coroticus. Patrick,
interestingly enough, saw himself in relation to the Irish to
whom he has been called to minister in somewhat the same
position as was Illich vis-à-vis the Puerto Ricans, one who
had the advantages of superior education and membership
of a privileged group. "I, a Roman citizen, gave up my status," wrote Patrick. "I made myself a barbarian so that I
could bring the barbarians to a knowledge and love of
Christ."

In a similar vein, Illich insisted that the missionary had to
divest himself of his own culture and incorporate himself
into that of the people to whom he ministers. It ran counter
to the whole practice of the Christian missions in Asia and
Africa during the long colonial period that was just ending,

and it was completely foreign to the presuppositions of New York's Irish pastors. Illich, nevertheless, succeeded in starting a radical change, persuading Cardinal Spellman to send half his newly ordained priests each year for a six-month course in Puerto Rico, three months' intensive study of the language and culture followed by three months' work in a parish. The impact, understandably, varied from person to person, but over a number of years the change in parish routine in New York was impressive.

Not less curious than the absence of Puerto Ricans from Catholic churches in New York was their flocking to the so-called store-front churches. In every neighborhood with any significant Puerto Rican population, one of their number would rent an empty store or basement and set himself up as a preacher. Some of the preachers got a summary theological education in a fundamentalist seminary. Others simply took the Bible and began to declaim and interpret it to their liking. All the participants were actively involved, with singing of hymns and public confessions of sins. The atmosphere was strikingly different from the silent congregation in a Catholic church watching a priest speak words only he understood (if he understood), his back to them. I was lucky to meet a young Chilean Jesuit priest, a graduate student in sociology at Fordham University, while he was studying the phenomenon, the only such study I know. Renato Poblete was to become well known in Latin American church circles as a theoretician for the Christian Democrats who came to power in Chile under Eduardo Frei in 1964. His halo was somewhat dimmed later—whether rightly or wrongly history may some day reveal—because of revelation of CIA covert support for organizations with which he was associated.

Renato, in any case, as a student at Fordham adopted the dress and manner of the typical store-front churchgoer and learned a great deal about the motivations and results. The basic cause of the phenomenon, he concluded, was *anomie*, the breakdown of traditional norms and values and the consequent sense of helplessness and terror that results when people—especially those with little education or other prepa-

ration—are uprooted from a fixed society and cast adrift in a
hostile milieu. The individualistic religion offered imperson-
ally in a strange language in the typical Catholic church in
New York provided no meaning for them in this condition.
But the preacher who talked to them at their own level in
their own language, offering them assurance of salvation
and a loving community, filled the emotional void. He made
them feel important by urging them to participate, so that
quickly they began to devote their major efforts in life to activities associated with their new community, visiting the
sick, helping those in difficulties, staying away from rum
shops, and even giving up the extraconjugal sexual activities which had been an integral part of their home culture.

   Although New York is probably the place in which the
store-front church solution for anomie was most openly recognized, the phenomenon itself is extremely widespread in
today's world, particularly in Latin America but also in
parts of Africa. The massive uprootings of long established
rural populations and the concomitant mushrooming of city
slums have everywhere had the same emotional impact. In
some places, as in Brazil, many have found for themselves a
solution in a revival of previously prohibited Shango and
similar rites, mixtures of African religions and Christianity.
Quite frequently, also, the solution has been similar to that
in New York. While the established Christian denominations are stagnant or decline, many forms of pentecostalism
flourish.

   As I describe this experience more than a quarter century
later, I am tempted to suggest that it forced me to challenge
injustices built into the fabric of American society. I recognize, nevertheless, that the immediate response was different. Specifically, I was quite sure that my own relegation to
a status lower than that proper to my background and experience was temporary, that I would quickly become the beneficiary of the upward mobility characteristic of the society.
The others would have to wait longer, but I still did not
doubt that ultimately they too would make it. A radical analysis and questioning of the system was still far in the future.
It would need much broader experience of the underside of
the American way of life.

My upward movement was for fifteen years within the complex of business dealings with Latin America centered in New York, my two primary activities being the editing of an agricultural magazine read by big farmers all over Latin America, and public relations for one of Latin America's principal coffee-growing countries. Both were activities which I believed advanced the development of Latin America. The agricultural magazine synthesized and simplified the latest findings of agronomic investigation, primarily in the United States but also in other parts of the world. Distribution of such knowledge was a significant benefit to a food-deficient area with rapidly expanding populations. It was helping people to help themselves. Or so we presented it, and so I then thought.

I found the challenge stimulating. The attitude of my business associates, with many of whom I developed enduring friendships, was one of an open frontier of opportunity, the particular frontier we were purportedly exploring, dominating, and exploiting being Latin America. They were satisfied they had something of value to sell, not only products and machines to make life easier and better but a complex of skills, better ways of organizing life by means of advertising, public relations and salesmanship: in a word, the extension of the American way of life in all its elements to the entire continent.

It was gratifying to my self-image to arrive on the scene from a very different background and experience and fit by my ingenuity and determination into the big picture, soon recognized by my peers as an equal. I was proud of my technical skill as an editor which enabled me to assume total responsibility for planning both content and editorial production of monthly magazines in Spanish and Portuguese, deal with the technicians who provided the information and with the translators who had to make it make sense to our readers. My content knowledge was minimal to start, my main advantage being the psychological one of having grown up on a farm and having in the process acquired some sense of the importance of modern techniques in agriculture from my father who had graduated from an agricultural college. What identifies the good editor most of all, in addition to the techniques of the craft, is the ability to identify the needs of his potential readers and know where to find the content to satisfy those needs. Among the acknowledgments of my success on that score I rank high an invitation from the head of the Division of Graphic Arts at Columbia University to develop a course on producing small magazines, a course I taught for ten years.

One problem that concerned me from the outset was that our publications had nothing to offer the small farmer, and I already knew that millions of such existed in Latin America and were in great need of help. There was a reason for this, a valid one as far as it went. The economic basis for the magazine was provided by the advertisers, predominantly from the United States, but also Canadians, British, Japanese, and West German (and more recently, also Russian). The magazine was a vehicle for selling sophisticated machinery, fertilizers, fungicides, insecticides, irrigation equipment and the like, because its editorial content demonstrated the value of such products and systems in cutting costs and increasing output. Changing mores in the 1970s and 1980s added yet another advertiser: the firms that do custom bullet-proofing of automobiles so camouflaged as not to be visible to prospective kidnappers.

Whenever I raised the morality and wisdom of servicing only the big farmer, my publishing colleagues and advertising representatives had a ready answer. Educating the peasants was the responsibility of the local governments. International business was of its nature not geared to perform it. I could only agree, without ever fully satisfying myself. I was stumbling into an area which advocates of big business prefer not to discuss: the technology of advanced, industrialized countries distorts the economy of poor agricultural countries because it tends to monopolize wealth, widening the gap between a few haves and many have-nots. Only much later did I realize that this problem is central to our growing world instability and hunger, and that we, the beneficiaries, are still far from facing up to its destructiveness.

Simultaneously, I was formulating a different but related issue. My search for editorial content led me to people in

many fields, researchers and professors in agricultural experiment stations, research scientists both in the United
States and in tropical countries employed by manufacturers
of the products we advertised, particularly those involved
with antibiotics, hormones and other chemicals designed to
speed up production of beef, chicken, lamb, and pork, and
those developing controls for fungi and insects. Then there
were the armies of public relations men seeking favorable
editorial mention for whatever product their employer was
pushing.

They were as pleasant a crowd of people as you would
want to meet at a reception in the New York Hilton after a
day discussing export markets under the auspices of the National Foreign Trade Council, or to join on a balcony of the
Tropicana Hotel in Miami Beach after a meeting of the
American Association of Food Processors, the public relations vice presidents of drug companies and can manufacturers happily signing the drink chits. There was a camaraderie
here. The newcomer was made to feel welcome to the club.
With my European background, I found the cooperation
among rivals astonishing, especially the willingness to discuss business details that would be regarded on the other
side of the Atlantic as supersecret. They could do business
with each other and you could do business with them with no
fear of being let down. Even if thousands or tens of thousands of dollars were at issue, once an understanding was
reached, it was perfectly safe to go ahead with the transaction even if the legal formalities might take a week or a
month. We were all gentlemen and traded as such.

The critical missing factor was the social impact of the
vast process in which we were engaged. Suavity and business honesty are poor substitutes for a social conscience.
These were typical products of an American philosophy of
education that turns out highly competent but morally neutral people, people with the sophisticated techniques to create a Watergate but no suspicion that their actions have si-
nister implications. I could discern no difference based on
the kind of schooling or the nature or level of religious practice. A monolithic professional molding seemed to overarch

and smother all such personal factors. So long as they could influence me (and people in positions such as mine) to believe that it was in the interest of my readers to use more of what their companies sought to sell, all means were legitimate. They would shower on me reports of scientific experiments carefully edited to stress benefits and downplay dangers. They would pay scientists to conduct experiments, knowing that some would shade the results in anticipation of upgrading from the modest payroll of a research institute to the rich rewards of company-directed laboratories.

Ralph Nader and his associates have thrown critical light on some of the techniques, but I had little such guidance except what my own instincts suggested and what I learned the hard way. Insecticides, fungicides, and herbicides were undoubtedly beneficial in the short run to the big farmer who could afford their cost and that of the equipment to apply them. But what about the dangers of poisoning by inhaling or skin contact on the part of the illiterate worker who operated the machines or later hand-thinned the crop or hoed it? Few researchers at the federal and state experiment stations concentrated on that aspect, in contrast to the multitudes who researched ways to increase productivity. And if the manufacturers had such information, it was locked in their secret archives. Even a passing warning that health hazards existed for workers who were not properly clothed and masked brought anguished protests from the advertisers, protests renewed by our own advertising salesmen whose concern was to keep the clients happy and their own commissions flowing in.

Drug manufacturers similarly pushed recklessly products that promised to speed the growth of chickens, hogs, cattle, and other livestock in every country that lacked legal controls, or whose legal controls they could circumvent, quite unconcerned that health authorities in the United States were not satisfied that they were free of danger. Robert J. Ledogar documented in 1975 the utter immorality of the sales methods of United States food and drug firms in Latin America in *Hungry for Profits* (New York: IDOC/NA). And we now know that even in the United States many products were given a clean bill of health, only to be withdrawn later as evidence mounted of a long-term danger of cancer or other ailments in humans.

Neither was any concern voiced about longer-term ecological and biological results. We seldom talked about the deterioration of the soil resulting from massive use of chemical fertilizers, about the development of resistance to insecticides, or the explosion of new pests as their natural predators were eliminated. If such issues were raised, they were quickly put to rest with the assurance that all-conquering science would never fail to find an answer. All we saw in the 1950s and 1960s were unlimited resources waiting to be exploited.

The same close links exist between state and federal government agencies and the complex of organizations and industries supplying the machinery and products involved in the growing and processing of food as are found between government and industry in general. Businessmen write the regulations governing their industry. Personnel move frequently from the public to the private sector, and vice versa. Rationalization and mechanization dominate planning, without concern for the impact on employment or on the quality of the tomato. When scientists prostitute their talents and manipulate experiments to reach the conclusions they know will ensure personal advancement, how can the editor distinguish the valid from the mirage? Lacking the data to make a firm judgment, he assuages his conscience with the reflection that the balance is favorable, because he is helping Latin America to grow more of the food its expanding population desperately needs.

Not till much later did I become convinced that even this argument lacked validity. By providing advanced technology accessible to and utilizable only by the few, we were continuing and expanding to a new area what has been a curse of Latin America from the European invasion and conquest: the accumulation of land, wealth and power in a minority, while the majority is destitute and powerless. One of the most persistent myths about Latin America is that the Spaniards concentrated all the good land in the hands of a small group of the King's favorites, and that from the time of creation of "national" governments in the early nineteenth century, public policy has sought land reform to achieve more equality of opportunity, a process significantly accelerated in more enlightened modern times. The concentration of land ownership begun by the Spaniards was intensified when the local oligarchs became sovereign rulers. Internal and international pressures, such as the Mexican Revolution in the first half of this century, and the Indian revolts in Bolivia following the Chaco War in the 1930s, and also programs of international agencies, brought a temporary halt or slight reversal of the process in some countries.

The concentration of power has, nevertheless, maintained the long-term balance in all Latin America in favor of the wealthy, the process of accumulation accelerated since World War II by rising land values and by minimal taxes that permit big landholders to keep vast areas of fertile land idle as a hedge against inflation. Actually, the economic processes at work are not significantly different from those in the United States, where since 1900 most independent farmers have been eliminated in favor of anonymous syndicates which in many cases acquired title by fraud and other illegalities.

New distortions further disadvantaging the poor have entered into Latin American land ownership and use since the 1960s with the expansion of United States agribusiness into Mexico, Central America, and Colombia to mass-produce luxury crops for export to the United States. Not only are peasants dispossessed but labor-saving machinery reduces the number of workers needed per acre, and land formerly growing grains and legumes for local consumption are diverted to beef, sugar, strawberries, and cut flowers, and such nonfood crops as coffee, cotton, bananas, sugar and rubber. Overuse of chemicals quickly depletes the land, and a further irony: output per acre is significantly less than under peasant cultivation.

An occurrence in the late 1950s gave me a further perspective on the techniques and structures that manipulate the Latin American economy for the benefit of a few at the expense of the many. I was caught in the middle in a struggle between the management and the majority stockholders for control of the magazines I had been editing for six or seven years. My support of the intrigues of management would have assured the success of their scheme. They were confident that I had no choice. They knew that I had just bought a house and was mortgaged to the hilt, and that I was in addition putting my son through college. Their confidence was misplaced. I simply refused to become a party to what I regarded as a piece of chicanery. And so one morning I was given three days' notice to get myself and all my belongings out of the office. Even that I am sure was intended as a bluff to bring me to my senses. I gathered up my things and walked out. Under the American system of free enterprise, the only employee who has any redress is the union member or the one with a specific contract. I belonged to the vast number with neither protection and consequently said goodbye to seven years of my life without a week's separation pay. It was a practical introduction to another facet of the American free-enterprise system.

Behind me I left a curious vacuum. My system of producing a monthly magazine called for the planning of at least six advance issues at all times, with three effectively ready to go to press. My departure consequently created no immediate crisis. But there was nobody on the staff with the know-how, the contacts, and the public identification among the advertisers and others whose support was in the longer run critical. It is true that in New York it is possible to find anyone or anything at a price, but I had a peculiar set of qualifications for the job required, and they were not readily replaceable at an acceptable price. Lengthy negotiations took place between representatives of ownership and the management, to which I was kept privy by the owners, and they also paid me my salary surreptitiously every two weeks while they hoped to straighten out the mess.

Meanwhile, I scrambled breathlessly to find a toehold elsewhere. A blind advertisement in the Bulletin of the Overseas Press Club, of which I was a member, led me to the International Coffee Institute, and through it to the

New York office of the National Association of Coffee Growers of Colombia, Latin America's second biggest coffee producer. It needed someone to write speeches and press releases, and ultimately to develop a major public relations program. The two top public relations men of the International Coffee Institute picked me as the best qualified of many applicants. The job paid nearly as much as my previous one, while calling for relatively little work and seldom involving office hours. Much later I discovered that the head of the office, a Latin American Catholic, had serious qualms about hiring me. The evidence of substantial writing for Catholic publications and concern with Catholic matters contained in my resumé, when translated into his cultural background, marked me as open to be swayed in my professional work by church interests. It took the two public relations men of the Coffee Institute, both Protestants, all their efforts to persuade him that things didn't work that way in the United States. Incidentally, he had no qualms about using my contacts some time later to arrange a society wedding for his daughter in St. Patrick's Cathedral.

Back at the magazine, the crisis dragged on for three months until the owners fired the management, installed a new publisher, and invited me to reoccupy my editorial chair with a fifty percent salary increase. Gratified as I was, I realized that the drawn-out conflict had weakened the magazine's economic base and its reputation. In consequence, I agreed to return only on condition that I retain the other job as well; and for several years I shuttled between the two offices which in good weather were within walking distance of each other, one on Wall Street, the other near City Hall. The coffee job grew in importance, in demands on my time and in remuneration, as the coffee-growing countries battled diplomatically with the United States. They wanted an international coffee agreement to level out the calamitous ups and downs that traditionally plagued the coffee trade. The United States preferred what it called a free market and what the Latin Americans called the game of shark and sardines. Dealing from economic and military strength with each producer separately, the United States could set prices

almost at will. What it feared—rightly, as the oil countries
subsequently showed—was a coalition of producers strong
enough to enforce the law of supply and demand.

I developed a series of position papers and pamphlets formulating the principle which ultimately was accepted by all
coffee-producing countries and which underlay the International Coffee Agreement signed under United Nations auspices by sixty producing and consuming countries in 1965.
The principle was not new, but this was the first time it had
been accepted—reluctantly, but in principle—by major industrialized nations who had hitherto dictated such terms of
trade with producers of raw materials as they saw fit. It is
that the actual price of a pound of green coffee is unimportant. What is important is the number of pounds of coffee it
takes to buy a tractor, that is to say, the relationship between the selling price of the exported raw material and the
buying price of the imported manufactures. Today, everyone is familiar with the principle, thanks on the one hand to
its insistent repetition by Dom Helder Camara and other
prophetic protestors against world injustice, and on the
other, to its application by the oil-rich countries when they
got the upper hand in the 1970s. But when I first met Dom
Helder in 1963, he was—as he himself told me with his typical humility—taking his first halting lessons in economics, a
branch of science in which he subsequently made marvelous
strides.

The organization for which I worked was not only an
agency of the government of Colombia but the country's effective government because it had for many years produced
seventy percent of Colombia's foreign exchange by its sales
of coffee around the world. The nature of my work involved
considerable knowledge of the inner workings and brought
me into direct contact with the highest levels of Colombia's
small and closely interlocked group of decision makers. It
also required me to study, both in books and by direct observation, the fascinating network of economic and social factors involved in the process of growing, depulping, drying,
storing and shipping the green coffee that is the product
traded internationally.

The arid south-eastern plains of Colombia stretching from the headwaters of the Orinoco on the Venezuelan border to the Amazon, barren and semi-desert, offered little to attract the Spaniards other than the legend of El Dorado, the man covered in gold from head to foot. The coastal plains of the Pacific and the Caribbean, marshy and infested with malaria and other diseases for which no remedies were then known, were likewise ignored except for the few harbors needed to transship the plunder of the Indies. The principal settlements were in the salubrious folds of the Andes, the spacious savannah of Bogotá, and the fertile Cauca Valley in the western range. Here the generals and courtiers carved out princely estates encompassing all the flat land. The foot soldiers and baggage carriers established themselves on the foothills, each acquiring squatter's rights to as much accidented terrain as he could cultivate with the help of an Indian wife and their mestizo offspring, the basis of the peasant stock in most of Latin America today. Introduced to Colombia early in the nineteenth century, the coffee tree grew well on mountain slopes too steep for annual crops and, thanks to the combination of volcanic soil and elevation, gave a superior product. A further peculiarity of the configuration of the Colombian Andes, involving significant differences in rainfall and in exposure to sunlight from one region to another, means that coffee ripens in some location at every season of the year, thus assuring a continuity of supply to the international traders.

The region prospered during the late nineteenth and early twentieth century. Large families grew to adulthood in the salubrious climate even before the introduction of preventive medicine stimulated a population explosion elsewhere. That meant a plentiful and cheap supply of domestic and field labor for the vast estates in the valleys. But the peasants were absolutely blocked by the *hacendados* from acquiring holdings in the valleys themselves, even though much fertile land lay fallow. The only outlet for children surplus to the labor need of the estates was to subdivide the existing small coffee farms or to squat ever higher up the mountains toward the frost line which is the ecological limit for growing the delicate coffee tree.

By the second world war, if not earlier, both these processes had been effectively exhausted, leading to an intensification of the social conflict which had earlier characterized Colombia. When similar conditions have occurred
elsewhere in Latin America, the normal response has been
to abandon the countryside and crowd into slums on the out-
skirts of the capital and other major cities. Colombia has
also experienced this trend, but there was a traditional alternative, withdrawal by young men into the mountain fast-
nesses to enjoy an exciting, sometimes rewarding, and
usually short life as a bandit. This practice had been encouraged by the two factions of the oligarchy, the Conservatives
and the Liberals, at least from the middle of the nineteenth
century. Through local bosses, they were able to manipulate
the bands of marauders to their own advantage, diverting
the frustrations of the peasants against each other and keeping them weak in their division.

The long-manipulated tradition of violence backfired in
1948 when the assassination of a popular leader in Bogotá
provoked a massive wave of irrational destruction by mobs
which spread from the capital to the entire country and gave
the Spanish language a new word, *bogotazo*. The damage
from looting, pillage, and burning in this first wave was estimated by the United States Embassy at $570 million.
Continuing violence cost an estimated one hundred thousand lives and led in 1953 to the establishment of a
dictatorship, and four years later to a coalition of the two
wings of the oligarchy, the Liberals and the Conservatives,
in a sixteen-year truce calculated—according to the rhetoric—to heal all wounds and finally bring not only order but
social justice to Colombia. My association with the Coffee
Federation began shortly after this shot-gun concubinage,
and in a moment of general hemispheric euphoria as President Juscelino Kubitschek of Brazil and a little later President John Kennedy of the United States called for a
continental partnership, a commitment of all the human and
material resources of America, north and south, to the building of a society free of ignorance, deprivation, and hunger.

From my vantage point, I had an exceptional view of what
that would mean. The Colombians who manipulated the

reins of power, and who alone spoke for Colombia through
the economically dependent local press and through their
spokesmen at the United Nations and elsewhere, depicted
the economy as traditionally based on a great number of independent small farmers, owners of the land on which they
produced the coffee and prepared it for shipment, while adding to their income by growing corn, plantains and other
vegetables. A cow or a couple of pigs provided additional income, and of course there was the mule, the only pack animal capable of carrying the loaded sacks of coffee down the
precipitous slopes.

The problem of modernization of Colombia, they insisted,
was simple. A better price for coffee in world markets would
mean better living conditions for these sturdy prototypes of
the best kind of private enterprise, more years of school for
their children, more rapid accumulation of capital by the
peasants to modernize their methods and to diversify from
the monoculture that was the curse of Colombia, as of so
many Latin American countries. With some pump priming
from the Alliance for Progress, Colombia could in a few
years reach the magic point about which economists in those
years were speaking with bated breath. In a mishmash of
mixed metaphors, once their pump was primed, they could
take off under their own steam and for ever after stand solidly on their own two feet.

Colombians are in my experience the most sophisticated
of Latin Americans, and with a celerity impressive even to
our fast-moving American businessmen, they compiled statistics, graphs, and blueprints to dazzle the bright young
men Kennedy had gathered in Washington, slick Harvard
types but sadly unequipped to evaluate the reality underlying the brilliant panoramas exposed to their admiring gaze.
The Colombians even had a project to parallel and work in
tandem with the Peace Corps. In fact, they got the first
units into training before we did. As living testimony to the
new partnership of equals, they would go out two by two
into the villages, as Christ had sent his first disciples, a
Peace Corps volunteer and a *promotor* (stimulator). Together they would dialogue with the hitherto voiceless and

powerless peasants, identify their needs, and show them how they themselves could with minimal outside help, simply through pooling their efforts and developing their sense of community, satisfy those needs, thereby creating a base for self-sustaining upward mobility and a place in the sun of the consumer society.

This is fantastic, I thought. I quickly developed an outline for a documentary film that would show concretely the first fruits of the Alliance in this joint Colombian-United States program to lift the peasants of the Andes out of their chronic poverty. The Kennedy enthusiasm had fired the American imagination, creating a public interest in Latin America to parallel which we have to go back to the charge up San Juan Hill in 1898 of Teddy Roosevelt and his Rough Riders. The film I proposed would have enormous appeal for high-school and college courses and would also get major television exposure on public service programs. The idea was enthusiastically approved, and I hired a production unit. We followed the progress of the first group of Peace Corps youth through their quickie courses in "native cultures" and in techniques of survival with intestinal parasites and contaminated water. They were college educated and highly motivated young people, and their instructors at Rutgers University confirmed them in their confident assumptions that the catalyst of American know-how was all that was needed to transform the stagnant societies below the Rio Grande, or I should say, the Rio Bravo, as they were taught to call it in deference to the idiosyncrasies and sensitivities of the Latin Americans.

Our next stop was Bogotá, Colombia, where we had further weeks of language study, indoctrination, and project-planning, this time in a single community made up in equal parts of Peace Corps and *promotores*. By now, production costs were mounting, so in proper film style, we faked the happy endings, taking selected pairs into selected villages where they sat in a hut or under a tree to learn from the villagers their problems and expectations, and explain to them in return that with their simple tools and the wood from the forest, they could build the bridge without which their children were not able to get to school, or erect a dirt dam to control the perennial floods, or cut a simple canal that would end the discharge of laundry suds or human excreta into the village water source.

The happy ending didn't happen. The Colombian village, like any Latin American village, or like villages everywhere in the world, looks simple and primitive to the outsider: smiling faces, cheerfulness, anxiety to please the visitor and nod agreement to whatever he proposes. The reality is more complicated than a precision watch. The network of human relationships requires years to unravel. Juan Peréz will tell you this is his five acres of land, a part in plantains, with chickens, a cow, three pigs, and a mule. But the title to the land is actually held by a dealer in the next town to whom the coffee is delivered and who decides what he gives Juan for it. The cow is owned by another dealer, from whom he buys his tobacco and a few groceries, and who gets half the milk and every second calf. As for the pigs, one of them is his, obtained as a piglet in return for his commitment to raise the other two. And so it goes, a network of debt—always with usurious interest—entwined with a network of human relations, bonds of marriage, memberships in a burial society, labor obligations to neighbors incurred by reason of an illness or a broken leg. And overarching all these relationships, which in their totality establish the pecking order and the social conventions, is the single decision maker, Don Jaime, Don Jorge, or Don Whoever. He is typically a big landowner, with a finger in commerce, trading, banking, and politics. He has the proper connections with the provincial and national authorities. Without his approval no cock crows. He has a monopoly on largesse, spending generously for the annual fiesta, for name-day gifts, for repairs to the church.

The local bosses welcomed the Alliance. It meant a flow of badly needed Yankee dollars, many of which would trickle down to their level—and stop there. As for the small army of do-gooding youngsters who were to spread out through the villages with their knowledge learned from books, they felt sure they could take care of them. And in fact, they could and they did. But not quite as easily as they thought. In some instances it was easy. The villagers, for example, decided their biggest need was drinking water. The project was worked out, and it was determined that all the labor could be donated and all elements except an inexpensive hand-operated pump were available.

For the Peace Corpsman that was no problem. He could requisition it through his authorities who were only too eager to help. "Let's start," he would say. "Not just yet," would come the answer from the village elders. "First Don Jaime must approve." Don Jaime normally received the delegation with open arms. "A splendid idea. I never knew you had this problem. Why didn't you tell me about it long ago? Just leave it to me. I'll take care of everything, and if there's anything else you want, don't be so hesitant the next time."

That left the two social catalysts back where they started. The village was materially improved by a supply of good water, but the whole concept of building community was in shreds. Instead, the paternalistic dependence on Don Jaime was reinforced, as was the peasants' sense of helplessness.

Many of the young enthusiasts tried to end-run Don Jaime, only to be denounced to the authorities as crypto-communists stirring up trouble among the simple peasants. That ensured immediate transfer and gradual reformulation of functions to ensure a bureaucratization of the program of community development and an end to the social objectives that were its heart and soul. All this happened so quickly that before the editing of the documentary had been completed, it was clear that the concept on which it was based had been repudiated by the Colombian authorities. The film was filed and forgotten.

To jump ahead for a moment, the Foreign Relations Committee of the United States Senate did an in-depth study in 1968 of the results of the first five years of the Alliance programs in Colombia, the country presented to the U.S. public as likely to show the quickest results. The Committee found that none of the objectives had been realized. On the contrary, Colombian governments had been enabled "to postpone making more basic reform in. . .public administration, taxation, local government, education and agriculture." No significant land reform was accomplished and there was no change in the rural power structures. The number of land-less families grew by 40,000 each year. An increase occurred in the level of illiteracy, in the incidence of unemployment, in capital flight. The social structures remained "essentially unchanged," with two-thirds of the population not partici-pating in any way "in the economic and political decision-making" process.

During these five years, in addition to the Peace Corps and hundreds of other consultants, advisers and investiga-tors, all paid from the Foreign Aid budget and many later identified as CIA operatives or specialists in counter-insur-gency who taught the local security forces sophisticated tor-ture for interrogating suspects, the United States loaned Colombia $732 million, repayable in periods of twenty to forty years. Practically none of this money trickled down to the poor, whom it was supposed to benefit. Much of it was used to repay debts earlier incurred for the import of luxury products from the United States. Large sums intended to provide credit to small farmers were diverted instead to big commercial farmers growing crops for export.

The end result was well summed up by Orlando Fals Borda, a distinguished and respected Colombian intellectual and one of the most influential progressive Protestant think-ers in Latin America. A former Director General of Agricul-ture, Fals Borda is Dean of the Faculty of Sociology of the National University of Colombia, a faculty Father Camilo Torres and he had founded in 1959. "What we actually did," wrote Fals Borda in an analysis of the Senate report, "was to mortgage the country in order to save a ruling class that was headed for disaster. It was already tottering when the stimulation came along to enable it to gasp out a few more breaths, the same kind of artificial breathing as that of a dying man who is fed oxygen, and equally expensive. The sad part is that this ruling class will not have to pay the mor-tage it incurred. It will be paid, perhaps with the blood, and certainly with the sweat of our children and the working classes, the innocent people who always in the last analysis pay for the broken plates."*

Cristianismo y Sociedad, #20. Montevideo, 1969, p. 29.

By that time, Fals Borda was not the only Colombian who had seen through the Alliance, the Peace Corps, and the rest of the neocolonialist invasion of their country. Raquel Cowan, in her moving account of her own experience in the Peace Corps, *Growing Up Yanqui*, describes graphically how she and her husband were chased from the student cafeteria of the National University of Colombia in Bogotá in October 1967 to cries of "get out, Peace Corps; go home, Yankees." By then, the popular antagonism had risen to such a height that United States officialdom had withdrawn Peace Corps members from the Colombian countryside and hidden them in government offices where they were supposed to be showing the local civil servants better ways to keep the inequitable system afloat.

I had not anticipated in the early 1960s such rapid and radical reevaluation of inter-American relations. I had, however, been traveling extensively in all parts of Latin America, from Mexico to Chile and Argentina, both while editor of *La Hacienda* and in my later work with the Colombian Coffee Federation. From talks with government officials, sociologists, political scientists, missionaries, and theologians, from direct observation of life in the mushrooming favelas and in the stagnant countryside, and from analysis of World Bank reports and other studies of economic and social trends, I had become increasingly distrustful of official professions of commitment to change. The experience of the first Peace Corps group in Colombia, which I have just described, did not consequently come as a total surprise. Rather, it confirmed what had long been coming into focus, that the overriding concern of the local oligarchies was to maintain the monopoly of wealth and status, to do which they were willing to act as the middlemen, the Herodians, in the foreign exploitation of their own people.

As this suspicion gradually acquired for me the level of a working hypothesis, I began to wonder if the Latin America situation was paralleled by that in the poor countries of Africa and Asia, many of them then in the process of acquiring political independence after a century or more of colonial rule. It was not that I had any desire to abandon my interest in Latin America. On the contrary, what I hoped was that I would be able to understand its problems better, and better help others to understand them, if I could put them in a world perspective.

One curious detail that encouraged me in this direction was the changed evaluation of Latin America by political and business spokesmen for the United States, on the one side, and by progressive Latin Americans on the other. When I first became involved with Latin America in the 1940s, Latin Americans stressed the major differences between their countries. "Argentina is not Mexico," they would say, "and Uruguay has more in common with Switzerland than it has with the predominantly Indian peoples of Bolivia and Peru." North Americans were then stressing the similarities of all their neighbors to the south, the lack of the Puritan work ethic, the mañana attitudes, the need for Yankee know-how.

By the 1960s, the roles were reversed. Thinking Latin Americans were pointing to the similarity of their structural defects, the lack of capital because of the centuries of export of their wealth, a process being speeded up by the efficiency of the twentieth century, the distortive effects of foreign control of resources and of the most dynamic sectors of the economy, the growing rich-poor gaps as progress and its benefits were concentrated on those already prosperous, the rising repression required to maintain a state of order without justice. The North Americans saw the threat involved in this growing sense of hemispheric identity. Once again, as in the days of Bolivar, they put their diplomatic, military, and academic power to work, enormously reinforced by their control of the sophisticated media of communications that today by radio, television, and the cinema, as well as print, reach to every remote corner of Latin America and of the world. They have learned from the Romans and the English that the first imperial rule is to divide; the next, to keep divided. They now talk about the differences, the impossibility of making decisions on a hemisphere level, the benefits of bilateral arrangements. In Latin American terminology, the shark prefers his sardines one at a time.

It is one thing to develop a desire to study at first hand the social and economic structures of Africa and the Near and Far East, quite a different thing to satisfy that desire. It so happened, nevertheless, that I had laid solid foundations for such a venture, even though my purpose in laying them had been much less specific. But my early experience of power-lessness when squeezed out of the seminary had concretized itself in the goal of achieving such independence as would allow me to express my beliefs and ensure the means to express them effectively. That meant for me in practical terms to establish myself as a freelance writer. The few people I know who make a mostly unglamorous living as free lancers usually combine a variety of activities to pay the rent, and I started from my arrival in New York to explore the entire spectrum, turning out magazine pieces, books, book-translations, ghosting, lecturing, and polishing up messy manuscripts for authors who sold but couldn't write. The fiction, both book length and short story, remains unpublished. In all other areas, I found a foothold. Probably the books, though seldom lucrative, were critical in establishing an identity and a professional reputation. The first to get widely and favorably reviewed in both the general press and the religious press was my third book, *Nothing Is Quite Enough*, published in New York in 1953, the following year in London, and also in Paris in a condensed version. The next major impact was *Latin America: the Eleventh Hour*, published in New York in 1962 and twice reprinted, and published in translation in France, Germany, and Italy. While I had occasional success with big-name publications, my bread-and-butter magazine work was with Catholic magazines, *America, Commonweal, Sign, Ave Maria, Catholic World*, and others. My success with the Catholic magazines was due—at least in part—to my involvement with the International Catholic Press Union (ICPU) at the United Nations and my simultaneous but unrelated involvement with the Catholic Encyclopedia. As both these experiences gave me unusual insights into the workings of the Catholic church and consequently helped to further the dialectical relationship in which I live with that institution, I should recount them briefly.

ICPU had been set up in Europe in the 1930s as a professional association to enable Catholic editors of different countries to exchange ideas and increase the professional and technical quality of their publications. Dormant during World War II, it was revived by the Vatican when the UN, UNESCO, and related structures began to operate. These organizations established machinery for the orderly collection and expression of the views of significant sectors of public opinion, as well as those of governments. Any international nongovernmental organization (NGO) whose aims paralleled in some meaningful way those of the UN was entitled to name a representative to the Economic and Social Council (ECOSOC), with the double function of keeping itself informed of current UN programs of professional interest or concern to it, and of feeding back to the UN its views on those programs.

Of particular concern to an association of journalists was freedom of information, a subject on which a subcommission of ECOSOC was laboriously drafting a Declaration in the 1950s, with endless conflict between the Soviet bloc members and what we used to call the Free World, over both the philosophic and pragmatic elements involved in the right to know. As religiously-oriented journalists, we were concerned more widely with human rights, on which both a Declaration and a Convention were being drafted, on issues of world development, hunger, population policy, and freedom of religion.

Those were the days of McCarthyism and the Cold War when every course of action was judged—as again by many in the 1980s—in terms of the relative benefits for the United States and for the Soviet Union. U.S. Catholics were even more suspicious of the UN than was the general public, and the Catholic press almost without exception either ignored the United Nations entirely or challenged its every initiative. The attitude of the Vatican and of the American bishops was somewhat more sophisticated. They could not challenge the organization's stated purposes: to save succeeding generations from the scourge of war; to reaffirm faith in fundamental human rights, in the dignity and worth of the human person; to establish conditions under which justice and respect for the obligations arising from treaties and other sources of international law can be maintained; to promote social progress and better standards of life in larger freedom; to employ international machinery for the promotion of the economic and social advancement of all peoples. Yet they feared that, as the UN was accorded a leadership role on world issues of right and wrong, the—largely imagined—standing of the Catholic church as the world arbiter of morality would be undermined. They feared in particular the opening up to rational discussion of the hitherto taboo subject of family planning.

The solution was to maintain a cautious, arms-length, and indirect contact, seeking to influence without adding to the prestige by official support. The American bishops sent observers to San Francisco to the meeting at which the UN was formally established, and these observers had a significant lobbying impact on the formulation of aims in the Charter. The bishops then set up an office in New York for UN Affairs. Since only international organizations could acquire official recognition, it had only subsidiary standing with the UN. With a symbolism that was plain to the male-dominated institutional church, its unimportance was underlined by placing it in charge of two women, Catherine Schaefer and Alba Zizzamia. Actually, a score of monsignori could not have done as much as these two highly intelligent, dedicated, and far-sighted women to prepare American Catholic opinion for the radical change that would come with the accession of Pope John in 1958 and his enthusiastic commitment of the church to support of the UN in *Mater et Magistra* and *Pacem in Terris*.

Meanwhile, the Vatican was busy promoting the creation or resuscitation of international organizations that were in principle citizen groups with various specialized interests, but which it counted on being able to marshall as a solid bloc in support of its positions. Bodies granted consultative status included the Catholic International Union for Social Service, the International Catholic Child Bureau, the International Catholic Migration Commission, the World Union of Catholic Women and Girls, Young Christian Workers,

Pax Romana, and ICPU. Catherine and Alba acquired an official status at the UN as representatives of two of the groups and arranged frequent briefings of their representatives to determine the issues on which each should concentrate, and who should present the agreed viewpoints orally or in writing to an ECOSOC subcommission or commission.

The Catholic Press Association of the United States, an organization of publishers of Catholic newspapers, nearly all of them diocesan-owned, and of Catholic magazines, devotional, fund-raising and opinion-making, self-satisfied in its ghetto, wanted no part of ICPU. What, its members asked, did they stand to gain from membership? Their superiority in every field was obvious. In particular, they did not want to give the UN the impression that they took it seriously by becoming involved in an organization that had formally subscribed to its basic principles in order to acquire official standing and participate in its deliberations. It never seemed to occur to the CPA that perhaps it had something to contribute to improving the quality of the Catholic press around the world, at least not until much later. In the early 1950s, I only knew of two active dissenters from what seemed a monolithic isolationism, Charley McNeill, then general manager of the George Pflaum operation and publisher of its extremely successful educational magazines, and Father Francis Lally, then editor of the Boston *Pilot*. Charley agreed in 1952 to share with a Canadian editor the representation of ICPU at UN headquarters in New York. And when Charley became president of the CPA shortly afterwards, he finally persuaded that body to affiliate with the international, but subject to the condition that only $100 a year should go from its well-lined coffers to help support the secretariat in Paris, a condition that was maintained for years.

But Charley was in Dayton, Ohio, and his associate was in Toronto, so that their presence was little more than token. In 1953, Jean-Pierre Dubois-Dumée, then secretary general of ICPU and now publisher of the Catholic news magazine, *L'Actualité Religieuse* (Paris), came to the United States and talked to Catherine Schaefer. Catherine was one of the first people I had met when I came to New York in 1949. On the recommendation of Father Raymond McGowan, head of the Social Action Department of the National Catholic Welfare Conference, whom I had earlier met at a hemispheric social action congress in Havana, Cuba, I visited her at Lake Success, Long Island, then the site of the UN Secretariat. She now put Jean-Pierre in touch with me, and I agreed to become permanent representative at UN headquarters, and to participate as fully as my work might permit, taking into account that the ICPU representation paid neither stipend nor secretarial or other expenses.

The constant flow of documents was enormous and meetings and briefings occupied an average of several hours weekly, often entire days. One of the first lessons a politician must learn soon became clear to me. A representative is only as strong as his constituency. The world Catholic press is in principle a respectable constituency. If it understands an issue within the field of its competence and concern, and if it is sufficiently interested to express itself on that issue, it can influence a substantial number of votes at the UN. But it is not enough for me or anyone else to stand up in the Commission on Human Rights and tell it that the views I express are those of the organization and of its affiliates in fifty countries, if these affiliates don't know what issue is being discussed, and consequently have never mentioned it editorially. And I was not long in office until I came to the painful realization that I was in that position.

At first I thought it would not be too difficult to establish an organized flow of information: reports flowing from me through the secretariat in Paris to the affiliates, and feedback from around the world to the secretariat where it could be collated and transmitted to me in the form of directives. The program never got off the ground. I spent years analyzing and synthesizing documents, isolating issues that seemed to me in the direct competence and concern of the Catholic press, setting up time-tables within which the feedback must come in order to be introduced into the massive and labyrinthine machinery of the UN while there is still time to make an impact. I got everything geared up at my end. But nothing ever happened. For years, often to the point of bitter verbal blows, I fought with Jean-Pierre and with his successor, Father Emile Gabel. The only benefit was the development of deep friendships based on mutual respect. They sympathized with me but they were even more in the middle than I was.

For one thing, most of the national affiliates were themselves façades, functioning—to the extent that they functioned—under the thumbs of local bishops, some as hostile to involvement in the UN as their U.S. colleagues, most working with limited resources and lacking the imagination to recognize that what happened at the UN might be of more lasting concern to their constituency than the storms in teacups at the local Chancery.

On the other side, as I was gradually and bitterly driven to recognize, the Vatican did not want the ICPU to acquire a life of its own. It wanted a puppet to manipulate whenever and in whatever direction the Secretariat of State judged God had directed it to intervene in the affairs of humans. The Vatican's concept of the function of the church press and its approach to the modulation of news I shall discuss in the context of my later experience in Rome during and after the Vatican Council. Here I confine myself to a few conclusions I reached from my ten years in the antechambers of the UN.

My colleagues representing other Catholic organizations, most of them volunteers, were people of high calibre, honestly committed to furthering the principles of the UN and as eager as I was to get their constituencies to realize the potential importance of the work. But we all shared the preconceptions and assumptions of the church before Pope John. If the Communist-dominated organizations supported a project, we automatically opposed it. The fellow-traveling peacenik Quakers were little better. And all Protestant groups were in principle suspect. I had increasing difficulty in swallowing all these party lines as I got to know the people I had been taught to see as enemies. Particularly after one intensive experience as chair of a committee representative of a cross-section of the NGOs charged with organizing a conference of NGOs, I acquired an insight into the mysterious way in which good and evil, love and malice, are distributed without regard to race, creed or national origin.

Officially, however, I wasn't supposed to recognize any of this, still less to act accordingly. The important thing for me was not to find out and express the nonexistent views of my paper organization, but to get the word—as did the other Catholic organizations—from the Vatican's liaison man who kept a deliberately low profile in Geneva. He was Henri de Riedmatten, a French Dominican priest. Most French Dominicans were progressives, but Henri belonged to the small but influential reactionary wing that saw Teilhard de Chardin as the devil incarnate and feared the slightest change would bring the church tumbling down in ruins. When he spoke, it was for us to caucus and agree how best to divide up the tasks he set us.

My contact with the Catholic Encyclopedia goes back further. I began to translate articles from Spanish for a supplement being produced in a tiny office in New York, shortly after my arrival in that city in 1949. It was, as I learned in due course, an amazing operation. The Encyclopedia had been conceived early in the twentieth century by a group of American scholars as an international reference work on the constitution, doctrine, discipline and history of the Catholic church. It dealt with art, biography, education, exploration, history, law, literature, nations, philosophy, races, religion, science, and sociology. The original editors were Charles G. Herbermann, Edward A. Pace, Conde B. Pallen, Thomas J. Shahan, and John J. Wynne, S.J. Helped by a top-level team of scholars, they issued the sixteenth and final volume in 1913. It was an outstanding work but marked by its period. The writers had worked under the restrictions of Pius X's condemnation of Modernism (1907), an action that ushered in for theologians a climate of fear comparable to that created for United States academics in the 1950s by McCarthyism. In addition, the world refused to stand still. World War I started kaleidoscopic change everywhere. A Code of Canon Law was published in 1917, the year the Bolsheviks seized power in Russia. Dictionaries still defined the atom as indi-

visible. Man had never flown the Atlantic, and not one person in a hundred believed he ever would. Neither comput-
ers, cybernetics, the movies, radio, television, nor
existential philosophy had become part of world culture.

In 1922 a one-volume supplement updated church affairs
to conform to the 1917 Code. Otherwise, reprints from the
1913 plates continued to be made into the 1950s. The reader
continued to be told there was absolutely no scientific evidence to support Darwin's theories of evolution or to refute
the constant teaching of the church that the world and
man—and woman—had been formed precisely as Genesis described the events. Not only were the language, style, and
concerns those of other days, but the questions answered
were no longer the questions being asked.

The original plans to issue regular supplements failed to
materialize because bad management brought reorganiza-
tions, compositions with creditors, and lengthy legal disputes. All that remained was the Gilmary Society as copy-
right owner, and Walter Magee to maintain token activity
until backers could be found to start afresh. Walter was in
his sixties when I knew him. He had joined the organization
as a youth and reached the top by surviving. After World
War II, he began a second supplement in loose-leaf form,
with enthusiastic but inexperienced writers and no ability to
handle translators or copy methodically. Soon I was busy
producing order from the chaos on his desk, cutting the hundred thousand words from an enthusiastic German missionary in Japan to twenty thousand, composing articles on the
religious, social, cultural, and economic life of the United
States from 1922 to date, a task for which I was ideally unequipped. After later work for several major encyclopedias
and reference books I felt a little better. My preparation
was about par for this course—a sweat-shop, production-line
subsection of publishing that depends on high-powered
salesmen to dispose of inferior materials. Walter's trouble
was that he had no high-powered salesmen.

Invited to join the board of the Gilmary Society, I pushed
forcefully the search for a sponsor in which Walter had long
been hesitantly engaged. We soon had expressions of inter-

est from Catholic University in Washington, Fordham University in New York, and Cardinal Samuel Stritch of Chicago. Stritch fancied himself as Maecenas in an American hierarchy that had forgotten, if it ever knew, that bronze and granite are not the most lasting monuments. Envisaging yet another possibility, I had John Reedy, editor of *Ave Maria*, approach the recently installed president of Notre Dame, Ted Hesburgh. Yes, he said, with typical incisiveness. Notre Dame would develop an institute to produce a totally new encyclopedia, but on one condition. It would move only if and when other interested parties withdrew.

That gave us leverage. We could now press the others to get in or out. Stritch was not ready to withdraw, however. He had in fact set up a committee in his diocese and allocated seed money to do cost and feasibility studies. At that point—it was March 1958—Pius XII named him to a post in the Roman Curia. Two months later he died on his way to Rome or just after arrival. Fordham was willing to take title to the Encyclopedia and its modest assets, but would give no commitments as to what more it would do. This we decided was a negative, leaving only Catholic University. Its interest was substantial, but we wasted months quibbling over legal details. I had developed a friendship with Bishop James H. Griffith, auxiliary of New York and the U.S. bishops' liaison with Catholic organizations at the UN. When I asked him to help cut the Gordian knot, he was in one of his frequent bilious moods and refused abruptly. Some weeks later, however, near midnight one evening, my telephone rang. It was Griffith and he wanted an immediate and detailed briefing. The bishops were meeting in Washington the next day to decide on the Encyclopedia proposal, and Cardinal Spellman had told Griffith to get all the facts. The upshot was the production of two encyclopedias: a new work of scholarship sponsored by Catholic University, and a shorter and less technical one for high school and college use sponsored by New York archdiocese. McGraw-Hill Book Company undertook the production and sale of both encyclopedias and made advances against anticipated profits to pay costs of editorial acquisition and editing.

I was immensely relieved at the resolution of this problem, for I had become over-extended in a plethora of activities. Two books published in 1962 involved time-consuming
promotion efforts, including a score of radio and television
talk shows, and negotiations with foreign publishers. As
head of the Inter-American Affairs Committee of the Overseas Press Club of America, I organized and presided over a
three-day seminar at the Club on the first anniversary of the
Alliance for Progress, with the participation of major states-
men and academicians from the United States and Latin
America. I edited the seminar proceedings, the first serious
book ever issued under the auspices of the Overseas Press
Club. I was still struggling, though ultimately unsuccess-
fully, to save from oblivion the already mentioned documentary film on the Peace Corps in Colombia. I was writing
the speeches and position papers to develop a common policy for the spokesmen of the coffee producer countries in the
approaching world conference.

I was still editing *La Hacienda*, and the reputation I had
acquired as its editor for more than ten years had brought
another chore, a Voice of America weekly script of practical
advice to Latin American peasants; elementary instructions
on sanitation, for example, the need to locate a latrine down
hill from the drinking water source; how to keep bees; how
to get rid of fire ants; the precautions essential in handling
chemical fertilizers, pesticides, and fungicides. I continued
to represent the International Catholic Press Union at the
UN. My diary records, for example, that in April I made an
oral intervention at the Commission for Human Rights. I
served as judge for the annual awards of the Catholic Institute of the Press. At least once a week, I presided over or
participated in some function at the Overseas Press Club as
chair of the Inter-American Affairs Committee, the most active Club committee during that brief flowering of United
States interest in Latin America. Simultaneously, I attended the frequent meetings of the executive committee of
the American Friends of Vietnam, of which I had been a
member since 1955 when I wrote two evaluations, one for
the United States bishops and one for Ngo Dinh Diem's gov-

ernment in Saigon on violations of the Geneva Agreements of 1954 which had effected the withdrawal of the French and the partition of Vietnam. I was particularly fascinated in my ringside seat that year (1962) as I observed changes, the meaning of which became evident only much later. After several years of being treated by Washington with attitudes ranging from indifference to hostility, and being completely ignored by the American public in our efforts to arouse opinion to the importance for us of the drama being played out in Southeast Asia, we were now being lionized by mysterious figures who recognized us as one of the few active American contacts with South Vietnam and who suddenly were able to guarantee us unlimited funds for educational and community development programs we had long been urging.

For a moment I persuaded myself that this was another of the miracles of the Kennedy Administration. Later it became clear that the CIA was starting the series of events that led to the assassination of Diem, the unnecessary deaths of tens of thousands of Americans and millions of Southeast Asians, the undermining of the faith of vast numbers of Americans in the validity of their institutions and the reality of their principles, and the first major defeat in war of the United States since the Declaration of Independence.

The American Friends of Vietnam were indeed being penetrated in those days, though I will not pretend that most of them did not deserve and welcome it. A few, like our long time chair, Joseph Buttinger, I am sure had no axe to grind. Buttinger, an active socialist in Europe before coming to the United States, was deeply committed to the creation of a democratic and socially progressive regime in South Vietnam. A gentle scholar, he is author of the definitive history of Vietnam from the earliest times to the present. But many of the others were "friends" of Vietnam, because they hoped to promote the business interest of the oil companies, banks, universities, or other institutions by whom they were employed. The academicians were particularly aggressive in pushing programs of university reorganization and expansion. It was only much later that it was established that such programs in Vietnam and all around the world were part of the information-gathering and opinion-influencing strategy encouraged and subsidized by the CIA and other Washington agencies.

In March 1962, I was not anxious for more work. Still, I agreed to meet him when Monsignor John H. Harrington of the New York archdiocese, editor-in-chief of the Catholic Youth Encyclopedia, called me. I had learned from a friend at McGraw-Hill that the Catholic University project was bogged down for lack of production know-how needed to ensure a regular flow of copy to the printers. From Harrington I learned that the same problem was plaguing the New York project, the basic reason being the allocation of titles and functions on the assumption—endemic in church structures—that ordination conferred on a priest the totality of knowledge and wisdom. Harrington, if inexperienced, was intelligent enough to recognize that he was in trouble. I, for my part, was not only interested in the challenge but finally had some spare time. *La Hacienda* had moved to Florida in February, and I had declined the invitation to relocate. So I undertook to edit copy at $8 per thousand words, delivering 30,405 words in April and 44,875 in May.

By this time it was clear to both Harrington and me that we were going round in circles. I had given him a small amount of material ready for the printers. But most of the manuscripts went back accompanied by lengthy memoranda indicating the need of more information from the author, or the need for checking by a content specialist for theological accuracy, or because they were internally contradictory. An encyclopedia does not have to have a monolithic viewpoint, but it must be coherent. Different writers on Scripture, for example, may have varying—even contradictory—views on the historicity of the Bible, its inerrancy, the meaning of inspiration, the function of tradition. But, particularly for young readers, their articles must be so correlated as to make meaningful the legitimate diversity of opinion within the overarching framework of orthodoxy.

A series of meetings with the top brass, including two attended by Cardinal Spellman, Monsignor (later Cardinal)

Cooke, and Harold McGraw, led to my appointment as general editorial manager with the duty of certifying each piece of copy as ready to set in type before release to the printers. This had been the job of the managing editor, a man of unrelieved mediocrity and total lack of understanding of what his function entailed, but supported by a self-image of inverse proportion to his talents.

My copies of interminable memoranda show that several more months were wasted in reaching agreement on procedures which the managing editor sabotaged as quickly as they were made, to the growing frustration of the McGraw-Hill people. I had inherited good editors, the names of Harry Cargas, Melissa Kay, Jacky Varriale, Cathy Hughes, and Sean O Criadain still remembered with affection and appreciation. Crushed by arbitrary assumptions as to what they should do and how much copy each should process weekly, they were delighted to deal with a professional. But I did not resolve their problems, because higher-ups constantly violated the procedures I quickly instituted. After several months of frustration, I finally notified Monsignor Harrington I was quitting. I cannot be professionally responsible for the quality of all copy, I told him, because CYE has not fulfilled its commitment to introduce the needed controls.

We parted without acrimony. I had no quarrel with him other than his inability to face up to a subordinate who happened to be a member of the same club, the Chancery mafia of New York archdiocese.

Having disposed of this detail, I drove home to find my wife mowing the grass, or mulching the roses, or staking the tomatoes, or engaged in some other of the many chores for which she had willingly assumed exclusive responsibility during the past hectic year. "How would you like a trip around the world," I asked her. "I'd love it," she answered.

It was typical of Jo. The uncertain life of a roving free lance held more allure for her than suburban comfort and security. She enjoyed travel as much as I did. In fact, she always made friends far more easily than I did. I could ride all day in a plane without exchanging a word with my fellow passengers. She would get home from a short bus ride with an interesting story from someone she had met. It was a facility that helped me often in my work. At a reception in Lima or Budapest she would find and bring to my attention people she knew I'd be anxious to meet. In Rome, in particular, where we had an apartment at different times, her contacts were invaluable for me. She enjoyed entertaining; she was at ease with people of all ages, races and conditions, and was constantly sought out by bishops, theologians, and others who had tired of pasta and hungered for their accustomed steak and baked potato.

"Very well, then," I said, "tomorrow we'll put the house on the market."

Rather than a spur-of-the-moment impulse, this was the seizure of a long-sought opportunity. Our son had completed four years of college and embarked on a career that required no further support from us. The house was bigger than we now needed, and a long trip would ease the wrench inevitable when an only child launches out. In addition, I had become convinced that if I was ever to make sense of Latin America, I needed to know more about Asia and Africa, to compare and contrast the economic and social situations, the impact of colonialism and neocolonialism on programs of development.

I had no way to determine what costs might be involved, but before setting out, I was able to plan some continuing income. Shortly before, in early 1963, I had been approached by one John McMeel who proposed a project on his own behalf and that of his friend, business associate, and former classmate at Notre Dame, James Andrews. The two had developed as a sideline a small feature agency to service Catholic diocesan weeklies in the United States and Canada, and several editors had expressed interest in a weekly column on Latin America, then in the news both because of the Alliance for Progress and the Vatican's appeal to U.S. bishops and religious orders of men and women to send ten percent of their personnel as missionaries to Latin America. I unhesitatingly replied no. The column might get ten or twelve subscribers, but in six months would be down to two or three. The current interest was a flash in the pan. North Americans didn't want to know the reality of Latin America, North American Catholics least of all. However, I would write a column on world affairs, and if it made editors happy, I'd devote ten or fifteen columns to Latin America before going on to other world issues. On that basis we reached agreement, and when I told them of my plans for a world trip, Andrews urged me to make Rome my first stop and report on the second session of Vatican Council II scheduled to start September 29. This, he said, would attract clients, an anticipation that proved correct. Before long, some thirty-five editors had signed up, ensuring me a weekly net of over $100.

Father John Reedy came in with another project which resulted in a survey of Catholicism in the United States published as ten articles in *Ave Maria*, each expanded into a pamphlet for church-rack sale, and the whole put together as a book, *New Challenges for American Catholics*. I completed the research before leaving, did the writing in odd moments as I wandered through Africa and sailed the oceans from the Mediterranean to Japan's Inland Sea. Later, a Spanish publisher brought out a translation, for which the only apparent rationale was that it let him express views on the rights of conscience, limits of authority, and basic human rights which neither the Franco state nor the ecclesiastical censors would have then approved if written by a Spaniard in a Spanish context.

Finally, the Spanish edition of Life magazine commissioned a study of the Latin American presence at the Vatican Council. With these underpinnings and the $15,000 realized from the sale of our mortgaged home and settlement of our affairs, I figured the worst that could happen would be that I'd have to go back to a desk job on our return. In September 1963, we sailed on the Italian Line's Saturnia for a leisurely sixteen-day sea voyage—with many intermediate ports of call—to Venice. A few days later the *rapido* deposited us in Rome.

7

Around the World
in Fourteen Months

My primary purpose in looking back across the Atlantic was to seek clues that would help me to interpret Latin America. Were its sociopolitical problems unique to the hemisphere, or rather one expression of a worldwide malaise? If such clues existed, they had to be in Africa and Asia. Europe was my first stop simply because my need to pay my way forced that option.

Rome, specifically, was one city that held no glamor for me. I had had my own experience of the Curia's insensitivity and its refusal to recognize human rights. Over the years I had seen good people destroyed by its legalisms. Pope John XXIII's brief pontificate had opened a few windows of hope. But that loving old gentleman, whose faith and affection for human beings had endeared him to the entire world had been frank about the limits of his power. *Sono nel sacco* ("I'm trapped": literally, "I'm in the bag") was his peasant formulation of the Curia's ability to thwart his initiatives. He had died before the Council had resolved a single one of the problems he had tossed to it.

His enigmatic successor's career—save for a few months in 1923—had been within the physical and mental prison of the Curia until he went as archbishop to Milan in 1954. It was not a life calculated to produce a crusading innovator;

and what little we had learned about the secret meetings of the Council's first session from Robert Kaiser in *Time* and from the semipseudonymous Xavier Rynne in the *New Yorker* had confirmed my own evaluation that nothing less could crack the fortress mentality that had dominated the Roman Curia for the four centuries since the Protestant Reformation. I had no doubt of the eager concern of many surrounding the new pope to pull tight and lock securely the windows his predecessor has opened.

In consequence, I anticipated no significant reforms from the Council, and I anticipated no significant impact on my worldview from my work as a reporter in Rome. The bishops I knew personally or by reputation in Ireland, the United States, and Latin America gave small indication as a group of any sense of need for substantive change. Rome's concentration of decision making and its ruthless suppression of all but its officially approved views had internalized in these elderly men, it seemed to me, the narrow legalistic mentality of the Code of Canon Law.

In some respects, at least, my anticipation was regrettably accurate. At times the collective mind of bishops drawn from all parts of the world was vastly different from the individual minds of the men who assembled for the Council, and the church's life and direction were drastically changed. But to what extent Rome was affected is still far from clear, just as it is still not clear whether changes presented as structural and organic were more than political and cosmetic.

What I do recognize is that, as so often in my life, an experience thrust on me proved more profitable than one I'd have chosen. My subsequent searchings in Africa and Asia were immensely more fruitful because of people I met in Rome. Even more important, in Rome during and after the Council I came to know scores, indeed hundreds, of people of all faiths and from all parts of the world who shared and encouraged my longtime dream that it is our destiny, our privilege, and our obligation to transform our world into something worthy of us and less unworthy of the Creator who initiated the process and turned it over to us to continue.

Many of these were people who, like me, had been raised in the blinkered ideology of post-Tridentine Roman Catholicism as crystallized in Pius IX's Syllabus of Errors, Pius X's anti-Modernism oath, the 1917 Code of Canon Law, and the quasi-divinization of the papacy by Pius XI and Pius XII. Many had risen high in the church's service, had much to lose and little to gain by challenging Rome's monopoly of truth and wisdom. They included bishops like Helder Camara of Brazil, Leónidas Proaño of Ecuador, Sergio Méndez Arceo of Mexico, Remi DeRoo of Canada, Maximos IV Saigh of Lebanon, Joseph Blomjous of Tanzania, Denis Hurley of South Africa. They included theologians and sociologists of world stature like Bernard Häring, Edward Schillebeeckx, Karl Rahner, Daniel O'Hanlon, Jean Pin, Hans Küng, Francois Houtart, Gregory Baum, Gustave Weigel.

Protestant counterparts, working in a context of equality that would quickly produce a radical realignment of the Christian forces frozen in conflict since the sixteenth century, included such talents as W.A. Visser 'tHooft, secretary general of the World Council of Churches, and José Míguez Bonino of Argentina, first official Protestant Observer from Latin America at the Vatican Council. Through them I would find my way to such committed Christians as William Wipfler of the National Council of the Churches of Christ in the United States, Julio Barreiro in Uruguay, Rubem Alves in Brazil, Joel Gajardo in Chile, and many other who were already quietly collaborating with Roman Catholics, people whose names would become household words in the 1970s as they projected from Latin America to an astonished world the first major innovation in theological thinking in centuries, the Theology of Liberation.

Then there were the great journalists whose world vision was paralleled by their commitment, John Cogley from the United States, Henri Fesquet from France, Giancarlo Zizola from Italy, Benny Aguiar from India, Jerzy Turowicz from Poland, and scores of others. In such company, I could be proud to be a member of a profession in which all too often the spotlight focuses on boot-lickers and charlatans.

I am not talking about people who shared a party line or

who were identified by a common rejection of conventional wisdom. On the contrary, there was wide divergence of attitude and opinion, some clear in their own minds about where they were and where they wanted to go, some struggling to break intellectual and emotional shackles that they sensed were preventing them from being fully themselves. What we shared was a dissatisfaction with the institutions that dominated church and society, a hope that humankind would take the great leap forward that had become technically possible because of our newly acquired control of our physical environment, and a belief that we could contribute to that transformation.

Few if any of us had much idea of how to go about the task. The first half of the 1960s, in particular, was a period of euphoria difficult for those who did not live it to comprehend. Decolonization was in full swing in Africa. Latin America was assured a totally new future in the Alliance for Progress. We had convinced ourselves that the leopard had changed his spots, that the rich and powerful had finally been persuaded by sweet reason and self-interest to share with the poor, the powerless, the voiceless majority of humankind.

After a stay of several months in Rome, I started in January 1964 on a series of travels that during the next two years would give me a kaleidoscopic view of the immensity and tangled complexity of the world such as I think few experience in a lifetime. More was crammed into them than I could then or perhaps ever absorb, yet enough clarified itself to help me gradually form a perspective and a worldview that I do not think I could have otherwise acquired. Later I shall analyze some of the issues with which these experiences brought me face to face, including the Orthodox church and the Christian missions. First, however, I trace the routes I followed and touch on incidents and experiences that remain vivid in my memory.

A sumptuous luncheon hosted by King Hussein of Jordan for the press corps accompanying Pope Paul VI on the first visit of a pope to Palestine since Peter was my introduction to the Middle East. The air grew oppressive as we drove to

the lowest point on the earth's surface to cross the Jordan
River just before it enters the Dead Sea, then lightened
again as we climbed the barren hillsides of Judea to view the
walls and towers of medieval Jerusalem gleaming in the afternoon sun. The Mandelbaum Gate opened easily to admit
the press from the Arab-held Old City to Israel, where over-
anxious public relations briefers spent two hours correcting
the distortions they assumed we had imbibed with Hussein's good food and wine.

We covered a lot of ground in the following days, and
much that before had been but familiar words took on shape,
size, color, texture: the hillside on which Jesus proclaimed
the Beatitudes; the inlet on the Sea of Galilee where Peter
tried—not too successfully—to duplicate the Lord's ability to
walk on the waters; the synagogue in Capharnaum, still impressive in its ruins, where Jesus taught as one having authority. But no moment remains more vivid in my memory
than one afternoon, again in the valley of the Jordan, when I
sat on a hillside alone on the West Bank, trails of smoke
rising off to the left from fires that prepared the evening
meal in a massive refugee camp. Suddenly silhouetted
against the sky at the summit of a nearby hill appeared a
shepherd who advanced with measured step carrying his
crook as might a king his scepter. Almost immediately there
came into view behind him the first of what proved a flock of
some twenty sheep. He did not look behind. Neither was
there a dog to round up stragglers as I was accustomed to
see in the mountains of Mayo in my youth and later in the
Peruvian Andes. This was a portrait of shepherd and sheep
far different from what I had heard in countless sermons
and read in many a book of asceticism. But it gave meaning
to the Gospel parable. The shepherd does not drive his
sheep. They follow him because they know his voice, because
they trust him to lead them to rich pastures.

The refugee camp and a divided Jerusalem were but two
of the myriad reminders that the land trod two thousand
years earlier by the Prince of Peace had ever since been
riven by conflict and hatreds. Perhaps nothing shocked me
more than the Moslem soldiers with automatic weapons in

the Church of the Holy Sepulcher in Jerusalem assigned to prevent Christians from slaughtering each other as they pressed their conflicting claims to tarnished ornaments and priorities in celebrating their liturgies. Presumably Israeli soldiers perform the same service of love in today's ecumenical atmosphere.

The thoughts I think and the images that give life what meaning it has come to me—as to all encultured in what we call Western Civilization—from the eastern Mediterranean. There I climbed on foot the rough road past ramshackle low houses and stores to the stately ruins of the Parthenon. I lay at anchor one night in the Gulf of Lepanto, a nondescript enough location for the pivotal event in which Don Juan of Austria broke the naval strength of the Turks and Cervantes lost the use of an arm. When my eyes were blinded by the brilliance of the Golden Gate, my imagination peopled its waters with countless tall galleons under full sail. And it called for no imagination at all to appreciate the glory of the Blue Mosque and of Hagia Sophia, its priceless mosaics recently again revealed after centuries under Moslem plaster. One could not be but grateful to the infidel for having dealt more mercifully with forbidden images than had been the wont of Christian iconoclasts.

Later I would see worse as I moved round the rim of Asia, but never till then had I seen such human misery as in Baghdad. It took strong stomach indeed to fight one's way through the hordes of hideously deformed and starved creatures who wailed piteously for bakshish in the narrow streets of the souk where merchants displayed fabulous carpets, exquisitely carved hardwood chests, intricately fashioned ornaments of precious metals studded with gems. Here, it would seem, everything had value save the human, an impression reinforced as one saw fleshless hands protruding in wordless appeal for a bit of bread between the iron bars of the tiger cages that remain scattered from India to Cayenne to South-East Asia as memorials of France's worldwide civilizing mission. Here, between the Tigris and the Euphrates, Jews and Christians had traditionally located the Garden of Eden in the most fertile area known to

them. The Hanging Gardens of Babylon were one of the
Seven Wonders of the Ancient world. It was all desert now,
desert as far north as the ancient capital of Samarra, today
to be visited only if one wants to see the single mosque in all
of Islam whose ruined minaret has an outside staircase. Not
that staircases matter any more in mosques. Today the mul-
lah reclines in comfort at ground level while proclaiming
through loudspeakers, as he summons the faithful to pray,
that Allah is one and Mohamet is his prophet.

Such is progress, a progress made possible by the electronic miracles of our age. But all our power and knowledge
cannot restore the fertility of paradise wiped out by the fire
and sword of the Tartar horsemen centuries ago as they
swept in wild abandon westward from their bare Siberian
steppes. The desolation I saw in the once fertile crescent became more meaningful for me a year later when for the first
time I visited Amazonia. As I crisscrossed that endless
green jungle by air, I saw the giant bulldozers repeat the
history of the Tartar horsemen, stripping away the timeless
cover to wrest a few quick harvests before the torrential
rains carried the topsoil into the Atlantic and the sun petri-
fied what remained into a hardpan unworkable for perhaps a
hundred thousand years. The disaster being wreaked by the
global corporations in Amazonia exceeds that wrought by
the Tartars in Mesopotamia by the scale by which their technology and power is superior to that of a barbarian horde.
They are capable in a generation, if unchecked, of so reduc-
ing the world's daily supply of oxygen produced by green
plants as to make uninhabitable Detroit, the Ruhr, and Yo-
kahama, poetic retribution to the countries that spawned
them.

The mummies in Cairo's museum left me cold, but the
pyramids compel admiration and wonder. What manner of
people dreamt such dreams? What was their knowledge of
mathematics, of astronomy, of physics? And what their understanding of human relations that they could sacrifice a
thousand or ten thousand to satisfy the whim of one? Perhaps the Sphinx has the answer. She does not share it.

Sunset at the confluence of the Blue and White Niles at

Khartoum restores one's awe before the mystery of nature.
But there was more than that to Khartoum. The English
had here, as wherever they had established themselves
around the world, encouraged conflict of race and religion to
facilitate control by keeping the conquered divided. And as
often, when forced out, they left the weaker of the enemies
to the mercy of the stronger. Here it was the Arabized north
of the Sudan to lord it over the rural south, part Christian,
mostly Animistic in religion, black skin as contrasted with
the lighter northerns. A chance meeting aroused my journalistic instincts. The south was sealed off as a genocidial war
was being waged. Posing as a retired American business executive with an insatiable love of the Nile, I persuaded the
Interior Ministry to give me a pass to visit Juba. There the
rebellion had been crushed. The young men who had survived had fled to Uganda where shortly I would find many
of them in internment camps. In the hotel, where lazy fans
stirred the languid air as they had done for the British officers and traders who installed them, I met a Greek merchant. We shared no intimacies, for a life here hung on a
careless word, yet we instinctively knew we had a common
interest. If Khartoum's purpose prevailed, Arab traders
would replace him and a thousand like him spread from the
Mediterranean to the Equator. World opinion was his only
protection, and he sensed that was my business. So for two
fascinating days he drove me hither and yon, pointing cas-
ually to one illustration after another of how the victors use
legislative, administrative, and military means to restructure a society and a civilization: the control of schools and
content of teaching, the transfer of trading concessions, a
special status for an unknown tongue, a disregard for traditional land titles. It was nothing new. It is the warp and web
of history. But here it was more real. I was present at the
becoming of what I had read about in the history of my native land and had seen in a more advanced and consequently
more static state in Trinidad.

Nothing substitutes for having seen with your own eyes.
Later in 1964, after I had completed the round of Africa on
which at this point I was just starting, one of my nephews—

a student then at Glasgow University—challenged me, as he had every right to do. "Was it not all a waste of time and money," he asked. "An entire continent. What do you know about it after three months?" He made me pause. "Almost nothing," I finally replied, "but more than nearly anyone else in the world." The answer has two meanings. On the one hand, I met on that trip people who had spent a lifetime in Tanzania or South Africa or Nigeria or Ghana, yet had not the slightest knowledge of Africa as a continent. On the other hand, my opportunity to see and hear and smell the fantastic diversity of the continent, to share the concerns and ambitions of those who sought to hold back and those who struggled for liberation, gave me a sense of the changing reality that I have seldom found among university professors who had given a lifetime to study of and teaching about Africa.

The dialectic became particularly clear in Tanzania. My first stop was at Arusha at the foot of Mount Kilimanjaro, where I stayed with a Scots friend with whom many years earlier I had explored the mountainous jungles of northern Trinidad, and who subsequently homesteaded in Tanzania. Combining advanced agronomic technology with cheap native labor, he had in ten or twelve years developed an extremely successful business as a producer of seeds for Europe. Because the vegetable and flower seeds with which he worked were not indigenous, he had none of the problems of avoiding cross-pollination from wild plants that add to the costs of Dutch and other European producers. Through him, I met several British expatriates, all equally successful in business and agriculture, thanks to the colonial structures that had lavished on them the wealth of East Africa.

They knew they were in the twilight of empire. Tanganyika had become a republic in 1962 and joined with Zanzibar in the republic of Tanzania just months before my visit. Kenya and Uganda had also become independent. Julius Nyerere, most moderate of the new leaders, had spelled out clearly his egalitarian goals. There was no way the handful of whites would long survive in the lands the dispossessed masses saw as rightfully theirs. All they could do was to extract as much of the wealth as they could and store it over-seas before the ax fell. And they were bitter. Over their eve-ning cocktails—the colonial ritual I had known in Trinidad—they bemoaned the ingratitude of the benighted natives who were still unable to see what blessings of civilization the Empire had brought them. They looked forward gleefully to the chaos that would surely follow their proximate expul-sion. Subsequently, my friend and others moved to the sym-pathetic climate of South Africa. Their homeland, they in-sisted, had betrayed them. I cannot but suspect that factors keeping them from returning to Britain were climate and loss of the status that allowed them as white settlers to lord it over inferior types.

Hamish took me to see some of the world's most impor-tant wildlife reserves. In the Ngoro-Ngoro Crater of a long extinct volcano we saw living in a stable ecological balance large numbers of elephants, rhinoceroses, hippopotamuses, lions (who recently learned to live in trees to escape the an-noyances of low-flying flies), wildebeests, zebras, jackals, monkeys, a dozen varieties of gazelles, and countless bright-colored birds, including a species that rides on the rhinoc-eros and keeps it clean by eating the ticks and other vermin that infest it. On the Serenguete Plain we saw the endless herds of wildebeests and zebras galloping toward the end-less horizons of Africa in search of food and water. We vis-ited the Aldubei Gorge where four years earlier Louis Leakey had unearthed the fossil bones of Zinjanthropus, one of our ancestors who had been sleeping there for over a mil-lion years. My next brief stop was at Mwanza, a Shangri-La of ineffable beauty on the shore of Lake Victoria, to visit a Cherokee Indian social anthropologist who was studying the lore of a traditional medical practitioner inaccurately de-scribed in our literature as a witch doctor.

From the bracing highlands down to the steaming humid-ity of Dar-es-Salaam and an evaluation of what was happen-ing in Tanzania and in Africa radically different to that of the expatriates in Arusha. My primary objective was to in-terview Julius Nyerere, who had already emerged as the outstanding statesman of postcolonial Africa. I had know

him, as I had known Ngo Dinh Diem and others, when they
had come as political exiles or opposition spokesmen to plead
at the United Nations for the right of their people to be
treated as humans. Before meeting Julius, I talked with several of his ministers who made a point of entertaining me as
their guest at the club where until a year earlier no black
African had set foot save as waiter, kitchen help, or worker.
They were not of Julius's stature. In a long lifetime I have
met few of his stature. Some were already interpreting the
national victory as authorization for their personal advancement regardless of who paid. Yet, given my knowledge of
the colonial system from my years in the West Indies, I
could only feel elation that black Africans were finally being
allowed to make their own mistakes. They couldn't do worse
than the expatriates.

Julius did not disappoint me. Success had not touched his
simple integrity. His office was modest. He wore an open-
neck, short-sleeved, flowered shirt and neat slacks. Behind
him, a silver spear and shield. His unlittered desk was polished. He gave the impression—as he always does—of being
shy, until he warmed up to the conversation, serious as he
studied a question, then breaking into a bright smile as he
developed the answer, his arms waving in fluid gestures to
stress his enjoyment of an intellectual challenge.

He has presented his basic political philosophy many
times in speeches, articles, and books. The world is divided
into a few rich and powerful nations and many poor and relatively powerless ones. If the rich and powerful continue to
use their wealth and power to maintain structures that benefit them at the expense of the others, the poor nations must
opt out of that system. They cannot compete within it. "The
choice is yours," he said to me, addressing me as a journalist
from a rich nation. "Either you change radically the terms
on which you trade with us, so that both parties benefit, or
we have to follow the example of China and cut ourselves off
absolutely. Given the low level from which we are starting,
the human suffering involved in this choice would be incalculable; but if you offer us no alternative, that is what we will
have to do."

These are words that constantly return to my mind as I study around the world the growing gap between rich and poor. Nyerere still struggles with the dilemma. I sensed from our conversation that he was aware that Tanzania could not establish an autarchy by itself, that the minimum living space for a China-style experiment would be half or more of Africa. In spite of his efforts toward African unity, the internal divisions continue to run deep. I doubt that anything will change until the bitter struggle to end domination of Southern Africa by a handful of white racists is first resolved. Today that moment draws near.

Salisbury, Rhodesia (now, Zimbabwe), gave me my first direct experience of apartheid. Over a period, laws and administrative practices had been changed to force all "Africans" (that is, blacks) out of the city. They could no longer own commercial property or homes, or even operate businesses, although of course they continued as work force and consumers. Access to secondary education was heavily biased. Every "European" (that is, white) child who obtained five credits in the entrance examination was automatically guaranteed a place, and those with fewer could be admitted at the headmaster's discretion. That year, 253 Africans had won six or more credits, but only eighty Africans were admitted. The Catholic church had an interesting rationale for one of its adjustments to society. Only Africans studied in its Salisbury seminary. European candidates went to an all-white seminary in South Africa. The reason, a Chancery official told me, was that it would increase costs unbearably if all studied together. They would have to be fed "European" food, to which the blacks could adjust, while the whites could not adjust to African food.

South Africa, however, made such discriminations seem trivial. I could not even have gone there if they knew I was a journalist. The necessary submission of a copy of everything I had published for several years would have ensured denial of a visa. But I had my own devices. Officially identified as a retired business executive, I whizzed through immigration at Johannesburg. Within hours I was in the home of two social workers involved with some 18,000 mine workers imported from what were then Portuguese colonies. They lived in closely guarded compounds. Each dormitory had forty to sixty cavities in its walls, each of size and depth to store a coffin. Like corpses in a morgue, the workers slept in these, their few possessions stuffed behind them for safety. Nearly all were under twenty. The nature of the work—descending each day in elevators as much as ten thousand feet to dig for gold in intense heat—limited the period a youth could endure to a year or a little more. Portuguese authorities got ten percent of their wages as "taxes" and the Portuguese church also got a percentage on the ground that all Portuguese subjects were Catholics, although it provided no priests or services for them while they were in South Africa. Tribal chiefs were allocated quotas, and the young men usually went willingly. It was the only way they could accumulate a couple of hundred dollars—their net savings from the tour—with which to buy a bride and start a home. But what a way to start life! What primitive tribal initiation could equal it? Thousands of young men drawn from the bush and crowded for a year in an exclusively male group are inevitably demoralized and corrupted by the experience.

For the South African blacks, life was little more human. I spent some hours with Stephen Wilges. Aged thirty, father of a three-year-old boy, obviously devoted to his wife and son, he was doing outstandingly well for an African. He spoke Zulu, Afrikaans, and English. His ability to articulate his hopes, fears, anticipations and prospects was impressive, much more so when I later learned he had only two or three years of formal education. He was a welder, a job category recently opened to Africans and rescheduled to pay half what Europeans had earned. The change had resulted from the scarcity of whites for the work, a scarcity intensified by the government's efforts to maintain the highest possible proportion of whites in the massive police and army. The police budget alone was twice the education budget for the blacks who constituted 70 percent of the country's population. The average black wage in Johannesburg was £4.7.6 (US $10.50) a week. Monthly rent absorbed one week's pay, and an equal amount was spent on travel from the living "location" to and from work. As a welder, Stephen earned three times the average. He owned an old car and lived in relative comfort. But it was a precarious life. He had no union, no compensation for injury on the job, was subject to arbitrary firing for any real or supposed insubordination, got no pay for sickness or other absence. And firing would mean banishment to a homeland, his "pass" automatically cancelled when he lost his job. Everyone had to have a pass, but the law was not even-handed. A white had a week to produce. A black standing outside his door would be arrested, not allowed to go inside for the pass in his jacket pocket, or to retrieve it from his car if he had carelessly stepped outside without it. And if a policeman wanted to be nasty, he took the pass and tore it up. The word of a black was not evidence against a white in a court of law.

I had met Stephen through a foreign social worker who lived in a "black spot," a Johannesburg slum area in process of being cleaned out by transfer of workers to "townships" outside the city and banishment of their families to distant homelands. The government assigned a homeland to the many who had long lost their tribal ties. Stephen's wife was a servant in my friend's home, and they lived in quarters at the back. This long tolerated practice was being stamped out under a recent law that had decreed that only one black servant, without spouse or dependents, could overnight in a white home. The police could catch up with them any day. Then Stephen would have to move to a township. The three-year-old child would be assigned to a homeland, and as they were not willing to abandon him, his mother would have to give up her job and go with him. Such was the logic of apartheid. It applied even to Catholic convents. Black sisters were being expelled from the servant quarters where hitherto they had been allowed to sleep.

I subsequently traveled extensively within South Africa and had the opportunity to talk frankly in their homes with typical educated whites. One of the things that most amazed me was that I had in my first twenty-four hours in the country seen with my own eyes more of the system that retains the vast majority as slaves, and learned more from black

people about their lives, their frustrations, and their sense
of helplessness, than whites who had lived there all their
lives. It did not seem possible. Yet I subsequently reflected
that their ignorance—essential to their emotional survival—
is no different than that of most whites I know in the United
States. People can live in a high-rise in midtown Manhattan
or commute from Westchester to Grand Central for a lifetime without once reflecting on or being affected by the
squalor of Harlem or the South Bronx. Or how many in
Phoenix, Arizona, regard as fellow humans the fruit pickers
who sleep without shelter or sanitation among the orange
trees at El Mirage a few miles away during the winter harvest season when temperatures often register ten or more
degrees of frost? What I found particularly distressing in
South Africa was to meet young professionals who within a
year or two of arrival from Ireland had effortlessly assimi-
lated the system.

A rail trip from Durban to Ladysmith added perspectives,
some absurd, others grim. A footbridge over the tracks at
the Durban station had separate entrances for whites and
nonwhites, but a common pathway. On the platform were
rows of seats for whites, not a single one for the nonwhites
who constituted 90 percent of the passengers on the train on
which I traveled. I had no choice but to travel "white" class,
had the luxury of an apartment all to myself. I paid twice as
much as the nonwhites but enjoyed at least ten times as
much space as each of them crowded into cars that were
little different from cattle carriers. It was a small instance of
how the rich exploit the poor. They were subsidizing my
comfort, paying five times as much per unit of travel space.
Or, as Archbishop Denis Hurley of Durban summed it up for
me, "An inhuman streak is conspicuous in every aspect of
this country's public life."

From South Africa my journey continued to the Congo
(now Zaire) on the west coast, then north through Nigeria
and Ghana to Morocco, and east through Algeria to Tunisia.
From Tunis I took the trolleycar one Sunday morning to
Carthage. Like Macaulay's twenty-first century Australian
sitting on the ruins of London Bridge, I found a grassy hill

overlooking the harbor that competes with San Francisco in my memory as the most exhilarating sight that nature has ever offered me. Other than the landlocked bay itself, ideal protection for a powerful navy, nothing remains to help re-create this one-time center of a vast empire. It was an ideal place to meditate on my recent whirlwind overview of the debris of another great empire—the British-French-German-Italian-Spanish-Portuguese-Dutch empire—which littered the entire African continent, and in particular on the ambiguous role Christianity had played in that sordid venture. One thing that was becoming clear to me was that this role could not be isolated from the long history of the expansion of the Christian religion.

From its infancy, Christianity had defined itself as a universal religion. By the fifth or sixth century, it had substantially achieved this objective—at least to its own satisfaction—by establishing itself as the official religion of the Roman Empire and by defining the limits of that empire as for practical purposes the limits of the world.

Subsequent missionizing was sporadic and in response to political stimuli, the northward thrust of Orthodoxy into Russia as part of the expansion of the Eastern Roman Empire, the evangelization of the barbarian invaders of Western Europe by Irish monks who served to restore the politico-cultural unity these barbarians had disrupted. The great geographic discoveries initiated by the Portuguese and Spaniards in the fourteenth and fifteenth centuries produced a series of brilliant but historically sterile adventures in China, Japan, and neighboring areas. The impact was more substantial in the Philippines and in Latin America, where the church accompanied the conquerors as part of their imperial apparatus and built enduring politico-cultural structures, the religious validity of which remains still ambiguous.

The massive missionary thrust, however, the one in which the churches of Western Christianity—Catholic and Protestant alike—became universally involved, occurred in the nineteenth century when the West set out on its self-defined civilizing task by carving up the rest of the world into spheres of influence, Britain, France, Germany, Belgium, Holland, and Italy imposing formal colonial rule, the United States generally choosing more subtle but ultimately equally destructive techniques. The churches undertook their task in formal separation from, and at times in highly visible—if superficial—conflict with, the colonizers. The de facto function and effect of these Christian missions was to identify christianizing with the introduction of the language, culture, and values of the colonizing powers.

For Catholics a further complication resulted from the popularity in the nineteenth and early twentieth century of an individualistic concept of salvation. This theology encouraged pietistic devotions and a mathematical concept of sin and forgiveness. The most obvious expression was the Saturday ritual of long lines of men, women, and little children waiting in church to report to a priest in a confessional cubicle the number and kind of sins committed since the previous confession, then speedily absolved by unintelligible words in Latin that sent the penitent off clean-laundered and ready to resume the sinful life that would lead back to another Saturday mathematical exercise.

The logic of this theology, which understood life as strictly a testing time for future eternal happiness or eternal punishment, had an overwhelming impact on the approach to the missionary task. Given that Jesus Christ had called all to follow him, those who rejected the call were automatically consigned to eternal punishment. Those who never heard it were excluded from his kingdom and its rewards. The first step in accepting the call was to be baptized. Most adult members of African tribes were slow to abandon their ancestral rites or unwilling to accept the monogamy imposed as an essential prerequisite. Many souls could nevertheless be snatched from the clutches of the devil and sent instead to populate the mansions of the Lord if the sanctifying water could be poured on the heads of dying infants. Similarly, children were ransomed from slavery and isolated in orphanages from corrupting pagan influences until they grew into true Christians. The potential of this practice as a fund raiser was quickly recognized. Much pious literature in my

youth encouraged the poverty-stricken Irish to give liberally of their pennies "to buy black babies."

Colonial systems needed schools, hospitals, and other
services for the military and civilian expatriates who civilized and exploited, and for the small minority of the indigenous populations needed for bureaucratic, peace-keeping,
and revenue-collecting tasks. The churches also recognized
the potential for their proclaimed purpose of making Christians, and incidentally for making money. The cause of God
and of Western civilization came together in enthusiastic
harmony, creating the illusion—still prevalent among Western Christians—that the churches played the predominant
role in preparing the benighted pagans of Africa and elsewhere for the day when they could assume control of their
own affairs in democratic and Christian freedom.

Let me give a concrete example. As a child, I read avidly
the magazines of mission orders and societies, in particular
one that extolled the wonderful work of Irish missionary
priests in Saint Mary's College, the most prestigious secondary school in East Africa. Established in the late nineteenth
century, it was presented as continuously engaged from the
start in providing advanced education to young Africans
who would otherwise still be running around naked and heathen in the bush. Inspired by such stories, the innocent Irish
poor contributed liberally to funds for its support.

Imagine my outrage when in 1964 I gazed on the magnificent block of buildings and learned from a priest long associated with it the facts. Up to the year 1960 no African child
had ever set foot in Saint Mary's as a student. It had served
exclusively to educate the children of the expatriate British
in the colonial service and in commerce, and of the British
colonists who had seized the rich highlands of Kenya to
make quick fortunes from export crops grown with ill-paid
native labor, a process it took the Mau Mau rebellion of the
1950s to end.

While helping to maintain the colonial system, Saint
Mary's was handsomely subsidized by the colonial government and had no need to look to Ireland or elsewhere for
charitable contributions. Indeed, it was the policy of the reli-

gious order that maintained it to levy an annual poll tax on all its overseas missions. Far from being a burden, they contributed to its flourishing operations in Ireland. Given such practices, one should not be surprised that new nations of Africa and Asia often identified Christianity with colonialism, and that some expelled missionaries and seized their properties. Saint Mary's survives, but its history is not forgotten by Kenyans. I recall a remark in the 1960s by a Kikuyu woman, a proud member of the tribe that produced the Mau Mau warriors. The British had withdrawn from the island of Zanzibar in 1963, passing control to a Moslem minority they hoped to manipulate for their purposes. The African majority a year later ousted the Sultan and joined Zanzibar with Tanganyika in what is since known as Tanzania. Referring to that event, my Kikuyu friend commented: "As my people walk past Saint Mary's, they tell each other: 'There stands Target No. 1 when we have our Zanzibar.'"

Self-identification with the colonizers led missionaries to errors with incalculable consequences. In Africa, they identified all native customs and beliefs with devil worship and demanded an impossible Europeanization as a prelude to acceptance as true Christians. One result was to retain control of all church policy. Even when lip service was paid to the idea of native clergy, the conditions imposed frustrated every initiative. Potential candidates were isolated from home and family from early childhood. They never learned the history and customs of their people and were not allowed to undergo the initiation ceremonies without which they were not accepted as tribe members.

Modeled on European practice and frequently provided in Europe, the seminary education deepened the emotional gap between candidates and their people. What emerged was a second-class imitation of a foreign model. Not until the 1950s, when the writing was clear on the wall, did Rome name black bishops. The first in West Africa was made an assistant in 1953, got his own diocese only ten years later. Not surprisingly, the quick promotions produced some startling results. One bishop in West Africa preached only in English to his tribespeople, an interpreter by his side translating into the vernacular the bishop spoke perfectly. After all, that was how bishops had always operated. Another, the papal nuncio who notified him of his promotion told me, immediately took a plane to Rome to be fitted for his episcopal robes by the tailor who had attired his predecessor.

Convent life for black African women was ghastly. In the early 1970s, a scandal made headlines in Europe when it was revealed that convents seeking unpaid labor were bringing girls from India to cook, clean, and housekeep. That practice has long been common in the southwest United States, where convent recruiters attract girls from Mexico with promises of a lifestyle in community bearing no relation to the reality. Nowhere, however, was this utilization of unpaid labor under the guise of religion so fully institutionalized as in Africa. Instead of admitting black applicants, the white missionaries from overseas created satellite communities in adjoining compounds, the administration selected and supervised by the "mother" convent. Following African practice, the black nuns worked the fields, and they also performed domestic chores for themselves and their white "sisters." Even more brutalizing was the rationale the foreigners offered. The African girls have no sense of Christian vocation, one was told, no ability to develop the spiritual life we practice. Their motives are primarily economic and sociological, the convent offering an escape from the drudgery and degradation of women's life in the bush.

Many missionaries were long frustrated by the vast gap between their profession and the results. But most had to suffer in silence. They knew something was radically wrong but lacked the knowledge to identify what it was or the power to change, even when their work was clearly counterproductive. An obstacle was built in from the outset, a missionary of long standing told me. Starting from the assumption that the Africans were ignorant savages, policy makers saw no reason to include studies of African cultures and psychology for future missionaries. On the contrary, they reasoned that they needed considerably less formal education than priests being prepared to work at home. The fact that lack of ability to control malaria, yellow fever, and other tropical diseases until well into the twentieth century gave the average missionary a short life expectancy further discouraged spending more than the absolute minimum on his education. The end result was a level of mediocrity that encouraged routine continuance of conventional activities and left unquestioned the total impact. If the records at the end of the year showed a satisfactory number of baptisms and of visits to outlying stations, that was proof positive that all was well.

World War II had ended the colonial domination to which the Christian mission world was organically linked. Many missionaries realized they were sitting on powder kegs, and Rome embarked on a crash program to "Africanize" the church by naming black Africans as bishops, conveniently forgetting its previous insistence that "they" were not yet ready. Other missionaries were too set in their ways to change. In the Sudan I met Italian priests who in their own minds were still legates of imperial Rome wearing the civilizing mantles of the Caesars and of Mussolini. Perhaps they had lived too long in the desert. Ostrich-like, they refused to see that Christianity was in headlong retreat since the Arabized Islamic north and center of the country had acquired from the withdrawing British total control of the national destiny. They could not make the cultural accommodations that had enabled the Copts—now finally emerging from the tomb of oblivion—to survive twelve centuries of Moslem domination.

In Southern Africa, some Roman Catholics like Hurley of Durban were drawing closer to some Anglicans in recognition of the absolute incompatibility of apartheid and Christianity, as Catholics and Protestants in Europe had recently come to recognize their Christian fellowship under the Nazi tyranny. But the overwhelming majority of Christians thought out of both sides of their head and spoke out of both sides of their mouth, like Archbishop W.P. Whelan of Bloemfontein who said: "There is no teaching of the church opposed to a state composed of national or racial groups. Apartheid has not been condemned by the church. Bishops in 1958 told people they were perfectly free to vote for any of the parties. It is common knowledge that the application of several provisions of our racial legislation involves hardship and injustice: conditions of African urban employment; unreasonable job reservation; restriction on the place of abode which separates members of the same family....It cannot be said that curtailment of an individual's rights necessarily constitutes an injustice."

The Italian missionaries in the Sudan and Whelan in South Africa were expressing in different ways the European arrogance that had assuaged consciences—and continues to assuage them—in the relations from the beginning of the colonial era of the militarily and economically dominant West with the cultures of America, Africa, Asia, and Australasia they had exploited and undermined for their own benefit. My Irish upbringing had given me a healthy scepticism about the white man's burden, and my work with the Caribbean Commission had provided hard data of continuing exploitation at a time when the imperial powers were publicly weeping at the enormous expense of their efforts to continue their civilizing task.

It took Africa, however, to explode for me another myth. The apologetics in which I had been saturated in all my education, in particular as a seminarian, had presented the enormous thrust of the Roman Catholic mission effort in Africa and Asia in the nineteenth century and the first half of the twentieth as confirmation of Rome's claim to a monopoly of Christianity. The lack of similar activity by the Orthodox showed what happened when a branch cut itself off from the trunk. The extent of the Protestant mission effort had been on the one hand minimized and on the other misrepresented as the sowing of cockle with the wheat. Now I had new perspectives. Having seen for myself something of the vigor of the Orthodox church within the constraints imposed by centuries of dominant Islamic culture, I could understand why it had not participated significantly in the modern expansion of Christianity. As for the shameful Catholic-Protestant contest for the "souls" of the "heathen" natives of Africa and Asia, it had been conducted with such obviously unChristian weapons as to make it extremely difficult for any thinking

African to accept the seriousness of the professions of either contender. Simultaneously, the insistence of both parties on selling their beliefs only within the cultural clothing of the colonizers encouraged Africans who had absorbed some of the spirit of Jesus to splinter off so that they could express their newfound beliefs in ways meaningful to them and their people, thus further rending the seamless garment.

I have already mentioned another problem that resulted logically from the assumptions of the mission planners. I got some sense of how widespread and significant this factor had been from discussions with friends during an extensive sidetrip through Nigeria, from Lagos to Onitsha, Enugu, Abakaliki, and the former slave port of Calabar. Once it is assumed that the "natives" are ignorant, the role of the missionary is reduced to eradicating pagan practices and substituting life styles consonant with conventional European moral codes. Apparently most mission societies limited the training and education of their members to preparing them for this task. Only the Missionaries of Africa (formerly, the White Fathers), a French group committed to establish a Christian presence in Moslem North Africa, early recognized that they were dealing with a sophisticated culture they had to respect, evaluate, and seek to absorb to the greatest possible extent. Elsewhere in Africa, the missionaries were not famed for their scholars, their sociologists, their anthropologists, their economists, even their theologians. Their ability to contribute to emerging Africa, or to attract the young intellectuals emerging from newly founded universities was proportionately limited. It was hardly surprising that so many African leaders were openly anti-Christian, amazing that some were not.

I need not linger on the details of the long journey east through the Suez Canal to Pakistan, India, Singapore, Vietnam, Hong Kong, Taiwan, Korea, and Japan. Enough to say that it confirmed in a thousand ways the catastrophic failure of Europe's multi-century effort to absorb the rest of the world, and the parallel failure of the Christian churches to rise significantly above the political objectives and strategies of the imperial powers whom they had accompanied in their spurious commitment to a civilizing mission. A particularly poignant experience was a visit to a village not far from Saigon. I had played a small part in arranging the evacuation of the people who now inhabited it from North Vietnam after the partition effected by the 1954 Geneva Agreements. There was as yet little evidence of the Vietcong activity that would a decade later hand the United States its first major military defeat. But these industrious peasants knew they would not long enjoy the prosperous community they had created, and their fears became more real to us as we drove back in the dusk and saw the flares and heard the exchange of small-arms fire in the forest that bordered our road. "You Americans persuaded us to leave our homes," they had said to me in our conversation. "Where can you take us from here—to Brazil, to Australia?" The issue was never faced. Instead, they became the boat people, the Wandering Jews of the twentieth century.

As I reached San Francisco in late 1964 on my way home, a new assignment was waiting for me, a book on Colombia, Venezuela, and the Guianas for the Life World Library. The research took me back to Trinidad and the three Guianas, still under British, Dutch, and French control respectively, including a tour deep into the Amazon basin of Surinam to visit a tribe consisting of a few hundred people who spoke a language otherwise unknown and who lived primitively by hunting and fishing with traditional implements. I took advantage of the opportunity for an extensive overview of the one big country in Latin America I had not previously visited. I saw slum life in the mud swamps of Belem at the mouth of the Amazon and in the green hell of the heart of Amazonia at Manaus a thousand miles up the river, the city that boasts of a magnificent baroque opera house in which Enrico Caruso and other contemporary opera stars sang during Brazil's brief rubber boom. I saw the spacious boulevards and modernistic skyline of the new capital, Brazilia, started a few years earlier in the wilderness by President Juscelino Kubitschek, startling beauty and opulence already knee-deep in surrounding slums before half built.

From Brazil I made my way north to another new city

being carved out in the wilderness, Santo Tomé de la Guayana, the projected Detroit of Venezuela, the steel mills fed by the limitless ores of the Iron Mountain in the background and run by the electricity generated as the mighty Caroni cascaded down from the Guiana Highlands to its confluence with the sleepy Orinoco. On the plains of eastern Colombia I stood on the field of Boyacá where the ragged survivors of a march over a 13,000-foot Andean pass, more daring than Hannibal's across the Alps, followed Simon Bolivar into a battle that broke Spain's hold on northern South America. By helicopter I viewed the oil camps and exploratory drillings deep in the Putamayo jungle on both sides of the Colombian-Ecuadorean border, recalling that the plight of the Indians had little changed since my compatriot Roger Casement had reported on it as British consul in Ecuador more than half a century earlier.

I talked to top government officials in half a dozen capitals, everywhere getting enthusiastic reports of how land reform and other social changes stimulated by the Alliance for Progress would get into high gear next year, and everywhere establishing by my own researches that the official stories were window dressing designed to ensure the continued flow of U.S. aid, aid that would go to make the rich richer and the poor poorer.

The fall of 1965, the Life World Library Book completed, found me back once more in Rome for the final session of the Vatican Council, on which I had now been commissioned to write a book that would in due course appear in English and German. To understand the Council and everything that has since happened and not happened in the Catholic church, one must begin with Rome. It is not the holy city of Christians in anything like the way Jerusalem is of the Jews or Mecca of the Moslems. For better or worse, however, it is the dominant city. And also very complex.

8

In the Shadow of the Vatican

When we first arrived in Rome, my wife and I rented a meagerly furnished apartment in a lower middle-class neighborhood within walking distance of the Vatican. It was a happy choice. Quickly we were neighbors among neighbors. Surrounded by eager helpers in the butcher shop, the grocery store, the hardware, or wherever, my wife—*la straniera*—was introduced to the mysteries of calculating in thousands of lire the price of miniscule quantities of meat, butter, vegetables, salami, cheese. If she didn't have the correct money, or if the woman—usually a woman—behind the counter wasn't sure of the price, no matter, take it anyway, pay the next time. When I returned the empties at the "wine and oil" store and picked up unwrapped two-liter flasks of red and of white wine, if the proprietor was not busy, he would insist on my sharing with him a glass of the best wine from his brother's or his brother-in-law's vineyard in the nearby Frascati hills.

Such were the marks of acceptance. Thus began many friendships in Rome and throughout Italy, developed in half a dozen visits that globally added up to more than a year. The Italians amaze and fascinate me. SPQR (*Senatus Populusque Romanus*: "the Senate and People of Rome") is stamped on every manhole cover in Rome's streets. Officials, both civil and clerical, in rundown and utterly dysfunc-

tional palaces, think and behave as though the imperial le-
gions still manned Hadrian's Wall and bivouacked in the
shadow of the Pyramids. But the people have no corresponding hauteur, no sense of superiority. One's first impression
is that their spirit has been broken by fifteen centuries of
barbarian invasions, Saracen incursions, French hegemony,
Spanish domination, finally oppression by native overlords,
sometimes temporal, sometimes spiritual, usually coalitions
of the two.

In fact, they are far from crushed. Rather, they are infi-
nitely patient, genetically adjusted to survival with minimal
material comforts. They have learned to stand together
against the *combinazione*, to share their poverty generously, outwit the wiles and torments of an officialdom arrogant in its weakness. *Francia o Spagna, basta se si mangia*
is the cynical yet dynamic response to each adversity. The
proverb recalls the centuries that France and Spain fought
over the bones of Italy with no compassion for the humans
whose bones cracked in the process. Few know the reference, but the meaning lives. So long as we have bread,
cheese and wine to satisfy today's hunger, let who will run
our affairs. Blank and unexpressive is the face to the outside
enemy, the judge, the priest, or *la celere*, the motorized riot
police molded by Mussolini, who still play the key role in
people control.

Such attitudes prevent reform, simply because nobody be-
lieves reform to be possible. In consequence, bureaucracy in
church and state throve and mushroomed in accordance
with Parkinson's Law for centuries before Parkinson formulated it. A Roman friend once regaled us at a reception with
the process of registering his child's birth. The baby had
been born outside the city, so he had to get the forms in
Rome, starting with the *carta bollata*, the official paper with
embossed stamp essential to every legal transaction, then
waste a day traveling to the clinic for signatures and seals.
Back at the Rome office, he worked his tedious way up the
long waiting line. With one quick glance, the official returned the papers, pointing to a blank space lacking a rubber stamp and signature. When my friend protested he

couldn't afford another day to go again to the clinic, the official obligingly scribbled on a slip of paper an address round
the corner where all such things were arranged for a small
fee. My friend rushed over, paid the fee, worked his way
back up the line. "This is bad," said the official after further
study. "I should have seen it. There's another gap—no witness to the birth." But he was not grasping. He was satisfied with the split he would later collect. "It's easy," he said
after some thought. "The man beside you has the same
problem. You sign for him, he for you."

A lawyer in our group laughed uproariously, drowning
the general amusement. "You missed a detail," he commented. "You certified you were present not only at the unknown infant's birth but also at its conception. The document states that X is the mother and Y the father."

Clerical bureaucracy welcomed me to Rome less hilar-
iously but equally characteristically. One of more than a
thousand international journalists, I came with credentials
from major U.S. publications. It was the Council's second
session, yet no clerk in the Vatican press office could tell me
how to get a *tessera*, the magic press card without which
nothing could be done, but with which—as I would learn—
nothing could be done either. Only the monsignor in charge
(any office above porter or filing clerk in the Vatican requires holy orders and monsignorial robes) knew. To find
him took two days, partly because I didn't know that Vatican officials spend only some morning hours in their offices,
a rule not to be changed because of a thousand foreign journalists eager to pry into church affairs they could not possibly understand.

When I finally waylaid him, my documents were worthless. I needed a certificate of good character signed by a
priest resident in Rome. For me that was a minor nuisance,
a wasted half-day going to the monastery of Irish Dominican
priests across town. For many from distant places, especially if not Catholics, it was a condition so arbitrary and irrelevant to their purpose as to be understandable only
within the cobwebby irrationality of the world's oldest bureaucracy. It was, however, a warning of things to come. To

survive, we had to learn who had reasonably priced rubber stamps, sign for each other without thought to the contents of the document.

Rome intensified the dialectical tension already existing in my relationship with the institutional church. It was not a challenge to my faith. The message of Christianity has never been more of a problem to me than other mysteries that surround and enrich my life. I have found no more attractive alternative. Most alternatives that have appealed to me mesh with the message of Jesus of Nazareth rather than conflict with it. My clash has always been with the structures: structures of power and insensitivity, of ambition, pride, and deception; of an inability to see either spiritual or human dignity not only in those who differ, but even in those within the institutions who lack power. Any who oppose are to be destroyed. The powerless inside are to be used. They are the foot soldiers of Pius XII's Catholic Action who execute orders without questioning their justice.

In Rome one could see how these distortions had occurred. Religion as a social phenomenon is incarnated in and expressed through a specific culture in each time and place. Rome's culture served that purpose for early Christianity. The Greco-Roman civilization enjoyed an advanced technology. The spirit flourished impressively in literature, the arts, philosophy, and law. Official Christian history presents Christianity as having withstood for centuries the savage persecutions of Roman emperors seeking to stamp out this threat to their values, then finally—and almost instantaneously—convincing its powerful opponents to accept it, on its terms, as the exclusive state religion. I suspect that the reality was more subtle. Pagan Rome had an uncanny ability to incorporate and domesticate religions from diverse sources containing contradictory principles. If Rome embraced Christianity, it was never converted to the spirit of Jesus Christ.

The Pantheon, the temple of all the gods, formally a Christian church, seems to me to express all the ambivalence of Rome's acceptance of yet another oriental cult. For several months I walked past it each morning to reach my office, and each time I smiled at the sign above its portals promising an *indulgentia plenaria diaria*, a daily remission of all the punishments to which my transgressions had exposed me, if I entered and made my obeisance in the home of all the gods. When I reached my office and looked out over the breathtakingly beautiful Piazza Navona to the monastery diagonally across from me in which the young Augustinian monk Martin Luther studied, I would wonder how he felt as he watched the basilica of Saint Peter rise triumphalistically beyond the Tiber, built with pennies extracted by equally ambivalent promises from Europe's superstitious poor.

Similarly ambivalent is the title of the successor of the Apostle who, tradition says, insisted on being crucified head down to stress how far he was beneath his Lord. The Pontifex Maximus combined civil and religious functions in the Rome of the Caesars, chief bridge-builder both literally and figuratively. That combination makes it difficult to obey the command to give to Caesar what is Caesar's and to God what is God's. It does not work well in our days of separation of church and state. Paul VI, its holder in those days, could be identified with the modern equivalent of bridge-building, namely the construction of apartment houses (ironically, one of them was the Watergate complex in Washington) and the creation of banks—activities that prevented his functioning as a bridge builder in the figurative sense. Indeed, as he himself asserted shortly after the Council, with perhaps some exaggeration, he had become a major obstacle ("undoubtedly the greatest" were his words) to building bridges between twentieth-century Christians.

Equally distorting was the church's absorption of the Roman concepts of human relations. Central to the teaching of Jesus is the theme that something intrinsically sacred, intrinsically deserving of respect, intrinsically calling for and entitled to love, is an integral part of every individual produced by the generative union of two human beings. That idea was foreign to Rome's mind-set, not only in its dealings with lesser breeds but within the complex of its own citizens—even in the heart of the family where the father had unbridled authority, not answerable in law for his treatment or mistreatment of wife and children. Nikilay Nikilayevich Vedenyapin expressed this philosophy and contrasted it with the Christian and human concept, in language of extraordinary poetic beauty and force, in Boris Pasternak's *Doctor Zhivago*:

"Rome was a flea market of borrowed gods and conquered peoples, a bargain basement on two tiers—earth and heaven—slaves on one, gods on the other. Dacians, Herculaneans, Scythians, Sarmatians, Hyperboreans. Heavy, spokeless wheels, eyes sunk in fat, bestialism, double chins, illiterate emperors, fish fed on the flesh of learned slaves. Beastliness convoluted in a triple knot like guts. There were more people in the world than there have ever been since, all crammed into the passages of the Coliseum, and all wretched.

"And then, into this tasteless heap of gold and marble, He came, light-footed and clothed in light, with his marked humanity, his deliberate Galilean provincialism, and from that moment there were neither gods nor peoples, there was only man—man the carpenter, man the plowman, man the shepherd with his flock of sheep at sunset, man whose name does not sound in the least proud, but who is sung in lullabies and portrayed in picture galleries the world over."

Rome served as vehicle to scatter this seed in Gaul, Germany, England, from where much later it crossed the Atlantic. The seed grew slowly and secretively, putting forth tender leaves of hope in Magna Carta, blossoming with blood-red petals in the French Revolution, and fruiting in the Universal Declaration of Human Rights of the United Nations. But Italy's own soil was stony. Its church remains a two-class culture, a class monopolizing rights with no corresponding obligations, a class subdivided into categories based on the Roman recipe for ruling—the subordinate and contingent privileges of each category minutely detailed in the Code of Canon Law.

Church historians long interpreted this Romanization, the shedding of the basically Jewish cultural dress that had kept early Christians warm in the catacombs, as a dispensation of providence. Today we are many who wonder if more was not lost than gained when in 313 Emperor Constantine imposed Christianity. Decked in its newfound paramount authority as official religion, it structured itself in the forms of Rome's civil order and absorbed its mentality. The church would project that class system forward into the nobility and serfs of the Middle Ages, finally crystallize it in the clergy-laity dichotomy we still suffer.

Ironically, Christianity identified with Rome just as the city was ceasing to be the hub of the universe. Alaric's Visigoths captured it in 410. Genseric's Vandals not only recaptured but sacked it in 455. And the deposition of Emperor Romulus Augustulus by Odoacer in 476 marked the formal end of Rome as the capital of the world. For centuries Rome fondly imagined itself to be the depositary of world culture, when it was at best one culture in a pluralistic world. Its limiting to expression in that culture what was by definition a religion for all was to invite the splitting of the church that occurred almost imperceptibly but projectably between the eleventh and fifteenth centuries into East and West.

Most Christians in the West know nothing about this horrendous rending of the Body of Christ by the Great Schism. The few with some knowledge of the event and its causes usually dismiss it as unfortunate but inevitable. That view I shared until circumstances took me to Palestine for the meeting of Pope Paul with Patriarch Athenagoras, then to Athens, Istanbul and other centers of Orthodoxy in the Near East. These experiences convinced me that, in spite of gestures, Rome still persists in its unrealistic and unChristian determination to force the East to capitulate.

I had no anticipation that such adventures were only months ahead when I finally acquired my *tessera* and with it the right to use the facilities of the recently opened press office. As a result of the outraged protests of journalists at the first session of the Council, the Vatican's information services had purportedly been modernized and streamlined. But the change was strictly cosmetic, and not much of that. Typewriters had been provided, almost all with Italian keyboards unusable by the rest of us accustomed to the keyboard elsewhere standard. Soap and toilet paper were almost invariably lacking in the toilets. When some of us protested, the problem was solved by locking the toilets. Fortunately the USO was down the street and never without soap and toilet paper. Whenever any interview or function worth attending was announced, one had to get a special pass. The *tessera*, it turned out, was mainly useful because without it one could not apply for special passes.

It took me some time to figure out that the set-up was not inefficient. Rather it had been carefully thought through, geared to a purpose other than the one it professed and we had expected. Unlike press facilities at the meetings of international bodies with which we were familiar, this system was designed to conceal from us what was happening and make selective disclosure of such facts as its manipulators either judged would advance the Vatican's interests—as they conceived them—or such facts as could be sold by insiders for cash or for balancing favors.

This concept of knowledge as power and as a salable commodity and of secrecy as a weapon of control was, of course, not new to me. It is normal in government and in the public relations departments of business and finance. I had seen for myself in New York how public relations manipulates the media and public opinion. Two elements in the Roman system, nevertheless, shocked me. The church is of its essence committed to honesty, justice, and morality. This institution lied shamelessly, deceived outrageously, sacrificed innocent people to achieve it purposes. Or as Charles Davis, a major English theologian who later withdrew from the active ministry, said in 1967, the church called to become "a zone of truth" had become "a zone of untruth." The other thing that shocked me was inefficiency. Professional training or experience was irrelevant. The necessary and sufficient qualification to hold an office was to have received the sacrament of orders, expressed publicly by wearing a cassock or Roman collar, with additional insignia to mark the upward movement to the dignity of monsignor, bishop, archbishop, cardinal. Only those within this hierarchy had rights. All outside approached as suppliants.

One experience encapsulated the system for me. Emile Gabel, a French priest, a former editor of the major French Catholic daily *La Croix*, was then secretary-general of the International Catholic Press Union. He later died in a plane crash at Martinique while on a duty tour in Latin America. Gabel was convinced that a free flow of information through professionally operated media was essential to the church's health, and he organized a seminar in Rome in an attempt to get the message across to bishops and other officials servicing the press at the Council. I had been representative of the International Catholic Press Union at UN headquarters in New York when Gabel became secretary general, and we had taken several years of sometimes bitter battling in three languages to reach a high level of mutual respect and deep friendship. At his urging, I agreed to analyze for the seminar the Vatican press office as seen by an American public-relations practitioner. What emerged from my typewriter shocked me. The notes I had kept day by day constituted a precise and documented expose of inefficiency and deception, but of inefficiency and deception so patent to any professional journalist as to defeat its ends. I sought out Gabel and insisted that he read. "It's all absolutely correct," he said, "but we can't say it. I know how Rome operates. There would be neither protest nor response. If you make this statement Saturday morning, however, under our auspices, the dinner being hosted Saturday evening by the Rome municipality for the participating journalists will be cancelled. That's how far the arm of the Curia reaches. It manipulates the civil as well as the religious authorities in this city. Then on Sunday morning the Pope will be indisposed, unable to say Mass, as arranged, and receive the journalists and their spouses in the Pauline chapel. We will simply have become nonpeople. That's how Rome sanctions violations of protocol. " "I'm not surprised," I answered. "I'm beginning to learn. But you know me. Either I say what I think or I say nothing. For your sake, I'll say nothing."

Such were my introductions to the official Roman mentality. But there was another and more positive side to the many dealings I had in Rome with church or church-related institutions. The first great breakthrough for me was the rending of the Velvet Curtain behind which the Curia had sought to hide the deliberations of the Vatican Council. It succeeded in retaining its formal mechanisms of news control. Journalists were excluded from the Council sessions, had the events interpreted to them after each session by written summaries and official briefings. But all the ingenuity of the Curia was unable to prevent the creation of a whole series of parallel information sources. One of the first was an information-documentation center (IDOC) sponsored by the Dutch bishops and Dutch radio-TV. It prepared background documents on upcoming issues, then organized open meetings at which cardinals, bishops, and theologians offered their views and answered questions. At first, only cardinals and bishops with major international reputations, most of them from Germany, France, Belgium, and Holland dared to deal with what had become a critical issue. This was the challenge developing within the Council to the program of the Roman theologians who sought a Council rubber stamp for triumphalistic reaffirmations of the monopoly of truth and wisdom conferred by God on the Roman Catholic church.

Gradually, many theologians began to say openly what they had long been whispering to each other. Some spoke because they knew their bishops would protect them from the heavy hand of the Holy Office. Others, professors in state universities, were not subject to economic pressures. Others combined an international reputation with a willingness to speak their mind regardless of consequences. If they had earlier been silent, it was not from fear, but rather because the climate had not existed in which their impact would be positive.

Sensitive to the importance of keeping good relations with the press, the U.S. bishops organized a daily briefing in the basement of the USO building on Via della Conciliazione, the broad artery cut through medieval Rome by Mussolini to mark the Concordat he signed with Pius XI and provide a spectacular view of Saint Peter's from the Tiber. The briefing lasted one hour each afternoon. Six to ten of the world's leading theologians, canon lawyers, scripture scholars, and sociologists formed each day's panel, the composition matching the issues that had dominated that morning's Council session or were expected to arise the next day. With room for about a hundred people, working journalists had priority and remaining space was allocated to theology students of both sexes who there found inspiration rare in the musty halls of their pontifical universities. Reporters for the wire services, major newspapers, radio and television, working against deadlines, asked their questions first. Then people like myself more interested in the underlying issues got our turn.

One scene remains indelibly etched in my memory. It was 18 November 1963, and the air was full of rumors. Angry exchanges had reportedly enlivened that morning's session when some Council members had urged a reversal of the canonical prohibition of participation in the religious services of other Christian churches. The Code of Canon Law and the standard theological manuals were very clear on the point. Active involvement by a Catholic in the worship of another church—technically called *communicatio in divinis*—was gravely sinful. To attend a wedding or funeral service in a Protestant church for social or business reasons required advance approval of the bishop; and the Catholic had to show that his or her presence was exclusively for nonreligious reasons by not joining in prayers or singing. Many popes had confirmed this "teaching." Gregory XVI in *Miravi vos* (1832) had denounced the claim that everyone should be granted and guaranteed freedom of conscience as "one of the most contagious of errors, false and absurd, or rather insane." And Leo XIII in *Libertas proestantissimum* (1885) called freedom of worship "a liberty totally contrary to the virtue of religion." To recognize the validity and virtue of worship conducted by "heretics" was to question the inerrancy of papal teaching, an issue Rome has always sidestepped.

It so happened that exactly a week earlier Cardinal Spellman of New York had made one of his several lightweight

contributions to the Council. Opposing the proposal for collegial government of the church, with the pope as first among
equals, he said: "The theology we all learned in the seminary teaches us that the pope alone has full power over the
entire church. He does not need the help of others." The remark had kept Rome sniggering all week, and I decided to
dramatize my question by referring to it. It was well I did,
because it gave me an unexpected bonus—a spectacular illustration of the extent to which fear of Rome's displeasure
dominated the judgment and action of those it had the effective power to discipline.

We were about a hundred people present, half being lay
reporters, probably as many of them being Protestant, Jewish, or agnostic as Catholic; the other half—some also journalists—identifiable as priests, seminarians, or nuns by the
cassocks or habits that were still de rigueur. The gentle, impartial, and ever-courteous Father John Sheerin, editor of
the *Catholic World* (New York), was presiding over a panel
of at least ten members. In due course, he recognized me,
and I began: "The theology we all learned in the seminary...."

A guffaw of laughter from fifty lay-garbed participants
drowned out my words, while not a single clerical muscle
moved. It was unbelievable, unbelievable yet a fact—a fact
that has to be absorbed to appreciate what an enormous
task of rehumanizing remains to be done within the clerical
establishment.

"The theology we all learned in the seminary," I repeated, "describes *communicatio in divinis* as one of the
most serious sins. Do I understand that the Council wants to
change all that?"

The question was not addressed to anyone in particular,
leaving every panel member free to reply. Usually several
were quick to show off their knowledge. But this was a hot
potato. The Holy Office's stand was well known, and the
partial clipping of its wings under the Council's pressures
was still far in the future. A theologian who gave the wrong
answer could find himself in disgrace, forbidden to teach or
publish, assured of no advancement in the only career for
which he was equipped.

Father Sheerin looked hopefully to left and right, but no hand was raised and no eye caught his. At the end of the table, seated inconspicuously as usual, was Bernard Haring. Only he himself seemed unconscious that he towered head and shoulders intellectually above most of his colleagues, seldom voicing an opinion unless addressed directly, always waiting deferentially for others to have their say before he intervened. When the silence had become deafening, Bernard seemed suddenly to realize what was up.

"I have no problem in answering that question," he said, his piercing eyes radiating from his ever-joyful face. "On the eve of battle, I would invite officers and men to join me. I would tell them that by the next day some of us would have penetrated the mystery of life. I offered my blessing and absolution as a priest to all who felt they had done wrong and believed my action could help them to make amends. I invited all who recognized the presence of Christ in the consecrated bread and wine to participate. I didn't ask if they were Catholics. I knew many were not. But as the only Christian minister present, I felt an equal obligation to serve each as he needed." Haring was then in the German army on the Eastern front. The Nazis did not allow chaplains but for a time tolerated off-duty chaplain service by clergy who had opted for noncombatant service. Haring was a stretcher bearer. As Hitler's persecution of religion intensified, all activity as chaplains was banned. Haring, nevertheless, continued to minister in secret.

"Later, when we went into a Russian village and the people learned I was a priest, they would come to me to celebrate the eucharist for them and to have their children baptized. I never refused. And, of course, I didn't ask if they intended to raise their children in a church in union with Rome. I knew they were Orthodox. For me the determining factor was simply that they needed a service I alone was in a position to provide."

That, as I was to learn, was typical Haring. The curialists hated him because he was not even marginally concerned about what they said or plotted against him, and because he was a better theologian than their most brilliant. In fact, he is a quite conventional theologian—and once accepted as a compliment my telling him so. His originality in theology, one that made him daringly progressive for many, was his clear understanding that the Sabbath was made for us, not we for the Sabbath. But what really distinguished him was unconcern for what others thought of him and his contempt for threats to his reputation or position. He was denounced as a heretic to the Holy Office several times, about the worst thing that could befall a theologian. When called by the Holy Office to explain or retract, he would storm into the grim medieval *palazzo*, the iron bars on its semi-basement windows grimly reminiscent of the dungeons of the Inquisition to which it was successor, angrily demand the names of his accusers so that he in turn might denounce them as the real heretics, then storm out again. It took time, but finally the Holy Office learned to leave him alone.

Of all the theologians I met at the Council, only one other gave me the same sense of saying precisely what he thought, without fear or favor. I do not mean this as a blanket indictment of the others, for many were honest, open, and courageous. But with people who are cogs or elements in a complicated machine, one prudently evaluates what is being held back, why a given point is stressed, who stands to gain or lose. The other person who gave me the same sense of unconcern for threat or promise was Gustave Weigel, the American Jesuit theologian. I had come consciously to this evaluation of Häring and Weigel long before I learned that the two had a transcendent experience in common. Both of them had already been through death.

Häring had assumed the leadership of a group of his German fellow soldiers when the German lines before Stalingrad had crumbled, and he led them back through Russian territory to a regrouping point, only to be courtmartialed by the Nazis and sentenced to death as a deserter. Miraculously, the location was overrun by the Russians before the sentence could be carried out. Häring escaped and joined another German regiment, now without papers or identification. This regiment in turn surrendered to the Russians in Poland, but by chance in a village where Häring had earlier been stationed and had made friends with the Polish resist-

ance. His Polish friends persuaded the Russian commander
to turn over this particular prisoner to them. They wanted,
they said, to make an example of him because of his earlier
behavior in their village. They then spirited him through the
Russian lines to safety in the West. Weigel's experience was
different. For ten years before I met him in 1963, he had
lived on borrowed time with a disease that ended his life
shortly after. But for both, the emotional passage had already been made. Ready to face God, they had the world in
its place.

Of the important theologians I met, the one I found hard-
est to figure out was Swiss-born Hans Küng, professor at
the University of Tübingen, Germany. Youthful, athletic-
looking, full of energy, he was in the midst of everything, always polite but always remote. He radiated a sense of being
free, yet simultaneously left one wondering if he wasn't too
cocksure about everything, too self-centered to see and respect different views. After several years my doubts were
resolved in a strange way. A young Irish priest, my distant
cousin, trained in traditional Irish schools and specialized in
the old-style Mariology that had become an ecumenical em-
barrassment, spent a sabbatical at Tübingen and followed
Küng's courses. The encounter tickled me, and when next I
went to Ireland my first visit was to my friend. "Tell me
about Hans," I urged him. "What sort of guy is he behind
that impassive face?" "Quite a guy," he replied. "I learned
one thing from him that more than justified the year—never
again to defend a position, but always to look for the truth."
Praise, indeed.

What most excited me intellectually and spiritually was
the daily discovery of openings in areas that had seemed forever closed. In a book I wrote more than thirty years ago, I
said I had from boyhood been convinced that Alexander the
Great must have been a halfwit if—as the story goes—he
wept because there were no more worlds to conquer. Yet we
Roman Catholics who tried to be people of our times and
read the signs of the times were in the same kind of box in
the dark ages preceding the Council. Some of us tried by
legal subtleties to find a living space within formulas that lit-

erally had ceased to make sense. Others withdrew into the Linus-blanket of mystery—an escape indeed but one that made religion progressively more meaningless and more marginal to living. And now we were meeting people prepared to face the facts head-on, come what may, not to defend positions but to seek the truth.

I recall my excitement as Dutch Dominican theologian Edward Schillebeeckx evaluated Pope Paul's encyclical *Mysterium fidei* at a meeting attended by more than a hundred bishops in a hall on Via Aurelia. Paul had tried time and again—with varying success—to head off discussion by the Council of issues particularly embarrassing to the Roman theologians. *Mysterium fidei* was one such effort. Issued in 1965, it tried to establish once for all that the Council of Trent had said the last word about the meaning of the change that takes place in the bread and wine at the commemoration of the Last Supper—a central religious ceremony for almost all Christian churches. Rejecting what it judged misrepresentations introduced by the Protestant reformers, Trent said that *transubstantiation* was the correct term to describe a change of substance with no corresponding change of the accidents (appearances).

Schillebeeckx did not challenge the term, other than to note that it assumes the chemical constitution of matter taken by the scholastics from Aristotle, a notion of substance and matter totally at variance with what scientists have established in our atomic age. All that was wrong with the word was that it no longer conveyed any meaning whatever to the believer or anyone else. Instead he proposed two words that express the purpose for which Jesus used these elements and asked his followers similarly to use them to express their unity with him, words that avoid a commitment to any particular scientific theory of the nature of bread and wine. They are transfinalization and transsignification. The bread and wine offered in the liturgy take on a new significance or meaning and a new finality or purpose, so that they become for the believers who share them the body and blood of Christ. The Schillebeeckx talk, one of a series sponsored by the Brazilian bishops, so offended the curialists that

Archbishop Pericle Felici, general secretary of the Council, went out of his way in Saint Peter's to stress that the talks had no official standing or approval.

These and similar experiences spread over several years gave me an understanding I previously lacked of the vast differences between the Roman façade—the only part of the church long visible—and the real thinking of serious and committed members. It helped me to understand something I had previously found incomprehensible, the intense hatred of Roman Catholicism as a perversion of Christianity that was seldom far from the surface in Protestant literature. The deeper I probed, the more I became convinced that Rome had indeed deeply distorted the message of Christ, that Martin Luther had seen accurately the reality of Rome from his vantage point on Piazza Navona.

Although it is more than a century since Italian society formally emancipated itself from church control, the church has retained enormous ability to manipulate Italy's economic and social policies, especially in the negative sense of preventing the normal evolution of the social order. Since World War II, Italy has experienced an almost uninterrupted series of government crises, yet has evolved politically at a slower rhythm than any of its neighbors. The "opening to the left," the obvious desire and need of the majority, is always about to come, yet never does. The country consequently flounders along under a load of archaic and meaningless legalisms that reduce productivity, create artificial and unproductive jobs, and inflate the egos of the countless officials paid to seek solutions for objectively insoluble situations.

A book published in 1976 has thrown important light on the church's role in retarding the evolution of Italy's political life.* Hitherto secret United States Government documents obtained under the Freedom of Information Act describe United States intentions for Italy as developed during World War II. The first policy line concentrated on transferring Italy from British to United States economic dependence. Later, as the Russians swept into central Eu-

*Roberto Faenza and Marco Fini *Gli Americani in Italia.* Milan: Feltrini, 1976.

rope and Yugoslavia became a part of the communist bloc, it
became clear that Italy could easily go the same way because of the enormous popularity of the communist guerrilla
movement against Hitler and because of the desperate social conditions. Priority was then given to a policy of blocking the Left. With the support of the Vatican and the Italian
bishops, the State Department developed and financed—in
part openly, in part through the CIA—the campaign that
put the Christian Democrats in power in 1948. The same coalition of interests kept them in power more than thirty
years and ensures them a continuing voice in government
out of all proportion to their popular base.

Cynicism inevitably thrives in this climate. Lack of confidence in the structures and in the professional politicians is
universal. Only careerists enter the party machine. Committed young people form politico-cultural groups to express
in small reviews their futile and negative criticism of the national inefficiencies and compromises. Having abandoned
hope of changing the structures, people find ways to live
with them. Birth control devices have long been universally
available. The church used all its efforts to prevent the re-
peal of the constitutional prohibition of divorce, and the biggest blow to its power and prestige in this century was its
defeat on the issue. All of its opposition, however, was for
the record and to maintain its controls over appearances.
The denial of divorce did not keep Italian couples together.
A weekly magazine made substantial revenue by running in
every issue a long list of "appeals from separated spouses"
for "friends of the opposite sex" with whom to set up a more
or less stable menage. And Rome's *Il Messaggéro*, a family
newspaper, could run equally long lists of "most elegant, re-
fined, and skillful" manicurists and masseuses who received
clients day or night in luxurious apartments with private entrances and were ready to hop in a taxi and perform their
services elsewhere.

The Vatican seems undisturbed by the behavior of Romans. They can break the rules but they must not try to
change them. It shows no concern when surveys establish
widespread lack of knowledge of the religion most Romans
profess and a near-universal belief that pope, bishops, and

priests are on the side of the rich. Nor are there many indications of rational efforts to change this situation by better
preparation of church leaders. For more priests, diocesan
and order, are assigned to vocation-hustling than to the psychological and pedagogical specialization needed to train
priests today.

Pope Paul VI exemplified the mentality. He loved spectacular gestures—traveling to Palestine, India and South
America, embracing the Patriarch, addressing the United
Nations. All the while he remained emotionally and intellectually locked into the world of his training and experience,
extremely intensive but equally narrow. His inability to
break out of the box on the use of contraceptives into which
he believed his predecessors had locked him was typical. His
speech to the first work session of the 1967 Synod of Bishops
gave another glimpse. He spoke of "scholars and publicists
eager to analyze the juridical aspects of this institution and
to determine, as far as they can, its form and function."
What could be more laudable? Not for Paul, however. For
him, such effort to ascertain the facts and place them in a
framework of meaning was irrelevant, if not impertinent interference in business that was none of their concern. Think
of the Synod as juridically unstructured, he told the bishops,
leaving it free to operate a rule of persons rather than a rule
of law. Such stress on the unaccountability of those chosen—
in fact, self-chosen—to rule was of the essence of Paul's self-
understanding. Speaking of change in the Curia as demanded by the Vatican Council, he insisted it must be slow
and partial "because of the respect the persons and traditions merit." That the "persons and traditions" were de-
stroying thousands of human beings, denying them their
dignity and their basic rights, seemed not to matter. A far
cry indeed from the use of authority prescribed by an earlier
Paul in II Corinthians 13:7, that there should be a primacy of
the objective good of the believers even at the price of possible loss of prestige to the ruler of the community.

*The Pope Speaks: Dialogues of Paul VI with Jean Guit-
ton** gives a unique glimpse into the Vatican mentality.
It shows Paul at age seventy living in a world as self-contained

*New York: Meredith Press, 1968.

and self-circumscribed as the seminary in which I lived in
the 1920s. He reveals himself as sensitive, spiritual, intellectual, but one whose contact with life is mediated through
books, and whose range of reading and consequently of concern and judgment is that of the traditional Catholic seminary. It is the pope's duty, he insists, not only to condemn
error but "modes of thought that could lead to errors, even
when they are themselves respectable." Only authorized
specialists should be allowed to discuss religious issues in
order to avoid not only errors but inexactitudes. That world
is one in which "the people" are children with nothing to
contribute, a world in which education consists of the one-
way transfer of fixed and eternally established truths from
those who possess them in their storehouse to the beggars
who accept them gratefully and passively. It is light years
from the society the Vatican Council had in mind when, in
its document on *The Church in the Modern World,* it told
the people "to realize that their pastors will not always be so
expert as to have a ready answer to every problem, even
every grave problem, that arises," but rather that they
"should not hesitate to take the initiative at the opportune
moment and put their findings into effect."

The authors Paul and Guitton discussed were almost all
from the past, many from a distant past: Newman, Mercier,
Lord Halifax, Socrates, Saint Augustine, Bossuet, Pascal,
Baudelaire, Dostoevsky, Bernanos, Flaubert, Huysmans,
François Mauriac, Simone Weil, Sigrid Unset, Gertrude
Von Le Fort, Dante, Romano Guardini, Shakespeare, Paul
Claudel, Vergil, Manzoni. And the context never changes.
In the style of the seminary manuals, the dialogue is always
defensive. Quotations overturn enemies or confirm one's
own commitment to perpetuate a past that was more dura-
ble and desirable than the fleeting, quick-changing, and an-
noyingly complicated present. There is no dialectic, no forward and upward movement through a reconciliation of
thesis and antithesis in a system that has discovered and
melded the good in each. In Paul's world, experience was
minimal and consequently suspect and undervalued. It was
a static world of unchanging categories. "You are right to

ask the church for a rule of human conduct," runs a typical reflection. "But you must not expect from her an instant automatic answer to the problems raised in our times, which are often so difficult, so little analyzed, so new, and so continually changing. The face of today's science changes so fast. And within ten years, yesterday's scientist must go to school and learn anew. Burning questions are also complex ones. Simple honesty demands that they be considered without haste. We should have respect for the complexity of things, listen, weigh them. If the past teaches us anything, it is that it is better to wait, to risk disappointing the impatient, than to make hasty improvisations. And the higher the authority, the more it must wait. It is easy to study, difficult to decide."

That passage revealed Paul as seeing himself living outside history, unconcerned with the needs of the real people who are suffering and cannot wait for an answer, if only an inadequate, improvised one. To that he was led by his concept of church teaching as also outside history, not bound by the social and cultural conditioning of the thinkers, the limitations of language, the impossibility of taking into account in one era a concept that had not then been conceived. "May I remind you of the teaching of the church from the beginning," he asks Guitton rhetorically, "which is essential, invariable. . .?" Essences being for him fixed are incapable of development. "They correspond to a design that is invariable although circumstances change." And that includes time, the acceleration of which as we have increased our domination of the material universe seems to have completely escaped his notice. "Fifteen centuries have passed, a brief interval."

In an essay on "The Style of Paul's Leadership," I commented on the paradox in this mentality. "For us who live in the accelerated and foreshortened time-space continuum of the twentieth century, it is not easy to comprehend the mentality that sees fifteen hundred years as a brief interval and that is therefore ready to allow a further fifteen hundred for changes that we feel cannot delay fifteen without building up explosive tensions. The contradictory message I hear is that the pope has the duty to protect us from error, and even from 'modes of thought that could lead us to error,' yet is unable to perform that task in a world moving at the speed of today's technology."*

Vatican II raised our expectations that the church was finally ready to face and dispose of this outmoded and dysfunctional concept of leadership. Church leaders from many countries put on the record abuses hitherto carefully concealed, arbitrary condemnations of and restraints on such orthodox intellectuals as Yves Congar, Karl Rahner, Edward Schillebeeckx, and Hans Küng. At a Council meeting, German Cardinal Frings called the Holy Office procedures scandalous. The Council documents, especially that on *The Church in the Modern World*, offered a concept of relationships within the church radically at variance with Rome's procedures.

The big question, of course, was what would happen when the bishops dispersed and the openly intransigent forces within the Curia mounted the counterattack that everyone knew was bound to come. Catholics all round the world had enormous if often ill-defined expectations. The substitution of the vernacular for Latin in worship meant active participation instead of passive presence at liturgical services. If most bishops were still remote on their pedestals, the gulf between the people on the one side and priests and nuns on the other was rapidly being bridged. All kinds of new structures were being discussed and in some places parish councils were being formed to give substance to the notion that all church members should participate in decision and policy making.

I was in a privileged position to observe and at times to participate in this making of history. During the six years following the Council I commuted almost constantly between the United States and Rome, with trips to many other countries of East and West Europe, Canada, and Latin America. At the close of the Council I was one of fifty theologians and journalists who incorporated IDOC (Infor-

---

*James F. Andrews, ed. *Paul VI: Critical Appraisals*. New York: Bruce Publishing Co., 1970.

mation and Documentation Service) as a nonprofit organization with headquarters in Rome to continue the excellent information service free from official restraints it had provided during the Council.

As it had long been de facto, IDOC now became formally ecumenical. A worldwide network of affiliates and associates would report to IDOC-International in Rome on implementation of the decrees and spirit of the Council and on related religious developments. The Rome center would collate the information, translate into many languages, and distribute directly and through its affiliates. Having survived many ups and downs, this center is now solidly established.

The national units have had more problems. Supported by Monsignor Richard Hanley, editor of the *Long Island Catholic* and a man who combined a world vision with rare executive talent, I inaugurated an IDOC-North America in 1967. As part of the process I returned to Rome for four months as general manager of the parent office, developing systems and procedures it needed as center of a modern publishing operation. My work involved renewal of contacts with many I had met in all parts of Africa and in Asia, from Baghdad to Karachi to Saigon to Tokyo, as well as with Europeans on both sides of the Iron Curtain and with the Latin Americans I had known for years. Unfortunately, Monsignor Hanley died before the United States project had been consolidated, and some years passed before it was revived by others. It then went through several years of successful publishing of important church-related materials, primarily in the social sphere, only to fade away again in the late 1970s.

I returned to Rome in 1967 for the Synod of Bishops, an event on which I coauthored a book with theologian Francis X. Murphy. At the urging of the Council, Paul VI had agreed to a periodic meeting in Rome of a small representative group of bishops to review the state of the church and become a consultative body more in touch with church life and thinking than the Curia. The Council had hoped that it would become the policy-making body for the papacy and reduce the Curia to its proper function as a civil service charged with the implementation of policy. The Synod as

constituted by Paul was accorded a purely advisory status
and had no control over its agenda. The optimists hoped that
it would gradually acquire greater powers. But that did not
happen at the second and third sessions which I also attended as a reporter in 1969 and 1971, nor in subsequent
meetings in 1974, 1977, 1980, 1983, and 1985. Instead, it
had become clear that the Curia had reasserted both its
policy-making and its policy-implementing roles.

The Curia's determination to minimize the impact of the
Council was equally visible at the Congress of the Lay Apostolate also held in Rome in October 1967, a meeting in which
I participated as the member of the International Catholic
Press Union Delegation designated to lead a workshop on
the function of the religious press in the conciliar church.
The Congress was a turning point in the life of the church to
a greater extent than is usually recognized. It brought together from 72 nations 1,415 national delegates, 261 international delegates, 88 observer-consultants from other Christian churches and bodies, 346 experts, 877 auditors, and 413
news reporters.

The membership of the national delegations had been
carefully handpicked by bishops or by committees named by
bishops in each country. Each national delegation was
headed by a bishop and had one or more priest advisers. As
many as six members could be "non-lay" (priests, seminarians, religious brothers, or nuns), and even this rule was not
strictly enforced. Clerics numbered eight in one delegation
of seventeen members, four of seven in another, one of two
in another, and six of thirteen in yet another. In addition,
many of the lay delegates were employees of the bishops or
so long involved in "official" movements as to reflect clerical
more than lay thinking. The organizing committee was composed exclusively of Vatican nominees. It named the five
presidents of the Congress, the twenty-five-member steer-
ing committee and the eighty presidents and rapporteurs of
the workshops. No precaution had been neglected to ensure
a rubber-stamp assembly.

From the very first day, nevertheless, as I wrote* at the

---

*Francis X. Murphy and Gary MacEoin, *Synod '67: A New Sound in Rome.*
Milwaukee: Bruce Publishing Co., 1986, p. 164.

time, "the Congress was dominated by a sense of destiny, a spirit of prophecy, demonstrating how deep is the power released in the church by the second Vatican Council and how universal the renewal of the face of the earth. Unlike the Synod of Bishops, the Congress showed little concern for the institutional problems of the church, apart from a stress on the urgent need to bring institutions into line with contemporary social forms, focusing instead on those of the world today."

In an opening address, Thom Kerstiens of Holland, general secretary of the International Christian Union of Business Executives, set the tone. Our contemporaries are concerned with war and peace, he said, with a world of haves and have-nots, with our increasing alienation in an economy of abundance. They seek to end racial prejudice, to understand why young people behave the way they do, why they look for a new economic philosophy "directed to man redeemed by Christ and. . .establishing a balance between economic efficiency and the full realization of the human being." They need a new morality of commerce and international exchange, a theology of revolution, a reflection on the field opened to Christians in a secularized world. Modern young people leave Christianity not because they find it too exacting, but because they find it too middle-class, not capable of galvanizing their generosity for worthwhile causes.

In spite of frantic behind-the-scenes efforts by the ecclesiastical supervisors, the Congress followed the road mapped by Kerstiens. It called for expansion of the recently formed Council on the Laity in accordance with democratic processes to make it truly representative of the multiple cultures, organizations and forms of the lay apostolate in all parts of the world, ensuring a fair geographic representation. It urged its members, when they returned home, to work consistently for democratically constituted structures of the laity at all levels and in all countries. On responsible parenthood, it expressed "the very strong feeling among Christian lay people that there is need for a clear stand by the teaching authorities of the church which would focus on fundamental moral and spiritual values, while leaving the choice of scientific and technical means for achieving responsible parenthood to parents acting in accordance with their Christian faith and on the basis of medical and scientific consultation."

The result of this confrontation might be described as a stand-off. The Curia failed in its efforts to censor the agenda or control the decisions of the Congress. But it succeeded in the sense that no implementation followed. On the contrary, the end effect was the withering away for lack of official encouragement of the worldwide network of lay organizations. No further Congress has been convoked, and the likelihood of one is minimal. Instead nonofficial groups began to spring up all over the place as an expression of the community that the liturgical changes had encouraged. In the United States, the National Association of Priests Councils became a progressive voice for priests, though from the start suffering the ambiguity that its membership was in part nonofficial and as such free to express itself, but official in some dioceses and there held back by rules and conventions. The National Association of the Laity (NAL) formulated programs matching Kerstiens' concerns and created so many foci that for a time it merited its self-description of "national." The National Association for Pastoral Renewal (NAPR) consisted mostly of priests who had left the active ministry and their wives, many of these former nuns. It included a small number of priests active in the ministry, as well as a few lay people committed to its objectives which on paper encompassed the entire range of pastoral renewal, although in practice it concentrated on creating a more sympathetic and understanding atmosphere within the church in favor of optional celibacy for priests. There was also the more radical Society of Priests for a Free Ministry which encouraged priests who had withdrawn from the jurisdiction of their bishops—usually in order to marry—to organize their own following and continue an active if canonically irregular ministry.

I became a director of NAL and of NAPR, and I represented both these organizations at a meeting in Rome in 1969 called to coincide with the Synod of Bishops and intended as a parallel synod. Most of the participants in this meeting were priests from Europe angered that the agenda and structuring of the second Synod of Bishops failed to show any advance over the earlier session. The newspapers quickly labeled us *contestatori* ("challengers") and that is what we were. For Vatican officialdom, such an open challenge in the Holy City was an insult. So all-pervading is the influence and power of the Curia that we were unable to rent a suitable assembly hall anywhere in Rome. However, the Waldensians, medieval "heretics" who have survived Rome's persecutions and anathemas, took pity on us and gave us the hospitality of their seminary just out of sight of the Vatican.

Unlike the *comunidades de base* ("grassroots communities") later formed in Latin American by peasants and slum dwellers, these movements in Europe and North America were principally a middle-class phenomenon; and after a brief moment of popularity and influence, most of them disappeared as quickly as they had come.

Several causes contributed to their decline. Middle-class priests from northwest Europe and North America had come together in pursuit of two goals: to make celibacy optional so that they might walk out with their wives and baby carriages like their bourgeois friends on Sunday afternoons; and to create a climate in which changing from the priestly ministry to a different career would no longer be considered a disgrace. As the second of these objectives was quickly achieved and the likelihood of attaining the other in the foreseeable future grew dim, many either withdrew from the ministry to marry, or established a secret liaison with a woman companion.

Socially concerned priests who identified with the workers and peasants, most of these in Italy, Spain, Portugal, and Latin America, grew frustrated at the slowness of the organized process and the unconcern of their bourgeois fellow-priests in the rich countries. They went their own way in labor unions, and in obscure political and social organizations, caring little for the protests of ecclesiastical authority but usually escaping formal condemnation unless they became excessively visible and politically challenging.

The crusading zeal of nuns, by far the most numerous element in the institutional church, and the one with least to lose and most to gain from change, similarly declined in the early 1970s as nuns split into three main groups and varied subgroups. Many found the pressures for conformity exerted by Rome and their local bishops intolerable, and most of these simply withdrew to make their own lives as lay persons, while some formed independent communities or communes no longer recognized as religious institutions under canon law. Others found sufficient elasticity within their own communities to permit them to lead their own professional and personal lives without a formal break with their superiors. Finally, not a few found the challenge to make their own moral and personal decisions too much for them. They were happy to cling to their established habits both vestural and personal, basking meanwhile in the approval of the old men in Rome who assured them that their unquestioning obedience and maintenance of tradition was preparing for them unending joy and reward in the life beyond.

Efforts by Rome since the election of Pope John Paul II in 1978 to return nuns to their pre-Vatican II subservience and lifestyle have, however, had the opposite effect. In many countries, and most notably in the United States, powerful coalitions of nuns have joined lay women in open challenge to male dominance of church life and institutions. Theology is no longer a male, much less a clerical, preserve. Far from being cowed by official efforts to silence them, nuns are again emerging as the leading edge of change in the church.

As the already mentioned Congress of the Lay Apostolate made clear, educated lay people, politically aware and accustomed to the conventions of good faith and fair dealing that make possible the functioning of contemporary society, expected at least a similar level of honor, truth, and equity in the operations of the church in which the Council had urged them to get involved. Instead, they were met nearly everywhere with evasions, unfulfilled promises, gross manipulation, naked use of power, and open deceit.

The challenge to Vatican teaching on contraception was for the Roman Curia the most unacceptable issue raised by the Congress. The challenge to clerical celibacy by the various organizations of priests described above was similarly unacceptable. Although intellectually quite distinct, the two issues have long been emotionally linked by a distorted theology of sex; and rational discussion of them was practically impossible because of the success of the church institution in creating a taboo atmosphere around them.

Ironically, the overriding objective sought by Rome in the Middle Ages was not a celibate clergy as such, but simply priests who could not lawfully marry and in consequence could not transmit to their children the properties which the church was anxious to accumulate under its own control. The idea that Catholic priests everywhere lived celibate lives from time immemorial is a pure fiction. Even within the Latin rite, "faithful concubinage" was never eliminated in many places, the Philippine Islands, for example, and various parts of Latin America. Elsewhere, the change was effected slowly and resulted from curious political pressures. Ireland, regarded in modern times as the paradigm of celibate virtue, held out tenaciously. Even married bishops were accepted into the sixteenth century, a practice facilitated by papal willingness to grant dispensations for a fee. In the 1550s, Pope Julius III granted dispensations to all the English priests who had married between Henry VIII's break with Rome in 1534 and Mary Tudor's accession as queen of England in 1553, allowing them to continue in the active ministry. And in the nineteenth century, Pius VII similarly gave dispensations to the priests and monks who had married during the French Revolution.

I have searched extensively but failed to unearth any statistics on the number of priests who profess to live celibate lives but in fact do not. Information from several friends in a position to know in a typical United States diocese has helped me to reach this guesstimate. Half of the priests are normally faithful to their commitment. Twenty-five percent vacation with a woman once or twice a year. Fifteen percent live in what is technically called "faithful concubinage," that is, they have a husband-wife secret relationship with one partner. And ten percent are homosexuals.

I suspect that the proportion of sexually active priests has grown with the development of a more relaxed attitude toward obligations imposed by canon law, thanks to the downgrading of legalisms by Vatican II. However, I do have some evidence that long before that time a considerable number of priests cheated. I have a story from an old monsignor about a banquet with a number of monsignori of the New York archdiocese presided over by Cardinal Spellman. The conversation got round to clerical celibacy, and there was universal condemnation of the moves then starting to make it optional. This monsignor, who insists that a lot of New York priests were then and had long been living in concubinage with the housekeeper or a woman in the parish, resented the hypocrisy. "It would be a shame," he interjected slyly, "when you think of all those fine old men who maintained their commitments, lived holy lives, and died with universal respect, men like Father X." Father X was a priest who had recently died. There was a chorus of agreement with this sentiment, the cardinal the most emphatic of all. Then the monsignor dropped the other shoe. "Yes, and you remember that at the graveside his wife and their seven children showed up." Sudden shift of conversation.

Why does the institution obstinately continue to link formal celibacy with authorization for a priest to function as such, especially after Vatican II spelled out again what has always been Catholic teaching, namely, that only celibacy chosen freely and maturely is virtuous? There are several reasons, quite different from those that introduced the aberration. An important one is the psychological attitude of the older clergy, those now wielding power, that the younger ones should be made to suffer the bitterness, the frustration, and the loneliness they themselves had to endure. That attitude is reinforced by the assumption that, if they now eased the rules, they would be held accountable at the Last Judgment for the "souls" they had consigned to eternal damnation by retaining unnecessary rules for centuries. A similar rationale has complicated the contraception controversy.

In addition, imposed celibacy functions as a powerful control mechanism. The mystique built around celibacy in the seminary and at priestly gatherings strengthens a class and club sense. It forms webs of relationships that guarantee steady advancement within the organization, and such recognition by one's peers is the sweetest music to those for whom ambition has replaced the pleasures of family associations. To leave the active ministry is to lose all the capital thus acquired over years of effort.

Yet another factor in the celibacy syndrome is the deeply ingrained antifeminism of the church. The Old Testament has a variety of cultural attitudes. In Abraham's time, the society was markedly patriarchal. In the Decalogue, the woman comes after the home, but before the male and female slaves, the ox and the donkey, in the list of a man's property. Yet many women excelled as prophets and leaders: Deborah, Judith, Esther. Gradually, however, women were downgraded to the level of children and slaves. Purification rites limited social contacts.

Jesus indeed made a valiant effort to change all that, and in the early church—or at least in some of the early churches—women were on a ministerial and social level with men. The spread of the church in the Greco-Roman world again lowered woman's status, a process culminating in the monopolization of ministries by male priests in the fifth century. By medieval times a theology was developed to support practice. The Scholastics "proved" that women were unsuited for exercising ministry. As St. Thomas put it, "because she is in a state of submission, she is consequently incapable of representing the authority and dignity of the priesthood." Add to this a literal interpretation of the Genesis accounts of woman as afterthought in the Creation and as temptress in the Fall, and you have a theological basis for indoctrinating aspirants to the priesthood with a distorted image of woman, a fear and an emotional withdrawal that leave them with the conviction that sex is dirty and that women exist to create problems for them in their chosen life.

Inevitably, all these myths and misinterpretations became part of the folklore not only of the celibates but of the community. They all served the institutional objectives of placing the clergy on pedestals and ensuring a public opinion that respected them for their celibacy and condemned them if they abandoned it. Women themselves were the most brainwashed of all. Various recent surveys show that the laity would resist women priests even more than the clergy, and that women would resist in greater numbers than men.

While philosophically and theologically quite unrelated, Rome's official teaching on contraception has been deeply influenced by the distorted attitude toward women. Even in Hebrew times, the function of the woman was seen primarily as the production and raising of children. This idea was incorporated into Christian thinking in the Middle Ages, though always with some questioners. St. Charles Borromeo, a leading figure in the final session (1560) of the Council of Trent, was one of these. In his *Catechism of the Council of Trent*, he gives primacy in marriage to the production and raising of children, but adds immediately: "Another and in a certain way primary (*quasiprimaria*) reason is the mutual perfecting of the spouses." Rigorist theologians in later centuries ignored the addition. The 1917 Code of Canon Law stated bluntly: *Matrimonii finis primarius est procreatio atque educatio prolis; secundarius mutuum adiutorium et remedium concupiscentiae.* The accepted translation was "The primary end of marriage is the procreation and education of children; the secondary purpose is mutual aid and the easing of concupiscence.*

The changes are significant. Now we have only one primary end. And Borromeo's "quasiprimaria" has not only been reduced to secondary but grossly distorted in the process. Instead of mutual perfecting, the spouses now help each other and keep each other from sinning by providing a permissible remedy for their lower instincts.

Underlying all of this is a progressive identification of sex with sin, an attitude further bolstered by the "discovery" of a natural law that decreed that the sex organs had one pur-

---

Codex Iuris Canonici. Westminster, Md.: Newman Press, 1944, Canon 1013. Translation by John A. Abbo and Jerome D. Hannan, *The Sacred Canons.* St. Louis: B. Herder Book Co., 1952, II, 164. The 1983 Code prudently gets away from the issue of primary ends. Marriage, it says (Canon 1055), is intended by its nature for the good of the spouses and for the procreation and education of offspring.

pose and no other, this in defiance of one of the most elementary and obvious natural laws, namely, that nature's genius is to endow organs with multiple functions, the tongue with participation in speech, in taste, in feeling, in cleansing, and a host more.

Even when I was a student of theology, I never found that argument intellectually convincing. Understandably, I never made an issue of it while in the seminary. But in the late 1930s, as a freelance journalist, I made several efforts to express my doubts. We Catholics were then so locked into legalisms that the only point I could question in print was the accuracy of the translation of the Code. Latin has no definite article. The text could consequently mean: "The primary. . ." or "A primary. . . ." While it ignored, it did not exclude Borromeo's "quasiprimary" reason or purpose. It is a rule of law that an ambiguity is to be resolved in favor of freedom. I argued, in consequence, that a procreative intention was not needed to justify marital relations of marriage partners.

A modest claim indeed, yet one for which I found little sympathy in the traditional Irish Catholic society in which sex and sin were practically synonymous, and in which it was widely believed that is was sinful for a wife and husband to enjoy the marital relations in which they engaged in order to produce children, and in which, in consequence, many believed intercourse was no longer justified once it was established that the wife had become pregnant. The only practice tolerated to delay a new pregnancy was to continue nursing the youngest as long as possible—not foolproof but worth trying. When the number of children had grown to more than the father's income or the mother's health could stand, all that was left was abstention. Instead of coming home from work in the evening, the husband stopped off at the pub and drank steadily until closing time. By then well soused, he lurched his way to the bedroom and snored drunkenly through the night. Not surprisingly, a human relationship seldom long survived, but the pressures of society usually kept the strangers living under the same roof for the sake of the children.

In Ireland, as elsewhere, the more sophisticated young

people were learning about the so-called safe period, the days in the woman's cycle in which conception cannot occur. But the level of knowledge was inadequate to use this method of contraception with any significant success, particularly when the woman's monthly cycle was irregular. In addition, its liceity was still widely questioned by Catholic theologians in the 1930s and 1940s. It was only in the 1960s, when the great birth-control debate hit the front pages of the world's newspapers and provoked the greatest crisis in the Catholic church since the Protestant Reformation, that Rome wholeheartedly espoused the "safe period" as its answer to the problem of family planning.

There were two major reasons for this change. The population explosion had reached such proportions worldwide that the traditional encouragement of big families had to be abandoned. The acceptance by Catholics of the use of contraceptives, thanks to the development of esthetically more acceptable and functionally more efficient techniques, was creating a yawning gap between official teaching and universal practice. The traditionalists saw in the "safe period" a tolerable compromise. Unlike contraceptive devices, it was not an artificial interference with the sex act to prevent the coming together of sperm and ovum. It merely took advantage of the knowledge that on several days of the menstrual cycle nature failed to provide the conditions for that union in spite of the efforts of the participants.

Many bishops at the Vatican Council, especially those from France, Germany, Belgium and Holland, were dissatisfied with this compromise. Quite apart from the artificiality of the reasoning, they knew that for most spouses, this system did not give the level of protection they needed, and that for many the limitations on conjugal relations it demanded were emotionally destructive. They wanted the Council to approve the radical change that would be needed to bring the church's stand into conformity with the practice of Catholic people. But the Roman Curia was too strong for them. It persuaded Pope Paul to announce that he was reserving this issue for himself. To placate the Council, he set up a series of study groups, including top specialists from all the areas of scientific knowledge involved.

The outcome was a report presented to the Pope in 1966, several months after the Council had ended. In it the vast majority of the experts challenged the basic assumptions, theological, philosophical, and scientific, on which the prohibition of the use of contraceptives rests. The report was, as usual, absolutely secret and confidential. But, as I was to discover once more when I passed briefly through Rome in mid-December 1966 on my way from Spain to Germany, such terms are relative. A friend who had obtained a copy told me he was giving it to *Le Monde* of Paris, hoping that its publication would force the Pope's hand. Like many others, he was frustrated at the months of silence since the delivery of the report and feared that the Curia simply intended to bury it.

His plan, I warned him, could backfire. This highly technical study would appear one day on the streets of Paris. Correspondents of the world news agencies would grab copies and write hasty summaries of a subject about which few of them knew anything. The result would be more likely to confuse public opinion further than to clarify it. Instead, I suggested, the document should first be thoroughly analyzed by people with both technical and journalistic skills who would prepare press releases to go with the text. Accepting my reasoning, he agreed to delay publication while I negotiated with the *National Catholic Reporter* (NCR) of Kansas City, Missouri, to copublish with *Le Monde*, having first made all preparations for release of the story to the wire services, *Time, Newsweek*, and major newspapers.

One major problem remained. Was the document authentic? I could only tell the NCR editors I had confidence in my source, though I could not disclose it. When they received the Latin text, they could use their own devices to check it out. And the price, they asked. To their surprise, I said the scoop was free. I was not involved for gain. I had not made the decision to publish. My concern was that publication should produce the most positive impact possible. And I never wanted anyone to be able to accuse me of making money on a purloined church document.

Publication caused worldwide sensation. Bob Hoyt, NCR's founding editor, regards it as the biggest story of his entire exciting and successful career. It resulted in many appeals similar to that of the Congress of the Lay Apostolate mentioned above. But Rome did not budge. In July 1968, Pope Paul VI tried to freeze the church's position on contraception for all time by reaffirming in *Humanae Vitae* the absolute prohibition of all methods of contraception other than the "safe period."

Seldom in history have Catholic and non-Catholic opinion been in such broad agreement, a combination of incredulity and outrage. The bishops of many countries wrote explanations that attempted to explain away the pope's words. Catholic husbands and wives went on using the prohibited contraceptive methods. Priests continued to give absolution in the confessional to those who told them what they were doing. But it was a time of anguish. Many who felt they had no choice but to use contraceptives, and many of the priests who absolved them, did so in bad faith. They did not have enough theology to justify what they instinctively recognized was their only choice.

Some far-sighted and progressive theologians were, nevertheless, happy. In the long run, they believed, Catholics would be shocked into realizing that each one has to make existential judgments on moral matters. They would come to see that the voice of the people—not the voice of the pope—is the voice of God. Rome's credibility was so shaken that it could never again re-establish the ideological consensus that since the Middle Ages caused the people to accept emotionally and psychologically whatever the holders of power imposed on them.

The most formal attempt to force Rome to institutionalize the changes voted by the Council was made in 1969 by Cardinal Leo Jozef Suenens of Belgium, whose personal contribution to the success of the Council discussions was perhaps greater than that of any other single individual. In an interview published in 1969 in a French Catholic newsmagazine and quickly reprinted in all parts of the world, he identified the tension on the issue of coresponsibility in the church since the Council as resulting from a conflict of theologies. For both ecumenical and theological reasons, he said, the pope should never be presented in isolation from the college of bishops he heads. Bishops, in turn, should recognize in theory and practice that many problems can no longer be solved by a decree of authority without the backing of priests and laity. All have to be involved—if not in decision-taking—at least in decision-making. Today we are dealing with a modern person with a different anthropology, a different scale of values, a different mentality, one conscious of personal dignity, of human rights, of the inalienable rights of conscience, of the right to be judged by one's peers. In all these respects, he concluded, the Roman Curia is an anachronism. It is not the pope's authority that is being challenged by the faithful but the "system" that keeps him prisoner, that makes him responsible for the smallest decision of any Roman Congregation, a decision the pope has not signed or even seen.

The worldwide response was enthusiastic. The *Times* (London) summed it up by saying that the Suenens manifesto gave new hope to the many Catholics who had lost faith in the hierarchy. Encouraged, Suenens carried his campaign to many countries, speaking to influential audiences and on general television. I helped to organize a tour of the United States and presided at a massively attended and reported news conference in New York. But Rome refused to budge. Pope Paul's health and vigor had declined, and all the Suenens open challenge did was to confirm that the Curia had recovered the strangle hold over church affairs that Vatican II had temporarily loosened. Disillusioned, Suenens abandoned church politics to concentrate his energies on the suddenly popular neopentecostal movement.

John Paul I, who succeeded Paul VI in 1978, did not live long enough to reveal his intentions regarding church reform, though rumors circulated after his sudden death that important curial figures were at least relieved at the intervention of providence. Hopes were again aroused with the selection of the first non-Italian pope in many centuries, an event widely interpreted as evidence that the Curia's control of the election process had ceased to be total. It did not take very long, however, to see that the Curia could live comfortably with the Polish pope. That he was a tough politician became evident on his first visit as pope to his homeland, when he answered the taunt made during World War II by Stalin by demonstrating how many divisions the pope in fact has. He made the same point on each of his unending round of visits to all parts of the world, especially in Mexico where tumultuous millions demonstrated to greet him and remind their government that a hundred years of anticlerical and antireligious governments had not achieved their objectives.

Obviously influenced by the success of the Polish church in maintaining popular allegiance and power in the face of a hostile regime, he seeks a monolithic, unquestioning unity as the basis for the church's survival. Since that scenario excludes the theological pluralism that is inherent in the mentality of John XXIII and Vatican II, it commits the church to a fundamentalist conservatism. It is, accordingly, not surprising that the Vatican again refuses to discuss such issues of human rights within the church as the ministry of women, effective family planning, optional celibacy, remarriage where an earlier union has died. It would set progress at the speed at which the most resistant can be persuaded to adapt. Given the acceleration of change as the central characteristic of our society, this means that the world will continue to move away faster than the church is prepared to run after it.

As a logical corollary of this mindset, John Paul II cannot envision a shift of the center of church power and decision making from Europe. The results show up in unlikely places. In one of his most important pontifical statements, for example, the encyclical *Laborem exercens* ("engaging in work"), one finds only a few passing references to the vast numbers, including more than half of all Roman Catholics, who live lives of desperation in the Third World of dependent capitalism. His expressed concern is for the millions of skilled workers threatened by automation and the exhaustion of natural resources. Nor is there any mention or even echo of the Liberation Theology that offers self-realization and dignity to the Third World masses.

John Paul's known aversion to Liberation Theology follows logically from his conservatism and commitment to monolithic unity. But political considerations reinforce it. At least since Vatican II, the church in Latin America has been agitated by movements to end the colonial control to which it has always been subject, movements expressed most concretely in Liberation Theology and the phenomenon of the *comunidades de base* ("grassroots communities"). In the late 1960s, this movement for local autonomy was encouraged by arrangements for greater consultation with bishops, clergy, and laity before a new bishop was appointed. The Curia, however, never reconciled itself to this watering down of its discretionary power. Paul VI's health forced him from about 1970 to withdraw progressively from making decisions, enabling it to regain full control. When Brazil's bishops notified the papal nuncio that they had set up standing committees in each region of the country to obtain input from clergy and laity and recommend candidates to be named bishops, he didn't even bother to acknowledge their letter. Before selecting a candidate to be appointed by Rome to a vacant diocese, he consulted only a few conservative archbishops, ignoring the president of the Bishops' Conference and other progressive cardinals. In this way two groups of bishops were named in 1978 before John Paul II's election. The new pope acquiesced in naming sixteen new bishops and transferring eight others according to the same procedures shortly after his election. One of those named had earlier had to leave his own diocese when it became known that he had denounced his bishop to the secret police as politically suspect. He is a member of the militant right-wing movement known as Tradition, Family, and Property.

"The entire affair," noted *Informations Catholiques Internationales* of Paris, "suggests that this policy of naming bishops constitutes, on the part of the conservative elements of the Roman Curia (and specifically Cardinal Baggio, a former nuncio in Brazil), a program of reprisals against the courageous stands of the Brazilian bishops in recent years." Among all the Latin American countries in which military dictatorships used torture, repression, and other violations of human rights as instruments of state policy, Brazil was distinguished by the solid opposition of its bishops to such atrocities. As such it earned the enmity of the reactionary secretariat of the Latin American Bishops' Conference (CELAM) headed for many years by Archbishop (now Cardinal) Alfonso López Trujillo, and of his patron, Cardinal Sebastiano Baggio, the Curia's watchdog over the church in Latin America. Both of these see the church's future as inextricably tied to the capitalist power structures that constitute for it a bulwark against the adventurous aggressions of "godless" communism.

That John Paul II is comfortable in this company was already clear from the events leading up to and following the meeting in January 1979 of the Latin American bishops at Puebla, Mexico. His major talks carried by world television echoed (and were obviously written by) CELAM's spokesmen. After the Puebla meeting, a still more reactionary CELAM secretariat was installed. One of its first actions was to write the Brazilian bishops assembled in plenary session that they should not arrange any discussion of the Puebla documents without first notifying CELAM and receiving guidelines from it. What CELAM and the Roman Curia fear is that a progressive Brazilian episcopate will come to dominate the Latin American church which in a few years will contain more than half the world's Catholics.

Vatican policies toward the church in Latin America since Puebla all indicate John Paul's agreement with the belief of López Trujillo and Baggio that firm controls must be maintained on the institution in order to prevent movements for reform and autonomy. Conservative clerics are singled out for advancement to the rank of bishop. At a higher level, John Paul restored a European majority of cardinal electors and increased the proportion of Italian cardinals. Latin America may have a majority of the world's Catholics by the year 2000, but it will have a long struggle to shift the locus of power across the Atlantic; and when it succeeds, it may find that it has merely transferred the final word from one self-perpetuating Curia to another equally self-perpetuating and unresponsive to the wishes of its constituents.

The curial attacks on Liberation Theology which made headlines in the world press in 1984 were undoubtedly motivated in part by Rome's determination to retain ideological control over the Latin American church. The protagonist was a conservative German cardinal, Joseph Ratzinger, whom John Paul II had named head of the Congregation for the Doctrine of the Faith (ex-Holy Office). His attack was two-pronged. He summoned to Rome two major exponents of the new theology, Father Gustavo Gutiérrez of Peru, and Father Leonardo Boff of Brazil, to explain certain passages in their writings that he regarded as unorthodox. Simultaneously, he issued a long document warning against dangers and deviations which he claimed existed in some Liberation theologians, though without naming any names or giving any citations from published works. The Pope, he stressed, had approved this document before publication. The Voice of America and other official and semi-official propaganda organs of the U.S. Administration (for reasons that will appear later) amplified the media barrage.

The assault was blunted, however, when after an inconclusive exchange between Ratzinger and Gutiérrez, the Peruvian bishops reaffirmed their confidence in Gutiérrez's orthodoxy. Ratzinger was further discomfited when Boff arrived in Rome flanked by two cardinals and all the episcopal members of the Brazilian Commission for the Doctrine of the Faith, an effective repudiation of his charges that Liberation theologians had invented "a popular church" at odds with the hierarchy. In Rome, the Brazilian cardinals further weakened Ratzinger's credibility and good faith by disabusing the Pope of the impression Ratzinger had given him that the Brazilian bishops had seen before publication and approved Ratzinger's document.

At the Synod of Bishops in Rome in December 1985, Ratzinger renewed his attack through several spokesmen who urged the Synod to condemn the Theology of Liberation. Two Brazilian cardinals responded with equal vigor, and the subject was not mentioned in the Synod's conclusions. The following April the Vatican published a long document on Christian freedom and liberation which suggested in a roundabout way that the church did not need the Theology of Liberation because its members had all the guidance they needed in papal social teaching. Then, quite surprisingly, a few days later the Brazilian bishops received a letter from Pope John Paul strongly endorsing their work, a letter that they and Catholic opinion in general took to mean that they could continue freely to develop the Theology of Liberation. The Ratzinger offensive would seem, at least for now, to be blunted.

It should by now be more than clear why all interested in reform of the church see the Roman Curia as the principal blockage. Self-centeredness, self-importance, and the inability to think of people except as things to be used and manipulated characterize its spirit at all levels. Even the pope's orders are circumvented when they do not suit. Pope John had stressed that he wanted a Council without condemnation, yet the curialists who controlled the preparations presented at the first session a series of documents bristling with anathemas and calculated to embitter relations with other Christians. Time and again at the Council, Curia members were caught in misrepresentations or in misuse of their office for partisan purposes, tactics that would have brought swift retribution if they were civil servants in a contemporary state. They altered Council texts surreptitiously. They distributed pamphlets with scurrilous attacks on Council Fathers opposed to their views. A release from the Vatican press office in October 1964 accused newsmen of having invented a letter that seventeen cardinals had in fact sent the pope.

In the already mentioned essay on the style of Paul's leadership, I described how I had occasion one day in 1969 to enter the Vatican, past the boy soldiers in fancy dress who guard the medieval gates. My destination was the Camposanto, once the site of Nero's Circus. It is directly behind the Palace of the Holy Office, now officially the Congregation for the Doctrine of the Faith. One enters the Camposanto through an opening in a fortress wall to a monastery garden that is also a cemetery. One walks on graves twenty feet deep. When the coffins pile up close to the surface, the lower ones are removed and the crumbling bones are relocated in urns cemented into the walls of the surrounding monastery.

There I met a grave monsignore with chiseled features. His rooms overlooked the cemetery, and he had spent a lifetime of prayer and study in this stylized yesterday, listening year after year to the ghosts of the martyrs sighing in the nerve-irritating sirocco and the rheumaticky *tramontana*. A New York publisher had asked me to get information about an enormous collection of commentaries on the Scriptures by early Church Fathers, a collection the monsignore had been translating for years. Graciously, he tried to explain what was involved, his didactic technique quickly revealing that he assumed me to be as ignorant of his world as he apparently was of mine. He talked down to me, as priests were long conditioned to talk down to lay people. All of the words in these commentaries that he was collating and translating, he assured me, with confidence in his voice that I would accept everything he said as coming to me from God through this chosen spokesman, all of them and every single one were inspired. The many sayings of Jesus that had not been recorded by Saint John or the other evangelists had been handed on orally from generation to generation, without losing or adding a word, until the Fathers put them in writing for us.

He recognized the incredulity in my face, for I made no effort to hide it. Apart from a multitude of other considerations, I knew as a one-time folklore collector how creative and developmental is the folk memory, how from generation to generation it embellishes what it has received. Yet to him the possibility never occurred that I might have a concept different from his, one more consonant with the nature and dignity of human beings, of the contributions the Fathers made to the growth of the church. For him there could be only one reason why I failed to assent. "Do you find it difficult to understand what I am saying?" he asked. Not *difficult to accept* but *difficult to understand*. With such intellectual snobbery dialogue is impossible.

As we paced back and forth, engaged in this incredible

conversation, on top of the twenty-foot-deep graves, in one of which he hoped to lay his bones one day to eternal rest, I was recalling a comment made the previous day at an outdoor cafe down the street by a priest long familiar with the Vatican scene but no part of it. Referring to the Synod of Bishops then in session, he said: "The bishops are talking openly in the pope's presence. He listens and he is impressed. But they soon depart, while he stays. What is important is not what he hears in the morning in the Hall of the Broken Heads, but what he hears last thing at night, every night in his life, as he goes to bed. 'Santo Padre,' says the self-assured and reassuring voice, 'do not be alarmed. The barbarians have always been at the gates, just as they are now. But providence has always picked the right man to deal with them, to out-maneuver them, and finally rout them. Fifteen hundred years ago, Pope Leo I met Attila the Hun, and the awe-struck savage backed away from the gaze of God's anointed. A thousand years ago, Emperor Henry IV humiliated Pope Gregory VII, and for that he stood three days barefoot in the snow at the gates of the castle of Canossa. Today we are still blessed, Santo Padre. The blood of Leo and Gregory runs in your veins."

No doubt the high curial official who lulls the pope to slumber with his reassuring rigmarole is influenced by his own vested interest. But his argument is effective precisely because the pope's conditioning places him on one side of an old philosophic concept that is of critical practical importance today: the Greek notion of history as circular, ever condemned to repeat itself, and the Hebrew notion of time as linear with man challenged by God to make history by struggling toward eschatological perfection.

For animals other than man, the past is totally conditioning. What the species learned for its self-preservation down the ages determines the response of the individual in circumstances that seem to duplicate that earlier experience. The salmon returning to spawn, faced by a barrier created by man or earthquake since its parents had mounted the same stream, will leap futilely against the unsurmountable object until it dies of exhaustion. We, on the contrary, need

not be captives of our past. Our present should determine
how we read the past, not the other way round. But it is only
to the extent that we are not blinded by the Greek error, to
the extent that we know and are prepared to function as the
makers of our future, of our own future and that of all humankind, that we can understand and interpret our past.
The captive of the past, on the other hand, is an oppressed
person with an oppressed consciousness. As Brazilian theologian Rubem Alves points out perceptively, Nietzsche's fu-
rious attack on Christianity and Western civilization was
based to a large degree on his discovery that they had eter-
nalized past values, transposing them into metaphysics,
thus forcing them on us as the only possible models for the
future.

Alves was in fact discussing the structure of Pope Paul's
consciousness when he made that observation. "The oppressed consciousness," he wrote, "is the one which is under
the bewitchment of the past; which lives in a world 'defined'
by the dead definitions which are legitimized as metaphysics, which become the laws of the present, which become
the models of the future. Definitions which, precisely because they are definitions, imply that history has come to an
end. Definitions which 'program' man in a way structurally
similar to the biological 'programming' which controls animals." His conclusion: for Pope Paul, "the past is master
over man."

As described earlier, I was raised in this tradition,
steeped in it so deeply that when I reflect, I marvel at the
resilience of the human mind that can literally detach itself
from itself and remake its own character. Plato, Aristotle,
Augustine, and Thomas Aquinas, read in the original and interpreted by men as sure of their inspiration as the monsignore waiting his turn to be buried in the Camposanto,
had—I thought—established for me for ever the superiority
of the deductive over the inductive approach to reasoning.
Once you started from axiomatic principles—and the church
was on hand to guarantee their accuracy—you had only to
follow them to their logical conclusions, the church holding
your hand meanwhile to safeguard the logic. If instead you

played around with fickle novelties, attempting to judge on the basis of observation and experience, you inevitably lost your way sooner or later in the uncertainties of the created condition.

In retrospect, I suspect that my internal assent was probably never as total as my formal acceptance of this philosophy. Aristotle himself insisted that in a chain of deductive reasoning, each link is weaker than the previous one. The certainty of the final conclusion is consequently less than that of the first principle. To surmount that obstacle, our teachers had worked out an elaborate theory of the inerrancy of the church's teaching on purely natural issues to the extent that they were related to revealed truth. In practice, this covered just about everything, Galileo notwithstanding.

Some years after I left the seminary, in my study of medieval literature, including the rediscovery of Aristotle in the West in Arabic translations, I came upon a point never mentioned in my philosophy courses. In his major studies of the natural sciences, Aristotle insisted that theory must derive from fact. Thus, when he set out to write a treatise on the crab, he did not start from first principles and build a series of syllogisms that would establish that the crab had to walk backwards. Rather he set off to the island of Lesbos and combed the beaches and rocks. An extended study of the actual structure and habits of crabs produced a theory to explain their peculiar form of locomotion.

Reflecting on this discovery, I began to ask myself if the limited knowledge and control of the environment achieved by humankind in Aristotle's time and for long after was not the real reason for such emphasis on theoretical analysis and deduction. Only in the relatively recent past has this situation been transformed. Our ability to establish facts, to analyze, to synthesize has now expanded to cover almost the whole of life, thanks to the microscope, the telescope, the airplane, the computer, and the many other inventions and discoveries that have made the life sciences possible and potentially beneficial. Lacking this knowledge, the ancients had no choice but to rely on deduction. The trouble with the

Curia is that it has not wakened up to the fact that now there is a better way.

To recognize the primacy of the inductive over the deductive method is a discovery of cosmic proportions. Sociology now becomes more important than philosophy as a tool for understanding the world of which we form a part. For the believer, sociology similarly replaces philosophy as a primary source of input for theologizing. Ironically, Rome of the Vatican Council and of the major church meetings of subsequent years was the catalyst that brought this revolution, this rebirth to me, as to many others. Part of the process was the physical and intellectual exposure to the Roman mind as I have been describing it, the gradual realization that its inability to deal with people as they are results from philosophical and theological distortions so imbedded as to be incapable of being exorcised by any rite so far developed. But an even bigger role was played by the people from all over the world, the participants in the press conferences and others, who had thought their way or were in the process of thinking their way to a new equilibrium that would give meaning to their lives both as humans and as believers.

9

Voices of the Voiceless

Such exposure to updated European metaphysics was enormously satisfying. It fulfilled, nevertheless, only part of the purpose that had led me back to Europe from America, and then to Africa and Asia. I had invested twenty years in Latin America, had acquired recognition in both the business and academic world, had moved from a euphoric confidence that I was part of a process of development and modernization to a state of uncertainty and confusion. I had no answers. I didn't even have neat questions. I had come on this quest with only doubts and gropings—obscure suspicions that I must go beyond Latin America to see Latin America, that the apparently disparate and conflicting political, economic, cultural, and religious phenomena could perhaps only be synthesized at the global level.

Gradually I discovered that many of the bishops and theologians who had come to the Council from the Third World shared my doubts and questionings. At first, they spoke cautiously and tentatively. After all, they were dependent on funds collected in the rich countries and channeled to them through the Rome-located and Curia-dominated Society for the Propagation of the Faith. Encouraged, however, by the criticism of the Roman system, both theological and administrative, in which the financially independent cardinals and bishops of Western Europe openly indulged, they gradually built coalitions. At first they were conscious mainly of their own institutional problems. Only later did the logic of their challenge open up broader issues. Starting with appeals to recognize that Jesus had always given preference to the poor, they formulated the theological and political reasons why the state of tutelage of the so-called mission churches should end. The Latin Americans, while conscious of their different historical experience, soon became aware that the practical issues for them were remarkably similar to those of the Africans and Asians. While Rome monopolized decision making, they would get European solutions that aggravated their problems.

An incident in which Dom Helder Camara, archbishop of Recife (Brazil), was involved in November 1962, illustrates the rapidity of the change. Asked to say Mass for the journalists covering the Council, he prepared a homily typical of the outspokenness which had already earned him in Brazil the name of the "slum bishop." His draft text protested the pomp of the Council's inaugural Mass as "difficult to justify in this age of television." It regretted that in six weeks the Council "has not yet touched on any of the major problems of our age," and suggested a penitential rather than a thanksgiving service as a fitting close to the session. The official press bureau insisted on reviewing the draft and rewrote it to eliminate these "inappropriate" comments. A newcomer to Rome with no influential following, Dom Helder had to submit. Two years later, by now vice-president of the Latin American Bishops' Council (CELAM) and recognized leader of a coalition of bishops of the poor countries of the world, he again addressed the journalists, praising the press, radio, and television "for their help to the Council." They deserved thanks, he said, "not only for reporting what is going on in St. Peter's but especially for not watering down the truth. The church has no need of our pious lies."

Contrary to the claims of the Roman curialists who sought to maintain their monopoly, theology is not a science that develops within its own closed confines. It reflects and expresses in each time and place the felt needs and identified awarenesses of those who theologize. The discovery by the bishops of Asia, Africa, and Latin America at the Council— or rather on the occasion of the Council (it is significant that Dom Helder never once opened his mouth at a meeting of the Council)—that their needs were not met by the theology they had inherited, started a revolution that continues to develop momentum.

Irrelevant to the churches of Asia and Africa, and— though in a different way—to those of Latin America, was the division of Christians into Catholics and Protestants, a problem resulting from and nourished by political, social, and economic differences of Europe's past. Far from creating emotional problems, ecumenical cooperation was seen by them as essential to survival. The resulting change in the alignment of religious forces was particularly striking and important in Latin America. Before the Council, Roman Catholics and Protestants constituted two monolithic blocs in total conflict on issues theological, political, and social. Just a few years produced a radical realignment that promises to endure indefinitely. On one side progressive Catholics and Protestants work together in harmony, while ranged against them is a similar coalition of reactionary Catholics and Protestants. The change is reasonable. The Protestant Reformation had occurred for specific historic reasons in Europe, and its importation to Latin America was a byproduct of European conflicts, a part of the process of the Conquest. The new division reflects the reality of social forces in the hemisphere.

Two events in 1964 and 1965 played a major part in moving the progressive church from concern with its institutional problems to a leadership role in the social revolution that was shaking the foundations of the status quo in every country of Latin America. With Washington's encouragement, the Brazilian army overthrew the constitutional presidency. The military dictatorship it substituted quickly rescinded social reforms introduced by the ousted regime and began a process of destruction of political parties, trade unions, and other expressions of popular opinion. And in the Dominican Republic, when indirect support failed, the United States sent in twenty-four thousand marines to block the accession to power of a constitutionally elected president. In both cases, the result of the U.S. intervention was to initiate a process of transformation of the economy to ensure greater benefits for the rich and greater suffering and deprivation for the poor, a repudiation of the Charter of the Alliance for Progress on which the ink was scarcely dry.

While these events were happening in Latin America, the church was attempting at the Council, for the first time in its history, to define its proper role in the common human effort to carry the world to the perfection envisaged by God and made manifest in the life and teaching of Jesus Christ. The results are found in the Council's last major statement, *Gaudium et Spes* (The Church in Today's World).

"The church sincerely professes that all people, believers and unbelievers alike, ought to work for the rightful betterment of the world where all live together." Human activity directed to improving living conditions "accords with God's will. Humans, created in God's image, received a mandate to subject the earth and all it contains. . . . This mandate concerns the whole of everyday activity. . . .The triumphs of the human race are a sign of God's grace and a flowering of God's mysterious design."

To the scandal of the Wall Street Journal, the Council went on to challenge several of the sacred cows of the American Way of Life. Justice, it asserted, gives top priority to the struggle to end the monstrous inequalities both within nations and between rich and poor nations. Not the search for power and profit, but the service of the people without distinction of race or geographic location is the fundamental law of economic progress. Private property is not absolute. It is good only to the extent that it furthers this objective. It can take many forms and must not be presented as an obstacle to public ownership when the common good so indicates. The huge estates in countries in which the peasants are landless and starving constitute a specific abuse of private property. Our realistic goals today should include a human level of comfort for the average person everywhere, democratic sharing of the orientation of national and world economies, and participation of organized labor in management of industry.

Latin American bishops lost no time in applying the new thinking to their own situation. Two weeks before the end of the Council in December 1965, Dom Helder—now spokesman for a coalition with worldwide support—described the challenge.

"Almost two thousand years after the death of Christ, at a time when the Declaration on Religious Liberty is to be promulgated, nearly two-thirds of humans live in a subhuman condition that makes it impossible for them to understand the real meaning of liberty. . . .Underdevelopment has plunged Latin America and the whole 'third world' into a situation unworthy of the human person; it constitutes an insult to creation. A revolt by Latin American Christians against the church is inevitable if the church sins today by omission, in an hour of oppression and slavery."

For me it was enormously exciting to have the opportunity to dialogue with Dom Helder and other Latin American bishops and theologians while they were engaged in this effort to chart a new course and define a new program for the church. Up to that time, churchmen had left economics strictly to bankers and other representatives of big business, contenting themselves with pious exhortations to the decision makers to share justly the fruits of joint enterprises, whether between employer and worker, or between dominant country and dependent country. Business wanted it to stay that way. And as the churches began to exhibit greater social concern and to ask hard questions about the growing gap between rich and poor countries, the world business community with its control of the media of information challenged the right of church leaders to get mixed up in things that were none of their concern. The rich countries, they insisted, were more than generous in their aid for the poor. All that was needed was patience until the benefits of development trickled down to the peasants and slum dwellers. It was the church's job, as it always had been, to preach patience. Besides, they ·argued, these church spokesmen didn't know what they were talking about. They had no training in the complexities of international trade and finance.

There was merit to the last argument. A sociological study I did in 1977 revealed that of the 120 cardinals who at that time formed the college that elects a pope, the overwhelming majority had been trained in philosophy, theology, and canon law. Absent from their studies had been any balancing exploration of the vast range of contemporary knowledge in art, literature, and the life sciences. Five had a degree in literature, four in sociology or other social sciences, one in political science, one in economics, none in biology, physics, computerization, cybernetics, communications, population, ecology, future planning, or other sciences that dominate contemporary thinking and are needed to make informed judgments on the issues that agitate the world today. This description is valid for bishops in general, from whose ranks cardinals are selected.*

Dom Helder was well aware of the dilemma. "I'm way out of my depth in this area," he once commented to me with characteristic humility and frankness, as we discussed a talk he had been asked to give in Brussels to an association of European businessmen. "But these things have to be said, and if no one else is ready to say them, I'll do the best I can—and learn as we go." Learn he certainly did, and he also persuaded many of his Latin American colleagues that the future of Christianity in the hemisphere hung on the church's response to the economic and social crisis that had been building up since World War II. Ten of the eighteen bishops who signed "A Letter to the Peoples of the Third World" in August 1967 were Latin Americans. The document would have a deep and lasting impact on the thinking of the poor countries, especially in Latin America.

Challenging the neocolonialist thesis that poor countries must accept control of their economies by the rich and materially developed nations if they wish to progress, they insisted that every country and people must liberate itself, that liberation from outside is at best a change of masters.

*Gary MacEoin, *The Inner Elite.* Kansas City: Sheed, Andrews and McMeel, 1978, p. xix.

"It is primarily up to the poor nations and the poor of the other nations to effect their own betterment. They must regain confidence in themselves. They must educate themselves and overcome their illiteracy. They must work zealously to fashion their own destiny.... Their pastors, for their part, must dispense the word of truth and the gospel of justice in its entirety.... The working classes and the poor must get together, for only unity will enable the poor to demand and achieve real justice.... It is our duty to share our food and all our goods. If some try to monopolize what others need, then it is the duty of public authority to carry out the distribution that was not made willingly.... We cannot allow rich foreigners to come and exploit our impoverished peoples under the pretext of developing commerce and industry; nor can we allow rich nationals to exploit their own nation.... The economic system allows the affluent nations to keep getting richer even when they offer a modicum of aid to the poor nations; the latter, in the meantime, keep getting poorer. These poor nations have the right to press, with all the legitimate means at their disposal, for the establishment of a world government where all nations without exception would be represented, and which would have the competence to demand and even force an equitable distribution of the earth's goods. This is an indispensable precondition for world peace....

"Governments must face up to the task of stopping class warfare. Contrary to popular belief, this warfare is often incited by the rich; and they keep it up by exploiting the worker through inadequate wages and inhuman working conditions. It is a subversive war that has been craftily waged throughout the world for a long time by money interests, annihilating whole nations in the process. It is high time that poor people, supported and guided by legitimate governments, defend their right to live. When God appeared to Moses, he told him: 'I have seen the miserable state of my people in Egypt, I have heard their appeal to be free of their slave drivers.... I mean to deliver them' (Ex. 3:7). Jesus took all humanity upon himself to lead it to eternal life. And the earthly foreshadowing of this is social justice, the first form of brotherly love. When Jesus freed humankind from death through his resurrection, he brought all human liberation movements to their fullness in eternity."

This document anticipated the essential conclusions of the Conference of Latin American Bishops held a year later at Medellín, Colombia. The Medellín statement introduced a significant new element, however, one now recognized as an integral part of Latin America's original contribution to Christian thought, the Liberation Theology that was then in the early stages of incubation. Departing from the characteristic style of papal social teachings and of traditional theology, the bishops at Medellín began with a sociological and historical analysis of the reality of Latin America, then proceeded to draw conclusions on the basis of that factual analysis. The detailed catalog of the evils crying for remedy was thus related directly to the causes of those evils: the dependent internal oligarchies in each country, the overarching external power structures of international monopolies and the international imperialism of money on which the system rested, the fact of intolerable institutionalized violence.

Once you reach this point of facing squarely the causes of the enormous and growing gap between rich and poor in our world, the external gap between rich and poor countries, and the internal gap between the few rich monopolizers of power and of decision making and the many powerless and relatively poor in the rich countries and the even greater numbers powerless and at a subhuman level of indigence in the poor countries, you have to make an option both as a human being and as a Christian. Do you, a beneficiary of the unjust structures, live as a parasite, enjoying your benefits as a mercenary, assuaging your conscience with the knowledge that your relative power and prestige enable you to ease the hardships of some, while your obvious lack of a real power base limits to the token or the quixotic your possibility to challenge?

And if you opt to challenge, what form can your challenge take? Indoctrinated over many centuries, and more insistently for the last century and a half, to regard as the natural order of things the division of humankind into rich and

poor, the Christian is easily tempted to reject any effort to
organize the poor in movements to change the established
injustice on the ground that such activity would constitute
an incitement to class war and as such be a direct violation of
the Christian law of love.

We have new goals. But we now have to reach agreement
on the means that are reasonably calculated to reach those
goals and are simultaneously morally permissible for us. In
the 1980s this issue of means still continues to divide Christians radically. Many of us, nevertheless, have transcended
the naïveté of the 1950s. We then shared Dom Helder's illusion that once the leaders of the rich countries were persuaded intellectually of the fact that the gap between a small
minority of high-living haves and a multitude of impoverished and impotent have-nots was growing dangerously,
they would recognize that equity and a sense of survival
would combine to make them accept the adjustments required to avoid global catastrophe. I remember how impressed I was by a statement Dom Helder made in 1965.
"The day North America decides to prevail upon all nations
to reexamine in depth the international politics of business—
the only way to the heart of the problem of harmonious and
overall development—the world will be nearer to peace than
if all the nuclear stockpiles were destroyed. . . . Political colonialism has ended but economic colonialism remains,
heavy and suffocating. The antitrust laws that exist in the
United States should be applied to commerce with the Third
World."

The Latin American bishops at Medellín three years later
had not moved beyond this position. As I noted above, they
broke radically from tradition by starting with a sociological
and historical analysis of the reality of the hemisphere, an
analysis that led them to identify and reject capitalism as
the root of their problems. But they added immediately that
if the solution is not to be found "in the liberal capitalist system," neither can it come from "the temptation of the Marxist system." The former they condemned "because it starts
by assuming the primacy of capital, of its power, and of its
right to indiscriminate use in order to make profits"; the lat-

ter, "because even if ideologically it can support humanist values it is more concerned with collective man, and in practice it ends up as a totalitarian concentration of power in the state."

What happened at Medellín is important, not only as illustrating the dynamics of the shift in the power balance within the church, but also as bringing into the open the concern of big business when threatened with losing the legitimation the church had long accorded it. The struggle for hearts and minds is one of the most fascinating aspects of contemporary life, and historically it is likely to prove more decisive than nuclear superiority.

Medellín's analytical documents were drafted by progressive priests, foremost among them Joseph Comblin, a Belgian-born sociologist, who enjoyed the confidence of those then in control of the Latin American Bishops' Council (CELAM). When the texts became known, they brought a torrent of denunciation from the institutional media. The Brazilian press dominated by the military dictatorship installed four years earlier called Comblin a bad priest, author of "a new *Mein Kampf*" (they probably meant *Das Kapital*), and "a Leninist theologian." The government was urged to exclude him from Brazil, where he was a seminary professor, "in order to save the religious patrimony of Brazil and its democratic security," an action the government in fact took at a later date. In Colombia, *La República* compared Comblin to Camilo Torres, the Colombian priest sociologist who had been killed while fighting with a guerrilla band two years earlier. The document, it charged, was calculated "to incite Catholics, on the occasion of the bishops' conference, to armed conflict and an alliance with Marxists."

The vast majority of the bishops buckled under such pressures. Comblin had once described the church as "one of the most underdeveloped of all Latin American institutions," a description that fitted the bishops precisely. Men of limited education and experience, most of them identified with the oligarchs who had selected them for office, and on whose favors they depended. They were adept as oratorical denouncers of sin, but they had no intention of promoting concrete programs of reform that might upset their privileged status. And so they defused the bomb Comblin had planted through a typical compromise. The economy, they proclaimed sententiously, should be restructured according to "the directives of the social magisterium of the church." Following Popes Leo XIII and Pius XI, they claimed that the monopolizers of wealth and power could be persuaded by appeals to religious principles and enlightened self-interest to change their ways.

"We make an urgent appeal to businessmen and their organizations, as well as to the political authorities, to modify radically their system of values, their attitudes and methods, as they affect the purpose, organization and operation of their enterprises. These entrepreneurs who individually or through their organizations try to operate their business in accordance with the directives of the social doctrine of the church deserve every support. Only through such initiatives can social and economic change in Latin America be directed toward a truly human economy."

An amazing statement. Purporting to offer a middle way between capitalism and socialism, it in fact repeated the capitalist rhetoric that a sound economy and well-being for all is best guaranteed by letting businessmen use their discretion and judgment. It parallels the "jawboning" approach to control of wages and prices of recent U.S. presidents.

Medellín, nevertheless, was a watershed. What the people heard and understood was the analysis. It changed them rapidly, and within a decade it had changed the balance of power and the dynamics of the church and had eroded the unjust structures of society. Most bishops remained bound in their emotional straitjackets. But the people had taken charge of their own lives as humans and as Christians, organized in a hemispheric network of *comunidades de base* ("grassroots communities"), backed by many priests, nuns, and other church leaders. Catholic and Protestant theologians had justified the shift in the power base by developing Liberation Theology, a radical departure in church thinking that swept from Latin America around the world.

Another experience in 1968 brought additional perspectives to my thinking. After participating in a world congress of the Catholic press in Berlin, I went with forty or fifty of my colleagues to Moscow, Prague, Budapest, and Warsaw. While that survey was too brief and superficial to support serious judgments, it challenged a number of assumptions. Destructive of the concept of a monolith was the enormous difference of style of the communist leaders we met in those countries, and the similar differences in their self-understanding of what they were trying to do. As a group of international journalists, we had doors opened to us that were normally kept locked and had opportunity to cross-question high officials, as well as spokespersons for both the Catholic and the Orthdox churches.

Only the Soviet Union appeared to conform to the model of a closed, suspicious, and bureaucrat-ridden society we in the West had been persuaded by the media of communications and propaganda to be at the heart of the monolithic communist system. Indeed, I left convinced that Russia's communists had failed to change significantly the system they had inherited. The mantle of the czars lies still heavy on them.

I interviewed more than a dozen of my tour companions, editors of Catholic publications from all the continents, on their attitudes to communism. They confirmed what had reached me from many sources while I was in Rome with IDOC the previous year—viewpoints far removed from those current in the United States. It was an insight into the density of the protective fog in which our supposed interests cause us to hide ourselves from what others are thinking. Enrique Maza, a Mexican Jesuit, turned the conventional assumption upside down. "It is we Catholics who have been the aggressors," he said. "When we are ready to make peace with the communists, they will make peace with us." He scoffed at the basic doctrine of the Washington creed, that the entire "free" world—especially Latin America—is under constant threat from an international communist conspiracy. Communist takeovers are possible in countries with huge sectors of misery, discontent, dissatisfaction, and inequality, he said, but the cause is to be sought in the internal conditions driving people to opt for what they see as the only viable alternative to capitalist oppression. That was in 1968. By the 1980s many were agreeing.

Another companion was Spanish theologian José María González Ruiz, whom I would get to know still better the following year in Rome at the second Synod of Bishops and the parallel "counter-synod" organized by progressive Catholics from several continents. As noted earlier, I participated in the counter-synod as representative of the National Association of the Laity and the National Association for Pastoral Renewal, two United States groups committed to speed up implementation of the letter and spirit of the Vatican Council. González Ruiz argued persuasively that one could not be a Christian without rejecting capitalism. He agreed with Pius XI's evaluation that it was intrinsically evil because based on greed and selfishness. As for the use of the Marxist or other analysis, he insisted that analyses don't belong to anyone or to any ideology to the extent that they are scientific and not subjective. A book he had just written* documented the extent to which Marx's rejection of God was motivated by the distorted and alienating notion of God presented in Christian theology and dominant in society. "One can adopt Marxism as a revolutionary praxis," González Ruiz concluded, "without professing the philosophy that historically gave its origin to that technique. The only problem a believer might have in espousing Marxism would arise if he had to accept tenets contrary to his own, for example, an ideology involving a denial of God. But as many Marxist thinkers recognize, this is not scientifically necessary."

Drawing together so many strands from so many sources, I was gradually forming for myself a clearer picture of the dynamic forces at work in Latin America, and the directions in which they were pushing and pulling the hemisphere. Dom Helder Camara has popularized a schematic simplification that can serve as a starting point, especially because of its influence on the analysis made at Medellín. First, you have the external overlords. Today, they are the Western

---

*José María González Ruiz, *Atheistic Humanism and the Christian God.* Milwaukee: Bruce Publishing Co., 1968.

industrial nations led by the United States. Through a combination of military might, economic leverage, and technological advantage, they dictate the nature of the economy in each country and the distribution of the benefits derived from the economic activities. The external overlords normally impose their will nowadays through conditions placed on loans offered by their government, by the World Bank, the Inter-American Development Bank, the International Monetary Fund (all dominated by the United States government), and by commercial banks. The global (previously called multinational or transnational) corporations, the major operating arm of the external overlords in dependent countries, usually prefer to hold in reserve the enormous power they wield through their worldwide holdings and operations. In an emergency, nevertheless, they show their teeth, as did the International Telephone and Telegraph Company (ITT) in the destabilization of Chile and bloody overthrow in 1973 of the Allende government. In that operation, as in many other interventions in the internal affairs of Latin American nations, the CIA played a major role with the prior knowledge and approval of the U.S. Administration. And when all else fails, Washington remains ready to use open force, as in the Dominican Republic in 1965 and in Grenada and Central America in the 1980s.

The domestic oligarchies in each country constitute the second tier of power. They form an upper class which—with the global corporations—monopolizes land ownership, industry, and commerce. Tied to them is a group of professionals, armed forces, police, and small business. Typically, the oligarchs and their supportive services (often but misleadingly called middle classes) account for fifteen to twenty percent of the population.

While absolutely dependent on the external overlords for their economic and political survival, the oligarchs have a monopoly of power within each country. The way this is exercised has changed substantially since World War II, and in particular since the triumph of the Cuban revolution in 1959. Increased social awareness on the part of the dispossessed, combined with rapid population increase without a parallel expansion of the economy, caused both the local oligarchs and U.S. policy makers to fear that other countries would follow the Cuban example. Their fears were intensified by a growth in the long endemic guerrilla activity—largely a product of frustration—in various countries. The power holders recognized that any change in the status quo would inescapably be to their disadvantage. The United States in particular also concluded, but not necessarily correctly, that change would benefit the Soviet Union in the contest for geopolitical influence in which the two superpowers were locked.

To maintain the status quo in the face of constantly increasing internal tension required the creation of strong repressive forces motivated to use whatever means might be necessary to stamp out opposition. Latin American countries had always maintained relatively strong military forces, the final arbiters in the internal struggles for power within the oligarchy during the long period in which its control of society was so absolute as to permit such family squabbles. Now the United States set out systematically to transform these armed forces into organs of domestic repression and oppression. To do this required first the creation of an ideology, a worldview that would convince the armed forces of the legitimacy and indeed necessity of the new role to which they were being elevated.

The theoretical framework was developed in the War College of the United States in the form of a rabid anticommunism that grew out of the Cold War policies with which the United States itself had buttressed its leadership of the West's coalition to stop Soviet expansionism after World War II. Brazilian General Golbery do Couta e Silva elaborated this into the Doctrine of National Security in the 1950s, drawing further inspiration from Italian fascism, German nazism, and the military theories of counterinsurgency with which the French tried to justify their efforts to reassert their control over Vietnam and Algeria.

This doctrine posits confrontation at the level of total war as the natural and perpetual situation both between nations and within nations, converting the world into a Darwinian nightmare. Whatever threatens the stability of the established order must be destroyed. Even development, though important, takes second place to security. And only the military possess the knowledge and judgment to determine the needs of security and, therefore, the national welfare.

This novel doctrine of a monopoly of wisdom, knowledge, and truth in the military establishment, a secularized version of the concept of infallibility, was ideal as a short-term rationale but ultimately could only prove disastrous. It made it easy for the military to persuade themselves that the universities, the intellectuals, the politicians, even major segments of the churches, had been infected by the Marxist virus, and could in consequence no longer be trusted to guard "traditional Christian principles." Only the military had the objectivity to make prudent judgments on education, social policy, and the direction of the economy.

We have here an obviously classist doctrine, with racist overtones. Privilege is reserved to the armed forces and to the moneyed classes who are obligated by fate and duty to support them in their Sisyphean conflict with the underprivileged. Ironically, the Vatican, while echoing Washington in continual denunciation of Lenin-style class war, remains silent about this equally pernicious classist and racist ideology propagated by the Pentagon in all its satellite armies.

To perpetuate the monopoly on decision making, the military had to destroy or domesticate all organs of opinion—political parties, legislative and judicial bodies, trade unions, student and other civic organizations. This process was immediately begun by the military dictatorship that seized power in Brazil in 1964. It was effectively completed in Brazil by the institutionalization of arbitrary exercise of power by dictatorial decree (Institutional Act #5) in 1968. Only some sectors of the churches succeeded in retaining a limited ability to escape the proletarianization, and it is these survivors who serve as rallying points for the continuing low-profile efforts to defend the poor and powerless against the structures of oppression and dehumanization.

Others quickly followed Brazil's example, notably Uruguay, Argentina, and Bolivia. They all imitated Brazil in in-troducing an economic system based on the theories of Milton Friedman and his so-called Chicago School of Economics. These theories are a warmed-up rehash of the dog-eat-dog approach of the nineteenth century Manchester School. Their application has enabled the global corporations to acquire the most dynamic and fastest-growing elements of the economy, and simultaneously to concentrate what is left in the hands of a much smaller part of the oligarchy. The workers have everywhere been squeezed by wage controls and inflation. In Brazil, for example, by the 1980s the industrial worker—the highest paid segment of labor—had not more than sixty percent of the purchasing power he enjoyed in 1964; and in 1964 he barely made enough to support his family.

Following the overthrow of Allende in Chile in 1973, Friedman's disciples developed an economic model for the country that provided for six million of the more than ten million inhabitants, making no allowance for work or sustenance for the "superfluous" four million. Within a decade, in spite of massive emigration to Argentina and other countries, a third of the work force was unemployed, and malnutrition of young children had risen to a level that threatened to lower drastically and irreversibly the national standards of intelligence. Simultaneously, ownership of property was further concentrated. In 1970, two hundred families controlled 80 percent of the country's wealth. A decade later, the same proportion was controlled by a mere fifty families.

The military regime established in Peru in 1968 was interpreted by many observers as representing a departure from the pattern. In its first years it made significant progress with land reform and devoted more effort to increasing the food supply for local consumption than to expanding exports. While I hoped the optimists would be proven right, I did not share their euphoria. "The historic problem of the military dictatorship," I wrote in 1970, "is that uncontrolled power corrupts. No matter how good the original intentions, the erosion of politics soon follows, especially in a small country which depends for survival on outside markets and suppliers."* The real function of the military regime was not

---

*Gary MacEoin, *Revolution Next Door: Latin America in the 1970s*. New York: Holt, Rinehart and Winston, 1971, p. 156.

to eliminate the oligarchy but to strengthen it by modernizing it. Peru in the early 1970s passed through the evolution
that most of Latin America experienced much earlier, a
transfer of the ultimate internal decision making from the
landed aristocracy to the urban business sector. Before the
end of the decade, it had bought the entire Friedman pack-
age, and with the same disastrous results as in the neighboring countries for the masses of the poor.

Colombia's oligarchy succeeded in maintaining the appearance of democracy longer than most of its neighbors.
But those appearances were highly deceiving. The grassroots pressures for social change that produced the wave of
violence known as the *bogotazo* in 1949 and caused a hundred thousand deaths in the civil war that followed were
contained for a time by a coalition of the only two parties allowed by the Constitution, the Conservatives and Liberals.
But during the 1970s this coalition had to depend progressively on open repression by the armed forces under a state of
permanent siege, so that by 1980 or earlier Colombia had become a military dictatorship in all but name, a dictatorship
fully committed to the Doctrine of National Security.

In 1969, a friend gave me a tip that seemed a lead to a
minor news story but in fact started a chain of events in
which I expect to remain involved as long as I live. A Brazilian Protestant minister, concerned for the safety of a friend,
Paulo Wright,* then being sought by the political police, had
smuggled out of the country a mass of documentary evidence of widespread use of torture by the political police.
Torture was being used not only on known opponents of the
dictatorship to extract information, but against demon-
strably innocent third parties. If a suspect failed to break,
his wife and children would be tortured in his presence.

My informant believed, a belief I have documented by
painstaking collection over the years of scraps of evidence
from many parts of the world,* that the torture was being

---

*Later captured by the Brazilian military and tortured to death. Richard Shaull
has dedicated *Heralds of a New Reformation* (Maryknoll, N.Y.: Orbis Press,
1984) to "Paulo Wright, 'disappeared' in a Brazilian prison, 1973."

---

*Gary MacEoin, *Northern Ireland: Captive of History*. New York: Holt, Rinehart and Winston, 1974, p. 218, p. 251 ff., and sources cited in Footnotes 6 and
7 to Chapter 12 and Footnote 15 to Chapter 14.

used systematically with the approval of responsible top officials, that specialists provided by entities of the U.S. government taught the torture techniques, and that employees of the U.S. government participated actively at times in the torturing.

In the course of my research on torture, I decided it was time for me to do another book on Latin America. In 1961 I had written a book, published in English, French, German, and Italian editions, that tried to show that Latin America, long static, was being subjected to tremendous new forces—many of them generated by the United States—that were cracking the old structures. "Our alternatives," I wrote, "are to channel that change constructively, a task that will require effort and sacrifice such as we have till now resisted; or let it develop away from us, so that it will destroy Latin America and surely destroy us too." I was then convinced that the United States had the ability and will to do what needed doing, that it was sincere when it committed itself in the Alliance for Progress to pool the resources of the hemisphere in a program to create decent living conditions for all its peoples. That book had been the first introduction to Latin America for many of the Catholic and Protestant missionaries from North America and Europe who flocked to Latin America in the 1960s as mission prospects dimmed in Asia and Africa. They had gone with innocence and enthusiasm. Like me, many of them were discovering the hard way that the programs they were promoting were poultices and aspirins for a patient suffering from leprosy and cancer.

In 1970, accordingly, I visited thirteen countries of the hemisphere, traveling twenty thousand miles and talking to opinion makers of all shades of the political and religious spectrum. In many countries the climate of oppression, fear, and terror was such that people no longer spoke their minds to a stranger. Here, the contacts I had made in Rome during the Council proved invaluable. I was able to dialogue freely with political scientists, sociologists, labor and peasant leaders, victims of torture inflicted by specialized units of the armed forces, people whose close relatives had been tortured to death or assassinated by Death Squadrons or other ultrarightist terrorists acting with official approval or toleration. I could sit in on clandestine meetings of peasants and slum-dwellers and hear them discuss their grievances and plan survival strategies. This on-the-spot survey, published in 1971 as *Revolution Next Door: Latin America in the 1970s*, confirmed my worst suspicions. Specifically, it led me to three conclusions, the accuracy of which subsequent and continuing events regrettably confirmed: that Latin Americans had abandoned hope of ever creating acceptable living standards for the masses of the people within the capitalist system, leaving them with the sole option of some kind of socialist society; that the United States was using all means at its disposal to prevent the necessary change, providing the military equipment and training to maintain order without justice; and that—following Newton's Third Law of Motion—every escalation of oppression brought a corresponding escalation of counterviolence. Many countries had reached the condition described in an Amnesty International report three years later: "Torture during interrogation, or as a disciplinary measure within prisons, is no longer even motivated by a desire to gather 'intelligence.'. . . Torture is widely used not only as an instrument of intimidation but as an end in itself,. . .in many instances no more or less than a matter of habit."

Humanity and religion alike shrieked out the need for change. The only visible alternative, nevertheless, still created problems for me and for many of my Christian friends. Papal teaching and much Protestant theological writing were incompatible with basic tenets or assumptions of contemporary socialism as influenced by Marxism. Even if one agreed with González Ruiz that the "god" Marx had described and rejected was an idol or distortion and consequently merited rejection, the central role given to class war remained.

Joel Gajardo, a Chilean Protestant theologian and social scientist, later exiled in 1973 when the CIA-backed generals overthrew Allende, started me on a line of thinking I have continued to pursue. "I now recognize that the class war is fundamental," he said. "We who have come to Marxism

after a long militancy within a Christian framework have
been ignorant of this dimension. We have stressed reconciliation, insisting that Christianity—and especially Christ—
has already overcome every difference; that for the Christian there is neither Jew nor Greek nor barbarian. Yet I
think that class opposition is something evident in Latin
America. The privileged classes have created for themselves a situation in which they will continue to enjoy privilege until the dispossessed classes acquire an awareness of
their own strength. This still creates problems for most
Christians, because they have not reflected enough on it to
develop a clear theology. When I say this, I am thinking not
only of Latin America, but of the total world situation. Even
the peace movements among Christians in eastern Europe
have not thought it through. I have had many discussions
with representatives of these movements, and they always
seem to minimize the enormous opposition that exists between classes."

Gajardo's challenge to study the cultural elements under-
girding the condemnations of socialism, particularly in its
Marxist expressions, which most of us had unquestioningly
assumed to follow inescapably from our Christian beliefs,
combined with my experience in Eastern Europe described
above to start me on a long historical review. I presented
my main conclusions in 1975 at Catholic University, Washington, D.C., under the auspices of the Bicentennial Committee of the United States Catholic bishops. By the mid-
nineteenth century, the capitalist system, solidly established
in England, was imposing itself rapidly throughout the
North Atlantic world that would remain its stronghold.
The peasants who for a thousand years had lived in relative
comfort, self-understanding, and dignity in western Europe
were being stripped by force, trickery, and political chicanery of their accumulated property and independent means
of livelihood. Nor was such human degradation confined to
the developing stages of capitalism. Rather, it is an insepar-
able quality and characteristic of the system, an antecedent
condition for the efficient supply of factory fodder, the number of work hours per month and the worker's life span ob-

jectively calculated to ensure maximum labor output per unit of subsistence input. Modified in privileged strata by the need to maintain consumption, it remains openly visible in the sectors of migrant labor and inner-city minorities in the United States, just as it does in Amazonia, Hong Kong, northern Mexico, and other "export platforms" developed by United States capitalists around the world.

The historic response in the nineteenth century to this monstrosity was the spawning of myriad approaches to a more human economic system and the popularization of such hitherto arcane words as anarchism, socialism, and communism. All who participated were undoubtedly neither saints nor heroes; human motives are mixed. But in the sweep of history, only one judgment on these pioneers as a group is reasonable. Men and women who risk and endure poverty, obscurity, exile, torture, prison, and firing squads in the conviction that they are defending the oppressed against their oppressors are in the tradition of the prophets. By promoting the purposes of the Creator and of creation, they stand in everlasting honor.

It is an elementary fact of life that if we want to change the world, we must start with it where it is. A particular type of economic organization is peculiar to each historic era. No other is arbitrarily substitutable. Catholic thinkers, nevertheless, when faced with the imperative need for change, long urged a return to a nostalgically mythicized system of economic organization they called distributism. People were happy in the good old days, they argued, in the days of Christendom when the social and political order recognized the hierarchy of values and of authority. But it is irrelevant whether or not the precapitalist system was more equitable than the capitalist. There is no going back. Capitalism was a giant advance by the human race in its thrust to unlock the secrets of the universe and utilize the riches of the earth to make possible a good life for all. The only way from here is forward.

The world, however, does not evolve automatically and continuously in a straight line. Iron determinism does not rule. Progress results from a dialectical struggle of opposites, in which the tide at times seems to be falling when in fact it is rising. We should not be surprised that the first concrete political counterform to issue from the noble theories of the anarchists, socialists, and communists was a state capitalism (called by Barbara Ward with typical elegance and accuracy a mirror image of capitalism), whose treatment of the powerless differed little from that of its capitalist predecessors. Whether that first experiment will result in a new and higher synthesis, or whether (as is statistically and historically more likely) it will prove to have been but one of the myriad abortive attempts inescapably preliminary to each evolutionary advance, the future will tell. At least it initiated flexible experimentation that could hardly have been possible without its countervailing power (second strike capability) to prevent the previously omnipotent capitalists from nipping every initiative in the bud. I think of such things as the ending of the colonial era, the rebirth of China, and the quintuplication of world oil prices.

Unfortunately, most church leaders lacked the global vision, the ability to read the signs of the times, needed to understand and encourage revolutionary change. Clinging pathetically throughout the nineteenth century to the shreds of a long-dead era of absolute monarchy, the crumbling ramparts manned with theological fulminations, the papacy openly rejected the people's claims to have a voice in their destiny. The Englightenment had more impact on Protestant thinking, but Protestantism's political and emotional identification with the major industrial powers inhibited efforts by individual Protestants to challenge capitalism's excesses, illustrating once again that where our treasure is, there also is our heart—and our theology.

The Christian refusal to examine on their merits the demands of the new prophets for radical restructuring of society has much deeper roots, however. The nineteenth century misjudgments followed logically from earlier errors. For example, a distorted concept of property, developed in the Middle Ages, was consistently supported by the church as a sacred taboo, religion being thus enlisted by the few who own property to protect them from the many they have despoiled and intend to despoil further.

In the process, the principles of law and morality were turned topsy-turvy. Lawyers and moralists universally agree that the wrongdoer should not benefit from his villainy, and that nobody can give what he does not own. Application of these two principles would wipe out practically every property title in the world. Because the United States is a young country, it is relatively easy to trace the origin of titles. One well researched example is the accumulation of land in California by the Kern Company through fraud, deception, and perversion of legal process. But the facts are well known more broadly: the rip-off of Indian lands as described in *Bury My Heart at Wounded Knee* and other books, the new assault today on reservations into which Indians were crowded on land believed worthless but now known to have oil, water, and scarce metals, the amassing of wealth by Harriman, Rockefeller, and others on which today's financial empires rest. Flowing from violation of law and basic human rights, all of these gave no title in law or morality to the present holders. Even an enormous increase in the value of the original rip-offs does not change the issue. Building a house or factory on ground to which one has no title does not give a title to the house or factory. That is basic law. Why is it not applied?

How much is enough? On this related question legal systems are less precise. The consensus of jurisprudence is that excessive concentration becomes antisocial—hence antimonopoly laws in the United States and elsewhere, laws more honored in the breach than the observance. Capitalist legal systems assume an absolute right of ownership of property, without any limit on the quantity, value, or use. Even the extreme case of total monopoly of the wealth and productive capacity of a community or state can be attacked only by the exercise of eminent domain, with "fair compensation." How provide fair compensation if the community or state has been completely despoiled? Yet that is the rationale for the U.S. resistance to land reform in the Third World.

Moral principles are clearer. The Jewish prophets unanimously condemned the rich who held as their own what was intended by God for the common use of all. Jewish lawmakers went further, formulating precise rules that prevented the rich from acquiring legal title to the land of the poor, thus blocking the accumulation that is basic to the dynamics of the capitalist system.

The early Church Fathers were extraordinarily explicit, too. "Tell me, how is it that you are rich," St. John Chrysostom asks. "From whom did you receive your wealth? And he, from whom did he receive it? From his grandfather, you say, from his father. By climbing this genealogical tree you are able to show the justice of the possession? Of course you cannot; rather, its beginning and root have necessarily come out of injustice." St. Jerome concurs in his comment on *mamona tes 'adikías* (Lk. 16:9), variously translated as "money of injustice," "tainted money," or "dishonest gain." "And he very rightly said 'money of injustice,' for all riches come from injustice. Unless one person has lost, another cannot find. Therefore I believe the popular proverb is very true: 'The rich man is either an unjust person or the heir of one.' " St. Ambrose agrees: "They [the philosophers] considered it consonant with justice that one should treat common, that is, public property, as public; and private as private. But this is not even in accord with nature, for nature has poured forth all things for all people for common use. God has ordered all things to be produced so that there should be food in common for all, and that the earth should be a common possession for all. Nature, therefore, has produced a common right for all, but greed has made it a right for a few."

The teaching of the Eastern Fathers was no different. St. Basil: "The beasts become fertile when they are young but quickly cease to be so. But capital produces interest from the very beginning, and this in turn multiplies into infinity. All that grows ceases to do so when it reaches its normal size. But the money of the greedy never stops growing." And St. Gregory Nazianzen: "After sin came into the world, greed destroyed the original nobility of nature and turned law into the handmaid of the powerful. But you, do look to the original equality, not to the later distinction; not to the law of the powerful but to the law of the Creator."

In the Middle Ages, an official and established church in a society that accepted private property and divided its members into rigid classes for the benefit of the rich, set itself a new task. Identifying with the system—as, sociologically, intellectuals do—theologians turned to Greek philosophers to salve the consciences of property owners by proving that Christianity did not absolutely forbid such ownership. St. Thomas Aquinas found in Aristotle three justifications of private property. The first would appeal to the contemporary supporter of uncontrolled competition, though I believe it rests on an arbitrary sociological assumption. It is that people take more care of what is their own than what they hold in common with others. The second—even more arbitrary—is that the affairs of society are conducted in a more orderly way when each member has the duty of looking after a particular thing. And the third either proves nothing or proves too much. It is that a more peaceful state is ensured if each is contented with his own. That logical apriorism flies in the face of all experience. Those who have, lust for more; and those who have more, lust even more for even more. If there is any argument here at all, it is that the present system—in which a few have more than they know what to do with while most lack the necessities—can never bring peace.

Far more important than Aquinas's attempted legitimation of ownership is his view on use of what is owned. The owner, he says, is bound to hold what he owns "not as his own, but as common, so that specifically he is ready to give to others in their need." Aquinas is talking here about what modern jurisprudence calls a trust. The "owner" of property does not have beneficial ownership for his own arbitrary use. He is obligated to allocate his property to others according to their need. Any other use or failure to use constitutes a violation of his trust.

That part was overlooked. What survived for centuries was the legitimation of private property.

In the eighteenth and nineteenth centuries, the Roman church's attitude toward property became progressively more distorted. The Protestant Reformation breakaway of much of northern Europe in the sixteenth and seventeenth centuries intensified Rome's centralization of decision making, in itself a major cause of the break. The papal states, politically, socially, and educationally backward, became the exemplar of Catholic society. As the gap between this backwater and Europe north of the Alps widened with the Enlightenment and the French Revolution, the church saw every modernizing movement as a threat. In reaction, it raised progressively higher the theological ramparts, its only defences as military power and world opinion defected.

Such is the context for the church's response to the challenges in the politico-economic order that surfaced in the second quarter of the nineteenth century after the Czar, the Kaiser, the Austrian Emperor, and the English King had, with the Pope's blessing, remade the map of Europe at the Congress of Vienna (1815) to banish for all time the pernicious notions of liberty, equality, and fraternity spawned by the French Revolution.

The challenge was groping and uncertain—a search for alternatives in the face of cruel exploitation of men, women, and children, rather than a formulated program with philosophic principles. The word *socialist* was first used in England in 1833 to identify the followers of Robert Owen, pioneer of the cooperative movement. It surfaced in France a year later in connection with the Saint-Simonians who advocated the abolition of private inheritance rights, public control of the means of production, and gradual emancipation of women. From that time, *socialist* and *communist* were long used interchangeably. Although the Communist League was created in 1847 and given its platform by Marx and Engels in the Communist Manifesto of 1848, the movement was generally known as socialism until the early years of the twentieth century.

Revolutionary outbreaks of socialist inspiration swept Europe in 1848, and riots in Rome forced Pius IX to flee for his life. He quickly abrogated the constitution he had earlier granted the papal states and reversed the liberal policies of the first years of his rule. In the encyclical *Nostis et nobiscum* (December 1849) he began to formulate what would long be the church's evaluation of socialism, a term that for him encompassed everything that threatened his divinely ordained temporal sovereignty. The Carbonari, the Garibaldians, the Freemasons, and the liberals, namely, all the groups seeking to unite Italy as a secular state, "everyone already knows," Pius wrote, "that their principal aim is to spread among the people—while abusing the words liberty and equality—the pernicious inventions of communism and socialism. It remains true that the leaders, whether they are communist or socialist, even though they proceed by different ways and means, share the common aim of keeping the workers and the men of lower orders in a state of continual agitation and gradually habituating them to ever more criminal acts, having first deluded them with cunning language and seduced them with the promise of a happier life." The faithful who allow themselves to be thus seduced will be "heaping up for themselves treasures of vengeance before the Divine Judge on the day of wrath," while in the meantime, "no temporal advantage will accrue to the people from this conspiracy, much rather an increase of misery and calamity. For it is not given to men to establish new societies and communities opposed to the natural state of human affairs."

In passing, I may note how close Pius was to contemporary Protestant thinking. A verse from a hymn popular in Protestant mouths in the nineteenth century is equally blasphemous in its understanding of God and equally rigid and unjust in its social determinism:

> The rich man in his castle,
> The poor man at his gate,
> God made them, high and lowly,
> And order'd their estate.*

In the Syllabus of Errors attached to the encyclical *Quanta cura* (1864), Pius IX spread the net still wider. Lumped together as "pests" with those who profess "these most fatal errors of socialism and communism" are secret societies, bible societies, and clerico-liberal societies.

As the headlong unfolding of history exposed the futility of this approach, Leo XIII and his advisers struggled franti-

---

*Cecil Francis Alexander, 1848, composer; W.R. Waghorne, 1906, arranger. *Hymns Ancient and Modern*, #573.

cally to modernize their arsenal. But the narrow angle of the beleaguered Vatican's intellectual vision handicapped them, as did the insistence of papal theologians that every official utterance of a pope was protected from error by the prerogatives of his office, and hence could not be reversed by a successor. This progressively narrowed the area of maneuverability. Feeling bound by the rulings of his predecessors, Pope Paul VI rejected the recommendation of his own theologians and other experts to modify the ban on artificial means of contraception. Other popes, more subtly, claimed to be repeating the former teachings while repudiating them. But such backdoor escapes from one's mistakes are psychologically destructive for those who practice them, and in addition they prevent healing of the wounds caused by the original error. The traditional formulation of contrition, confession, and satisfaction as needed for forgiveness of sin in the sacrament of penance is psychologically sound, provided these three elements are not seen as following in a time sequence. The reeducation processes developed in Mao's China for enemies of the regime, bringing them to acknowledge and repudiate their errors, followed a similar logic. Healing demands admission of wrongdoing and commitment to make amends.

Blinded by his principles, Leo XIII could see no error on his side. His first contribution, in consequence, did not carry him far beyond Pius IX. The conspirators known as socialists, communists, or nihilists were spread all over the world and bound together by the closest ties in a wicked confederacy, he lamented in *Quod apostolici* (1878). They were now openly preparing what they had long plotted in secret, "the overthrow of all civil society. . . .They leave nothing untouched or whole that by both human and divine law had been decreed for the health and beauty of life. They refuse obedience to the higher powers, to whom—according to the Apostle's admonition—every soul should be subject, and who derive the power of governing from God; and they proclaim the absolute equality of all men in rights and duties. . . . As the recruits of socialism are especially sought among artisans and workmen who, perhaps tired of labor,

are more easily allured by the hope of riches and the promise of wealth, it is well to encourage societies of artisans and
workmen which, set up under the guardianship of religion,
may tend to make all associates contented with their lot and
urge them to a quiet and peaceful life."

Supported morally and financially by big business, the
church set out enthusiastically to create worker organizations that would persuade their members to earn spiritual
rewards by accepting inhuman working conditions submis-
sively. The resulting ideological conflicts still plague the labor movement, especially in Europe and Latin America. The
mindset of *Nostis et nobiscum* and *Quod apostolici* survives
at least at the subconscious level, preventing an objective
reading of the signs of the times. Its first assumption and af-
firmation is that the Western capitalist system—the rest of
the world ignored as impertinent—has been fixed for all
time by God's inscrutable decrees, the divine purpose placing a few rich and powerful over the many poor and powerless to ensure the necessary testing in preparation for eternal bliss. Such a formulation is obviously a caricature, but
the caricature is not mine. In 1939—so long was the stereotype openly proclaimed—Pius XI in *Sertum letitiae* wrote
the bishops of the United States that God "had determined
that there should be rich people and poor people in the world
so that virtues may be exercised and merits proven."

How different the actual signs of the times in the second
half of the nineteenth century, not merely in the hindsight of
a century later, but as then on the public record. Apart from
other obvious facts that a church with its own worldwide
network of informed reporters was ideally equipped to establish and evaluate, Karl Marx had eleven years before
Quod apostolici published in *Das Kapital* a mass of specific
data drawn from official English sources in the British Museum on the condition of workers in Great Britain and Ireland. It required voluntary blindness not to see that the
order proclaimed by Pius as fixed by the eternal and immutable decrees of God meant that in the home of capitalism
women and eight-year-old children worked twelve and more
hours a day and were paid—as determined by the natural

law of supply and demand—just enough to keep enough of them alive long enough to ensure smooth and uninterrupted production.

In Ireland, a million starved to death and a million and a half fled the island while wheat to feed all of them was exported. Peasants were chased like wild animals from Scotland's Highlands to create grouse ranches on which London bankers could enjoy two weeks of legal slaughter each August. In the New World, Indians were being cheated, tricked, killed like vermin in the name of progress; and such freebooters as Carnegie, Rockefeller, Mellon, and Harriman, repeating and perfecting the techniques that had impoverished Britain's masses, were assembling the wealth and power that still dominate the United States. Australia's natives, by all equity the country's owners, were being fed the poisoned carcasses of sheep. And the rapacious carpetbaggers of Christian Europe were carving the helpless body of Africa into bits and pieces that made neither cultural nor linguistic sense, designed exclusively to satisfy their greed.

No hint of an awareness of these glaring signs of the times or concern for the victims is found in contemporary papal documents. Instead, they denounce as wicked conspirators inspired by hatred of religion and envy of those to whom God had given the mandate to rule the visionaries and prophets who chose obscurity, poverty, persecution, and imprisonment because they were torn by human suffering and were convinced that the human condition deserved and was capable of better. The lower orders were *naturally* content with their lot. If they manned the barricades across Europe time and again, it was because they were deceived by wicked counsellors. To attempt to establish any other system was to violate the natural state of human affairs. The judgment of the ruler, whom God had chosen, may not be questioned. And the function of religion is to confirm the legitimacy of the socio-economic system. By bringing the workers together in church-controlled associations and teaching them to accept their condition as willed by God, it will solve the problem. As for the notion that all have equal rights, absit omen.

By 1891, Leo XIII and his advisers had a better understanding of the enemy. Friedrich Engels had in 1885 published the second part of *Das Kapital*, using the notes and outlines left by Marx at his death two years earlier. Leo's judgment that the church should concentrate its fire on Marxism was, from his viewpoint, correct. It was the leading socialist theory and in the ascendant. In *Rerum Novarum*, accordingly, he challenged some of its major theses. Its theory of collective property, he argued, would upset the social order, lead to slavery of the citizens, eliminate economic stimuli, deny the natural rights of property owners, involve the state in activities foreign to its purposes, and reduce all citizens to an equal level of destitution. Interestingly, the capitalist media continue to propagate these assumptions as articles of faith, ignoring the vast accumulation of experimental data now available for scientific judgment. Not until recently—still mostly in the counterculture—has it been noted that monopoly capitalism has itself produced precisely these results.

Only obliquely did Leo deal with another cardinal element in Marxism, the intrinsic injustice of the wage system. While admitting frequent abuses by employers, he insisted that the system is legitimate when profits are held within "just" limits. The reformist or developmentalist stand to which this judgment committed the church remained an axiom of Catholic social teaching until challenged in the 1970s by Latin America's Theology of Liberation.

Forty years after Leo and in a vastly different world context, Pius XI returned to the issue. The Great Depression had brought universal impoverishment to the capitalist world. A regime claiming to express faithfully the principles of Marx ruled the Soviet Union, and Marxism was spreading in most European countries. Germany, Italy, Spain, and Portugal were seeking in corporatism a formula to replace both capitalism and communism. Following the church's longstanding preference for the middle way—an attitude derived not from Jesus or the prophets but from Greek and Roman philosophers—Pius backed cautiously away from his predecessor's support of capitalism. He condemned the system to the extent that it retained for itself excessive advantages, and he disassociated himself explicitly from the philosophy of the Manchester School which claimed that objective economic laws allocated all accumulation of riches to those already wealthy, allowing the worker only the minimum needed to survive. But Marx's claim that only work produces wealth and that consequently all profits of production should go to the worker was, he added immediately, equally wrong, "an alluring poison."

Pius was ambivalent about the reformability of capitalism. "Leo XIII's whole endeavor was to adjust this economic regime [i.e., the capitalist system] to the standards of true order; whence it follows that the system itself is not to be condemned. And surely it is not vicious of its very nature." Yet he agrees with Lenin that "free enterprise" must evolve into monopoly capitalism, "an international imperialism whose country is where profit is," a system not able to control itself, or to direct economic life, and in consequence ultimately self-destructive. The free market "of its own nature" concentrates power in antisocial types, in those "who fight most violently and give least heed to their conscience." It is Darwinism gone mad.

Pius opened up a new area of maneuver by stressing the split of the social movement into "a more violent section, communism; and a more moderate section that retains the name of socialism." He could now modify the previous absolute condemnation of all forms of socialism. The moderate form offered programs that "often strikingly approach the just demands of Christian social reformers" and consequently contain some Christian values. But the corporate state, he insisted, was a better way to realize those positive values. That brief aberration, fortunately, did not survive World War II.

A previously overlooked indictment of communism—soon to achieve pride of place in *Divini Redemptoris* (1937)—premieres in *Quadragesimo anno:* its preaching and practice of militant atheism. Pius, moreover, accepted the claim of the Soviet leaders to own a single and coherent philosophy that meant precisely and only what they said it meant, a counterorthodoxy. In Christian terms, this is the Anti-Christ, the beast of the Apocalypse enthroned with power and able to deceive even the elect. That aspect was central to conflict in Russia, Spain, and Mexico in the 1930s. It has since dominated the institutional church's attitude to communism, as the earlier concerns of Pius IX and Leo XIII grew less important. With many nations of western as well as of eastern Europe today calling themselves socialist, the only serious remaining question for most Christians is whether Marxism is intrinsically atheistic in a sense incompatible with Christianity. The cold warriors of the West, whose philosophy and ideology are as remote from Christianity as those of their adversaries, make much of it.

Not knowing how to respond to this reality, Pius XII adopted an intransigent fort-holding stand. To inspire his supporters, he encouraged a cult of personality, a form of protection that seemed directly inspired by the self-divinization of the late Roman emperors—and equally futile.

It took the genial genius of Pope John XXIII to escape from the impasse. *Mater et magistra* (1961) recognizes and describes the social reality. "While a few accumulated excessive riches, large masses of working people daily labored in very acute need. Indeed, wages were insufficient for the necessities of life, and sometimes were at starvation level. For the most part, workers had to find employment under conditions that endangered health, moral integrity, and religious faith. Especially inhuman were the working conditions to which women and children were subjected. The specter of unemployment was ever present, and the family was exposed to a process of disorganization. As a natural consequence, workers indignant at their lot decided that this state of affairs must be publicly protested."

Pacem in terris (1963) was John's dying appeal to the church to accept the actual and objective impulse of contemporary society, which he correctly described as an intense drive to socialization, collectivization, and planetarization. Here he was light-years away from the world of fixed essences and the socio-economic system immutably determined by God in which Pius IX had lived. Opinions differ as to the extent of John's knowledge and acceptance of the Teilhardian worldview, but he was clearly conscious of the dynamic of change that characterizes contemporary life.

John criticized neocapitalism: lack of social progress to match the obvious economic advance, escalating concentration of wealth caused by auto-financing of industry at the consumer's expense, denial to workers of any real voice in decision making. John was reading the signs of the times, as the socialists had long been doing. With capitalism approaching self-destruction, we had acquired a control of the material world that could not be left in private hands: nuclear energy, genetic engineering, automation, cybernation, conquest of space, instant communications. The inheritance of all, their control and benefits should be shared by all.

Regrettably, John felt compelled to follow papal protocol, pretending to repeat what his predecessors had said, when in fact saying something radically different. Paul VI in *Populorum progressio* (1967) and *Octogesima adveniens* (1971) followed John's lead, while—like him—ignoring the conflicts within the corpus of papal social teaching.

If anything, *Octogesima adveniens* compounds the contradictions. Pius XI and John XXIII had admitted that moderate socialism had good elements. Paul apparently recognized that history was on Marx's side, making further concessions necessary. If I understand the document, Paul admits the validity of the Marxian analysis of capitalism, including the stress on class conflict. But the language is so Delphic that any conclusion from it remains open to challenge.

Having noted "a certain splintering of Marxism," Paul distinguishes four kinds. "For some, Marxism remains essentially the active practice of class struggle. Experiencing the ever present and continually renewed force of the relationships of domination and exploitation among people, they reduce Marxism to no more than a struggle—at times with no other purpose—to be pursued and even stirred up in permanent fashion. For others, it is first and foremost the collective exercise of political and economic power under the direction of a single party, which would be the sole expression and guarantee of the welfare of all, and would deprive individuals and other groups of any possibility of initiative or choice. At a third level, Marxism—whether in power or not—is viewed as a socialist ideology based on historical materialism and the denial of everything transcendent. At other times, finally, it presents itself in a more attenuated form, one also more attractive to the modern mind: as a rigorous method of examining social and political reality, and as the rational link—tested by history—between theoretical knowledge and the practice of revolutionary transformation. Although this kind of analysis gives a privileged position to certain aspects of reality to the detriment of the rest, and interprets them in the light of its ideology, it nevertheless furnishes some people not only with a working tool but also a certitude preliminary to action: the claim to decipher in a scientific manner the mainsprings of the evolution of society.

"While, through the concrete existing forms of Marxism, one can distinguish these various aspects and the questions they pose for the reflection and activity of Christians, it would be illusory and dangerous to reach a point of forgetting the intimate link that radically binds them together, to accept the elements of Marxist analysis without recognizing their relations with ideology, and to enter into the practice of class struggle and its Marxist interpretations, while failing to note the kind of totalitarian and violent society to which this process leads."

Only one thing is clear to me about this passage. It does not provide me with "a working tool" or "a certitude preliminary to action." It is Hamlet-like in its evasion of issues and its range of ill-defined options. It is consequently divisive of people who know that exploitation and oppression are rampant, and that as human beings and as Christians they should fight for change. It is ammunition for the exploiters who use it to rally support for palliatives that can no more cure the sickness than aspirins can cure cancer. Ultimately, it is this kind of splitting of Christians, through unwillingness to admit error and face reality, that enabled Kennecott and Anaconda and the ITT and the CIA to detach the Christian Democrats from their commitment to socialism and enlist them in the campaign to destabilize Chile and overthrow Allende. Such fence-sitting neutralizes most of the support the church could give to the poor who everywhere struggle for a better society, one consonant with the basic concepts of religion and providing conditions in which people can live religiously.

Reflection on these facts has led me to conclude that the church's refusal to recognize its involvement in wrongdoing, its prostitution of its power for personal and institutional benefit, accounts for its lack of credibility and consequent marginal impact on events. It was the Soviet trials of the 1930s that started me on this line of thought. Although the methods Stalin used to force his victims to confess before he killed them were then little understood, it was obvious that enormous energy and effort were invested in the program. What seemed the most logical rationale was that when leaders exhibited weakness by repudiating publicly the things they had stood for, the allegiance of their followers would be undermined. Stalin did not want to make martyrs whose cause would continue if they died unconfessed and unrepentant. Instead, the self-humiliation of the public confessions destroyed the faith of the group. The same principle was applied more constructively and on a vaster scale in Mao's China. Millions went through a process designed to effect a true interior conversion in the belief that a change of heart is a prerequisite to the creation of the New Human promised—each within his own vision—by Saint Paul and Karl Marx.

Any thought of self-humiliation, however, runs counter to Rome's perennial triumphalism. I know of only one pope who tried to break that tradition. It was at one of the two or three most critical crossroads of history. If his orders had been obeyed, the reasonable reforms demanded by Martin Luther in the first stages of his protest might have been implemented without splitting the church. Within months of his election, Pope Adrian VI wrote in November 1522 to his nuncio at the Diet of Nuremberg. Tell them, he said, that we frankly acknowledge that God permits this persecution of his church on account of the sins of men, and especially of prelates and clergy. "We know well that for many years things deserving of abhorrence have gathered around the Holy See; sacred things have been misused, ordinances transgressed, so that in everything there has been a change for the worse. We all, prelates and clergy, have gone astray from the right way;. . .each one of us must consider how he has fallen and be more ready to judge himself than to be judged by God in the day of wrath."

Adrian, interestingly in the light of the Dutch leadership in updating the church during and after Vatican Council II, was a Dutchman, the last non-Italian pope until John Paul II. He was no match for a pleasure-loving and high-spending Curia. His instructions were ignored. His message was never conveyed to the Diet. And when he died less than a year later, Rome rejoiced.

The issue was resurrected at Vatican Council II when many Fathers sought a specific admission of shared guilt for the division of the church in the sixteenth century. The outrage of the Curia was no less than when Adrian made the same suggestion 450 years earlier. In the end, a typical—and typically inadequate—curial compromise was adopted. "If we have in any way offended you . . ." Pope Paul addressed a group of Protestant leaders. When wrong is evident, conditional apology is salt in an open wound.

[10]

Central America Enters History

Like most observers of Latin America up to the mid-1970s, I believed that Central America and the Caribbean were doomed to experience history, not make it. Even Castro's success in the 1960s did not change this view. A standoff between the superpowers saved him, as long as the Soviet Union was willing to pay the price. History and geography had split the region into microcommunities radically estranged from each other and manipulated by outsiders. Only events elsewhere, it seemed, could bring meaningful social and political change.

Since the early nineteenth century, the United States has asserted rights at variance with the concept of national sovereignty. The Monroe Doctrine was a unilateral warning against new European interventions anywhere in the Americas. Teddy Roosevelt went much farther when he asserted a U.S. right "as a policeman" to maintain order in Latin America. William Howard Taft agreed, while stressing the job could normally be done by the diplomatic leverage of the dollar, keeping in reserve the "moral value" of the navy.

Woodrow Wilson believed in using force if necessary to ensure to Central America the benefits of the U.S. system. FDR's Good Neighbor policy, as seen from Mexico, guaranteed the permanent slavery of Central Americans under a league of mestizo dictators. The Miller Doctrine, enunciated by Assistant Secretary of State for Inter-American Affairs Miller in 1950 and updated by President Johnson for the 1965 invasion of the Dominican Republic, was adopted by the Russians as the Brezhnev Doctrine in 1968 and used by them to justify collective "socialist" intervention to protect the Soviet Union from Western adventurism.

In the 1960s and early 1970s, the United States seemed to be extending to all of South America the level of hegemony it had long exercised over the Caribbean and Central America. Brazil, Chile, Argentina, and Uruguay were ruled by military regimes committed to the Doctrine of National Security and to an economic model that transferred decision making to global corporations. Survival of these unpopular regimes required U.S. economic and military support and involved a progressive lowering of the living standard of the masses and the importation of "dirty" industry without regard for worker health and ecology.

The claim of the military dictators and their U.S. advisors that austerity was a stepping stone to a better life for all did not stand the test of time. By the second half of the 1970s, the failure of the model to provide human decency for the masses was building up extreme pressures in the Southern Cone for a return to civilian rule and for punishment of the military and the paramilitary death squads who had defended the system with wholesale torture, assassinations, and disappearances. Gradually it became apparent that the ability of the United States to dictate the form of government of these nations and to control their economies was declining. Instead, the huge debts they had accumulated had become a threat to the survival of the international banking system.

Simultaneously, a new threat emerged in Central America. After the major earthquake that in 1972 destroyed Managua, Somoza and his cronies overstepped themselves in diverting to their own benefit—and to their Swiss bank accounts—the millions of aid from around the world. A broad coalition of middle-class and wealthy Nicaraguans joined with the Sandinista revolutionaries and in 1979 toppled the dictatorship. It was a hard-won victory, with 50,000 killed in the final struggle and twice that number wounded out of a population of 2.6 million. But it gave new enthusiasm to the revolutionary forces in neighboring El Salvador and Guatemala, forces who had been driven to armed conflict by savage repression of their movements for constitutional reform.

Given the universal abhorrence to Somoza, the United States was reluctant to move openly against the Sandinistas. It was determined, nevertheless, to prevent the overthrow of neighboring satellite governments. The most immediate threat was in El Salvador, and the flow of U.S. arms and advisors was quickly stepped up, an inflow that was soon paralleled by an outflow of refugees fleeing from the savage attacks of armed forces and death squads.

It so happened that I was particularly well located to observe and evaluate this new stream of refugees as it mingled with older ones in its movement across Honduras, Guatemala, and Mexico in search of asylum in the United States. In 1974, I had moved for family reasons to Tucson, Arizona, a state that until last century was a part of Mexico. Many of the region's inhabitants are Spanish-speaking, emotionally as well as linguistically identified more with Latin America than with the dominant Anglo culture. Migration from Mexico to work as stoop labor in the fields and to pick citrus and grapes is an old tradition, but since the mid 1970s, there have been important changes. Deterioration of Mexico's economy has increased the numbers of Mexican migrants enormously. And the civil strife in El Salvador and Guatemala has driven half a million or more of their peasants into the ghettos of Los Angeles, San Francisco, Chicago, Boston, New York, Washington and Houston.

My first involvement in Tucson, however, was with none of these but with some Chilean victims of the Pinochet dictatorship. In the last three months of 1973, I had written *No Peaceful Way*, a book that placed in historical perspective the attempt by President Salvador Allende to implement a socialist program in Chile, and described the CIA-ITT conspiracy that led to Allende's overthrow and death in September 1973. I was able to complete this work so fast because of help from colleagues in an informal ecumenical group of Christians and Jews professionally involved with Latin America. In 1976, a member of this group asked me on behalf of a resettlement agency if Tucson could provide sponsors for Chileans jailed or interned by the Pinochet dictatorship. Pinochet had agreed to expel those who could find a place of exile, and Washington had finally been persuaded to accept five hundred and their dependents.

There was still a catch. Unlike refugees from East Europe or Cuba (or more recently, from Southeast Asia), the United States would pay nothing toward transport or resettlement. A European agency would advance transport costs. The rest would be the sponsor's responsibility.

Helped by David Sholin, pastor of St. Mark's Presbyterian Church, and Nivita Riley, then director of religious education in St. Pius X Catholic parish, I started a process under which individuals and churches sponsored more than thirty Chileans who in due course became part of the Tucson community. Concerned Anglos and Chicanos joined with them in several complementary organizations that would continue to service the economic refugees from Mexico and the political refugees from Central American who were soon flooding into the Southwest.

Even before the actual arrival of the Central Americans, however, another development involved me in the situation that was creating this new wave of refugees. In 1977, Larry Simon went to work for Oxfam-America. As associates at Fordham University in the early 1970s, Larry and I had arranged lectures and seminars on world development featuring such authorities as Gunnar Myrdal, Paulo Freire, Celso Furtado, Paul Lin and Dom Helder Camara. Now assigned to develop educational programs for Oxfam support groups around the United States, Larry asked me to join him in strategizing. Previously, Oxfam-America, like the original Oxfam in England and Oxfams in Belgium, Australia and Canada, had concentrated on famine relief and on projects calculated to improve food production and storage and the quality of life in poor countries. Larry sought a new dimension: the exploration by Oxfam supporters of the systemic sources of hunger and, in particular, the extent to which the United States is a cause rather than a solution to hunger in the Third World.

The first concrete result was a conference in Putney, Vermont, of more than two hundred concerned persons: officers of national and community-based service organizations, economic analysts and international development specialists, community organizers from overseas development programs, campus-based clergy, high school and college faculty and students, religious leaders and representatives from hunger action projects. I drafted a statement on "universal justice in human development," which the conference adopted after long discussion with several strengthening amendments. It called for a process of education to accompany a radical restructuring of society, a process involving "an examination of our basic assumptions about ourselves and our relationship to the world around us."

Of many programs sparked by this statement, I have been principally involved in organizing and leading groups to the Caribbean and Central America. Some tours were designed exclusively for journalists, for whom our contacts provided a well-rounded look at people and issues in Nicaragua after Somoza's overthrow and in El Salvador after Archbishop Romero's assassination and the explosion of government sponsored or encouraged repression that killed as many as a thousand innocent people a month and has driven between a quarter and a third of the population into refugee camps or exile. Most groups, however, have been Oxfam activists anxious to see for themselves Third World living conditions.

The formula was simple. A quick briefing in New York or Miami for a group of twenty-five to thirty-five preceded a week each in two countries that had adopted significantly different prescriptions for creating a better life for their people. We chose small countries so that observers with some background could in a week acquire a meaningful overview. At first, we concentrated on food and such closely related issues as nutrition and sanitation, but soon realized that quality of life is a more meaningful measure, embracing health, education, opportunity for self-realization and self-fulfillment.

We chose countries reachable without excessive cost, countries where we had contacts to ensure exposure to a cross-section of life, countries with a level of civil order that allowed people to express their minds without fear of punishment and did not expose our students to physical danger. We did bring some small groups of journalists to El Salvador but decided against taking study groups to El Salvador, Guatemala, or Haiti. Each tour consequently went to two of the following: Dominican Republic, Jamaica, Cuba, Puerto Rico, Honduras, Nicaragua, Costa Rica. In every case we included either Cuba or Nicaragua, the two countries attempting an approach to the quality of life radically different from the others.

Participants varied widely: college and graduate students, professors, political activists, community organizers and others involved in social change in the United States or in the Third World. Every group included some with experience in the Peace Corps or as mission workers, always enough Spanish speakers to facilitate informal exchanges in stores, workshops and homes. We had formal sessions with government officials, professors, leaders of peasant and women's organizations, and field trips to compare for ourselves theory and practice. Our youngest participant was fourteen, and we had several in their seventies or eighties, people with a vast store of knowledge and experience that enriched all of us. Most were between twenty and thirty-five.

Among all the learning experiences in which I have participated, these study tours gave the most dramatic results. "I have never learned so much in two weeks," one participant wrote me afterward, "I think (I hope) I will never be quite the same." From continuing correspondence and visits from many participants, I know that they will never again be the same.

By this time, we in Tucson—as in other border cities—had become deeply involved in helping Central American refugees, Salvadorans at first but later many Guatemalans also. Those intercepted by the Immigration and Naturalization Service (INS) border patrol went to a detention camp at El

Centro, California, four hours from Tucson, while awaiting deportation. Mexicans, for whom the camp was a revolving door as they were shipped back across the border only to return immediately, gave the Salvadorans a phone number to call in Tucson. For them, detention was very different. Repatriation could mean persecution or death, and the INS was abusing their ignorance to have them waive their rights and be shipped back by plane.

A 1951 UN Convention and subsequent protocol, having been signed by the President and ratified by the Senate, are under Article VI of the U.S. Constitution the supreme law of the land on equal level with the Constitution itself. Incorporated into domestic law in 1980, they forbid the United States to expel or forcibly return a refugee who has a reasonable fear that life or freedom would thereby be threatened because of race, religion, nationality, membership of a political or social group, or political opinion. The UN High Commissioner for Refugees has ruled that anyone who left El Salvador since 1980 has a prima facie claim to political asylum under this Convention. He has at least twice warned the U.S. Administration that it is in violation of its obligations under the Convention. Nevertheless, the INS—following a pattern established at the top level in the Administration—pursues policies in callous disregard both of equity and of law. The U.S. Administration cannot admit that governments it supports militarily and economically violate the human rights of their own citizens. It accordingly insists that all who leave El Salvador, Guatemala, or Haiti do so only to seek economic advancement, not because they fear for their lives.

I helped to form a Task Force of the Tucson Ecumenical Council to work at El Centro with legal groups from Tucson, Los Angeles, and San Diego. We raised considerably more than half a million dollars in cash and collateral to bond several hundred Central Americans out of the camp. Nivita Riley and I authored the first major factual study of the situation, *No Promised Land,* distributed by Oxfam. "The situation confronted by those hundreds of thousands of refugees in the United States is critical," we wrote. "Whether measured in terms of human lives or the irreparable loss of legal rights inherent in current INS policy and practices, illegal deportations of frightened unrepresented refugees to countries where they face torture and death have reached crisis proportions. These unfortunate persons are arrested by INS agents, placed into incommunicado interrogation, and cajoled or coerced into agreeing to summary removal by way of 'voluntary departure,' a procedure whereby the refugee waives all procedural and substantive rights to remain in the United States and avoid deportation into the midst of turmoil and civil strife. Although the life-threatening situation in their home countries is a matter of public knowledge especially in regards to Haiti and El Salvador, refugees arrested by the INS are seldom advised of their right to seek political asylum. Even if summary deportation is avoided, illegal treatment of these refugees continues. Although charged with no crime, they are herded into detention centers that are less adequate than most of our overcrowded and understaffed jails for convicted criminals. Bail is often set at a level that forces most refugees to wait indefinitely for a ruling on their application for asylum. These long-term detainees are denied reading materials, often given inadequate food, clothing, and medical attention, and can be put in solitary confinement at the whim of their guards."

In addition to reading hundreds of reports from lawyers and other refugee helpers, preparation of this study involved interviewing displaced persons inside El Salvador, refugees in Honduras, Nicaragua, Costa Rica, Mexico and the United States, participation as an expert witness in deportation hearings in the United States and visits to detention centers in the United States and Mexico. Combined with what I had learned on the Oxfam study and news tours and on visits to Central America and the Caribbean for other reasons, it gave me a clear up-to-date picture of what is happening to individuals and society in the area of the world most totally controlled by the United States, our "backyard." A brief talk to an Oxfam study group in a hotel lobby in Havana, Cuba, sticks in my mind as encapsulating my essential conclusions. We were waiting for the airport bus at the end of two weeks spent studying two contrasting approaches to the task of creating society, a human society.

The two units we had just observed, I said, small though they were, were representative of broad areas of the world. I had first visited Cuba in 1945 and Puerto Rico in the same year. When I worked with the Caribbean Commission in the late 1940s, we were deeply involved in the development of Operation Bootstrap. Dreamt up by Rexford G. Tugwell, Luis Muñoz Marín and other Rooseveltian New Dealers, this program was designed to show the world how a U.S. territory would prosper under Washington's benevolent guidance. It included tax and other incentives to U.S. industrial entrepreneurs, and a detailed plan to make the island—which then grew 60 percent of its food needs—completely self-sufficient in food within twenty years.

Thirty years later, Puerto Rico produces far less food than in 1950. A third of the best agricultural land is under concrete. The factories built on the island are not geared to its needs, are not owned by Puerto Ricans, leave little benefit in Puerto Rico. Many of them have already moved to the Dominican Republic or Taiwan to cheaper and more docile labor, leaving twisted remnants of their steel shells jutting from crumbling concrete. Effluvia from oil refineries and pharmaceutical plants have polluted much of the island's water and adversely affected the remaining agricultural land. The coastal mangrove swamps, breeding grounds for the fish that are one of the major potential resources, are similarly polluted. In spite of the escape valve to the United States, where two fifths of those born on the island live, those who stay have little work. Sixty percent of families receive food stamps, and a further ten percent are eligible for them. So much for Operation Bootstrap.

While in 1950 the outlook for Puerto Rico was bright, the prospects for Cuba were depressing. I visited half a dozen times in the years preceding Batista's ouster in 1959. Ever since the U.S. occupied Cuba in 1898, it either directly or through surrogates controlled all aspects of life, dominating the economy and substituting export crops for local food production. By the 1950s, unemployment was massive, and half the agricultural workers were employed only for the few months of the sugar harvest. Corruption dominated the society, as Las Vegas gangsters built hotels and casinos for wealthy North Americans and made prostitution Havana's most flourishing industry.

When Castro clamped down on the prostitution and set out to restructure the economy, the United States responded venemously. Even after the defeat of the Bay of Pigs invasion in 1962 showed the commitment of the overwhelming majority of Cubans to their reforming government, the United States has continued up to the present time to maintain and underwrite a potential invasion force in Florida, a force that in violation of international law constantly engages in sabotage inside Cuba and in attacks on Cuban officials and property in many parts of the world, forcing Cuba to remain on a permanent war footing. The U.S. embargo has denied Cuba equipment, spares and service for its factories and closed to it its logical market. Since 1950, one million Cubans have emigrated, most through such abnormal channels as the Mariel sea-lift of 1980. That represents ten percent of the population, whereas nearly half of Puerto Rico's population has left that island.

In spite of all these negative factors, limitations on normal growth that were an intended result of U.S. policy, the progress Cuba has made since 1959 has been spectacular. Ownership of resources is today completely Cuban. The national priorities are the equitable provision of food, clothing, shelter, health and education to all citizens, regardless of ability to pay. Involuntary unemployment does not exist. Free health care is everywhere available. Education at all levels has so flourished that after all domestic needs are fully met, a significant surplus of doctors, teachers and other professionals is available to help other poor countries.

I am not happy with many things in Cuba, and I believe that Cubans and their government are not happy with some of the same things. I believe, for example, that they would prefer to be less dependent on one of the great powers. But that dependence must be placed in a double perspective. By its embargo and other overt and covert belligerent acts, the

United States left Cuba with no option but to seek Soviet help. Besides, the impact of the Soviets on Cuba's life is significantly less than the former U.S. impact. They have not simply substituted one master for another. The new one is far less oppressive than the old.

Russian purposes and objectives are not necessarily more noble and altruistic than those of the United States. The objective reality allows the Russians to get value for their money without imposing limitations on Cuba's economic development. The economic development fostered in Puerto Rico was transitory and predatory. The parallel development in Cuba is geared to needs and resources; and by the 1980s it is paying off in a remarkably improved quality of life, Availability of consumer goods has increased significantly. Rationing has become marginal.

What is least attractive about Cuba is the monopoly control of the communications media and of all social organization. I believe that a society lacking free exchange of ideas and open criticism of social and political systems is less than human and soon stagnates. As in Eastern Europe, the pressures for more freedom of expression have grown with the improved economy. Distance limits the Soviet Union's control over such movements in Cuba. The restricting factor is Washington's unchanging commitment to returning Cuba to its former satellite condition. Were the United States to recognize that the Cuban revolution is irreversible and come to terms with it, as it has with the Soviet Union and China, I believe Cuba would quickly replace the Marxism-Leninism to which it subscribes mechanically as part of its defence against U.S. imperialism with an ideology cognate to its history and culture.

Washington's behavior in Central America in the late 1970s and early 1980s shows, however, that it has forgotten nothing and learned nothing. A series of grossly rigged elections in El Salvador in 1972 and subsequent years produced no protest. The Carter government, elected in 1976 on a platform of human rights, was undisturbed in 1977 when the military not only brazenly rejected the popular will but reaffirmed control by widespread torture and killing of unarmed opponents. After a large part of Nicaragua's oligarchy, backed by world opinion, had joined with the Sandinistas to isolate and repudiate Somoza, the Carter Administration desperately sought a compromise that would have blocked social change: a reshuffling of the old guard and retention of the bloody armed forces who symbolized the forty-year tyranny of the Somozas.

Although supported by Archbishop Obando y Bravo of Managua, who would later emerge as an open enemy of the Sandinista program of social reform, the Carter project failed. Somoza fled the country and the National Guard crumbled as the revolutionaries entered Managua to be hailed by the people as liberators.

The date was 17 July 1979. It was near the end of the planting season, and in addition to the longer-term crises facing the new regime, the lack of seeds threatened a devastating famine within a matter of months. Oxfam had been following sympathetically the evolution of events, and it organized a major provision of seeds to meet the emergency.

It soon became apparent, however, that the U.S. propaganda machine was hard at work presenting to the U.S. and world public a distorted picture of the Sandinista program for a new society. I, accordingly, went to Managua on behalf of Oxfam. My assignment was to make arrangements for journalists to interview representatives of government, church, business, cooperatives, small farmers, and others, so that they could see for themselves and present informed reports on the rapidly changing situation.

On this and nearly a dozen visits during the subsequent five years, I met many of the people who play key roles in the process. None impressed me more than the Maryknoll Sisters living in a shack indistinguishable from its neighbors in Ciudad Sandino, the newly acquired name of a slum relocated from Acahualinca when Lake Managua rose and wiped out the original site during the 1972 earthquake. Their neighbors loved to recount stories of the ingenuity of the Sisters in protecting them from the incursions of Somoza's National guard. On one occasion, they formed a human chain as guardsmen came running down the dirt road. The Sisters held back the attackers long enough for the young men of the section to escape but they paid a price. The angry soldiers tossed them one by one across a barbed wire fence, leaving them with torn clothing and deep gashes on their bodies.

I was fascinated by the impact of his involvement in the liberation movement on Miguel D'Escoto. I had known him when he was Director of Communications for the Maryknoll Fathers, a very pleasant, outgoing man, a dynamic and creative worker, but within the paternalistic and conservative framework of a wealthy Nicaraguan family and a pre-Vatican II missionary formation. Now he had made an irrevocable option for the poor, an option based on a solid analysis of the structural causes of their poverty. This is what has made him the convincing advocate of the Sandinista government and has caused the Reagan Administration to elevate him to the position of Enemy No. 1.

Unlike D'Escoto, who revels in his work, Ernesto Cardenal is a reluctant bureaucrat. His true vocation is poetry and his ambition is to go back to Solentiname to meditate and to add to his already impressive output. "It all depends on Reagan," he says with his disarming smile. "While he attacks us, I have to stay." A visit with Ernesto is a unique experience. Within minutes you have the feeling that you have been friends for life. I'll never forget one occasion on which I had brought a group to visit him. Jean-Pierre, a French student at a U.S. college, got into a discussion. "But Ernesto," Jean-Pierre was expostulating. I know no other world-famous poet and cabinet minister with whom such familiarity would not be an unacceptable breach of etiquette.

Ernesto's brother, Fernando, is a very different person. Nothing of the dreamy poet about him. Rather, his Jesuit training shows in his precise, ordered appearance, manner and mode of operation. I first met him when he was organizing the literacy campaign, the remarkable success of which is a measure of his energy and talent. Almost from the outset he was under extreme pressure from elements in the Vatican to leave the government. I can well believe that the reactionary Opus Dei organization, a major power in Rome since John Paul II became Pope, used him as a pawn in its efforts to replace the Jesuits as the dominant ideological force in the church. Just how much he suffered comes through in the beautiful statement published after his official separation from the Society of Jesus in December 1984. His anguish was already apparent when I had talked to him shortly before. I could see in his face and his gestures the profound struggle in which he was involved. But I also divined the decision he had already made, a decision he later formulated in these words: "In all sincerity I consider that before God, I would be committing serious sin if in the present circumstances I were to abandon my priestly option for the poor, which is at this time being concretized in Nicaragua through my work in the Sandinista people's revolution." At least he has the comfort of total support of his fellow Jesuits with whom he continues to live and who regard him just as fully a member of their family as before.

An important part of the contribution of these priests to the Sandinista government has been their analysis, on the basis of their Christian principles, of U.S. policy toward Nicaragua. As D'Escoto in particular formulates it, behind all the propaganda the real objective is to restore the control of Nicaragua's economy and political life long exercised either directly or through puppets.

The vendetta against the Sandinistas, accordingly, did not begin with President Reagan. The alarm sounded the very moment the Sandinistas gained control and set out the program they intended to implement. It was a modest and moderate program. The economy would satisfy the basic needs of all citizens before providing luxuries for any. It would be mixed, 60 percent private sector, 20 percent cooperative, 20 percent state. The private sector, guaranteed credit, fair profits, and freedom from expropriation, would be controlled to the extent necessary to ensure the first objective: basic needs before luxuries. Trade would be spread among as many nations as possible, thus diversifying and lessening dependence. The program was simple, modest, limited, but for Washington intolerable. If it worked, who would not want to imitate?

The first step was to prevent the popular forces in El Salvador from repeating the Sandinista victory. Otherwise, the
virus would immediately spread. In October 1979, accordingly, young Salvadoran officers with Washington's encouragement substituted a five-man junta for the President in a
bloodless coup. Overriding the choice of the officers, Washington imposed as junta member a hard-line colonel and
picked another hard-liner as Defense Minister. Both were
previously associated with U.S. business interests, as was
the representative of private-enterprise groups in the junta.

At Archbishop Romero's urging, the popular movements
suspended agitation to give the junta a fair trial. Within
three months, however, Romero had to admit that it was escalating violence while pretending reform, and he called on
the United States to stop supporting the murderers. The
Carter Administration ignored his appeal, continuing its aid
even after Romero's assassination while celebrating Mass in
March 1980.

I date my personal involvement in this process to February 1979 when I interviewed Archbishop Romero at the
meeting of Latin American bishops in Puebla, Mexico, for
Canadian television. What first struck me about him was his
gentleness and lack of pretension. Although he had already
emerged as the principal voice of the voiceless peasants and
slum dwellers, he stressed his role as a listener and
spokesperson who followed and supported the people in the
decisions they took. I found him very open, ready to have his
views questioned, yet at the same time resolute once he was
convinced of his duty. Just after he left El Salvador for
Puebla, a death squad had announced it would kill him if he
returned. He did not take the threat lightly. Too many of his
associates had been killed. But it did not affect his decision.

It was only when I visited El Salvador a month after Romero's assassination, however, that I got a real sense of
what was happening. Even in the capital city, rifle shots
punctuated one's sleep, and bursts of machine-gun fire substituted for an alarm clock in the early morning. A chance
encounter with a Canadian TV crew, one of whose members
I knew from Puebla, made the savagery visible, as they

filmed five bodies scattered over an eight-block area in Soya-pango, a town on the eastern fringe of San Salvador. Most looked as if they had been running from an enemy, only to turn a corner and meet a short burst or a single shot from a waiting executioner. The performance was highly profes-sional. No bullet missed its target to spatter nearby wall or ground. The newspapers carried no mention of the five dead, thanks to the state of siege and censorship. One rumor said they were the mayor's bodyguards; another, popular leaders killed in revenge for the killing earlier the same day of the mayor of Soyapango, himself reputedly slain in retal-iation for the assassination of Archbishop Romero some weeks earlier. The mayor was identified with ORDEN, the ultraright terrorist organization.

In the grounds of the Catholic seminary and of other churches, a thousand persons, mostly old people and chil-dren, squatted in conditions of extreme misery. They were the beginning of the mass flight that scattered more than a million Salvadorans between 1980 and 1985. Half of them are displaced within El Salvador, the rest in Honduras, Nic-aragua, Mexico and the United States. The flight began with the introduction by the United States of a process that had been tried and failed in Vietnam, land reform combined with a state of siege, the reform being used to identify and kill all suspected of opposition. Their stories were gruesome beyond belief. One sobbing woman's fifteen-year-old daughter, member of a high school mutual defense group, had been carried off by two truckloads of National Guards. After mul-tiple raping, they chopped off her arms and legs, then killed her by driving a stake through her head. An old man re-called a conversation between two soldiers in his village. "We have to kill the children as well as adults," one told the other, "because they are bad seed."

The national university was still open. (It would have been stormed with much loss of life and closed down by my next visit a few months later.) To enter from streets in which tanks and personnel carriers constantly prowled was to find a different world. I had already been amazed, as I drove through the city, at the proliferation of slogans

painted on walls and billboards, painted by people who knew
they would be shot if caught in the act. They were evidence
of a level of community commitment that has been confirmed in the following years by the refusal to be cowed by
the might of the United States. Inside the fragile sanctuary
of the university, the graffiti and posters took a quantum
jump. Every available space carried a message of encouragement, of hope, of warning to the oppressors, of denunciation of torturers and killers. Most striking was a poster that
carried the protest, not of the students, but of the governing
board of the university. Its dominant feature was the Stars
and Stripes. The lowest stripe was dissolving into bomb-
shaped blood-red globules dropping down on the cities of El
Salvador. "No to imperialist intervention!" screamed the
text.

In the months and years that followed I witnessed in various places and at various levels, the progressive escalation
of U.S. directed violence and savagery. I was again in San
Salvador in July 1980 when the editor of *La Cronica* and one
of his top helpers were abducted in broad daylight from a
mid-town restaurant. Their tortured and mutilated corpses
were lying in the street the following morning. That was the
end of *La Cronica*. The only other opposition newspaper, *El
Independiente*, closed down in 1981 after the army arrested
the staff and destroyed the physical plant. The editor, who
had evaded the police raid, fled into exile. A church-owned
weekly has been constantly harassed ever since a bombing
attack in 1977. The only radio transmitter not controlled by
the government is also church-owned. It was bombed five
times after the 1979 coup and put completely out of commission for an extended period in 1981 when its transmitter was
destroyed. Since 1979, also, at least 26 journalists, domestic
and foreign, have been assassinated. The security forces actually circulated a death list of 35 journalists just before the
March 1982 elections.

Also in preparation for the 1982 elections, the armed
forces and their rightwing associates murdered 1,500 unarmed civilians in less than three months, bringing to some
30,000 the number of such murders since late 1979. These

were the elections which the United States administration had planned in an effort—highly successful thanks to media cooperation—to persuade the U.S. public that the Salvadoran peasants supported the regime that was assassinating them by the thousands.

The exercise was an extremely sophisticated one, and it followed a script that had worked in the Dominican Republic in 1965, in Vietnam in 1967, and in Zimbabwe-Rhodesia in 1979. In addition to eliminating opposition media of communications and terrorizing the people by mass killings, all popular and private organizations in El Salvador had been gutted. Such intermediate organizations are essential to involve the citizen in politics, to protect those who take independent positions, to bring organized pressure on the state, and to restrain arbitrary state power. Assassinations in El Salvador had included several thousand leaders of civic organizations, among them more than a hundred officials and organizers of the peasant union sponsored by an arm of the AFL-CIO. The teachers union listed 292 teachers murdered, 16 disappeared, 52 jailed and 1,200 schools closed by government repression since the 1979 coup. Most of the teachers killed, according to Amnesty International, had been active as organizers or union officials. Other trade unions and professional organizations had similar experiences.

In early 1980, all the parties and organizations that had given up hope of reform by the electoral process came together in the Democratic Revolutionary Front. It included a part of the Christian Democratic Party, the Social Democrat Party, the University of El Salvador, the Catholic University, the Association of University Students, the Association of Women Market Vendors, the Federation of Food, Clothing and Textile Workers, the Workers Union of Private Industry, the United Federation of Trade Unions of El Salvador, the National Federation of Small Business, the Independent Movement of Professionals and Technicians, the Revolutionary Democratic Movement of Retired Military, and many others. As representative of almost the entire spectrum of organized Salvadorans, the Front was the primary target for the death squads. In November 1980, its six top leaders were seized at a press conference in a Catholic high school in San Salvador, tortured, mutilated, and killed. In April 1981, the army published in the press a death list of 138 of its leaders. Since then, all leadership has been clandestine and much of it in exile.

A further necessary step in the preparation of what Edward Herman, a professor at the Wharton School, has aptly called "demonstration elections" is to build up the secret police, the army and other cooperating organisms into pervasive instruments of terror. A twenty-fold increase in U.S. military aid between 1979 and 1985 is reflected in a vast expansion of the army, the National Guard, the Treasury Police and the National Police, and even more progress in their training, equipment and weaponry, including napalm and white phosphorus for aerial attacks on villages. Working in coordination with them, as U.S. spokesmen have repeatedly admitted, are many death squads, including the Maximilian Hernández named for the dictator who in 1932 slaughtered 30,000 peasant leaders. Most important of these is ORDEN, a network of spies and assassins numbering many thousands and spread throughout the country. Originally sponsored by the army, and the security establishment, it was formally outlawed after the 1979 coup. It not only survives, however, but flourishes, and it has now been integrated by U.S. strategists into a sophisticated counterinsurgency program similar to the Phoenix program in Vietnam under which thousands of peasants were assassinated to root out a radical "infrastructure."

For meaningful elections, all significant currents of political opinion must have the right and ability to field candidates. In the Salvadoran elections of 1982 and again of 1984, this condition was conspicuously unfulfilled. Even when José Napoleón Duarte, its leader, was a Junta member and later President of El Salvador, the Christian Democratic party did not escape repression. An April 1981 human rights report recorded the death by assassination of forty Christian Democratic mayors and scores of other functionaries. In a three-week period in May 1982 six more Christian Democratic mayors and a number of other party activists were killed.

During the two following years the violence of the death squads, working in cooperation with the armed forces, continued unabated. Even after the 1984 elections, which finally gave the presidency to Duarte but without affecting the army's power base, the human rights situation did not improve. As in Guatemala under General Ríos Montt, the number of assassinations in the cities declined. This was more than balanced, however, by an intensification of the ground and air attacks on the civilian population in villages where it provided the infrastructure for the insurgents, an operation for which the United States provided the gunships, the chemical and other weapons, and the technical training and guidance.

To conduct such policies in Central America, the Reagan Administration needed and overwhelmingly obtained the support of the major communications media, both written and electronic, in the United States. In reporting on the elections in El Salvador, for example, the media slavishly followed the Administration line. And in overall reporting, statements of U.S. ambassadors and officials tend to dominate, even when reporters have easy access to contrary facts. A not untypical example was a story in the New York Times a few days before the 1984 Salvadoran elections. It presented the contest for president as between "a moderate leftist and an outspoken conservative." The computerized information available to the editors of that article establishes that Duarte, "the moderate leftist," is in fact far to the right of center on the political spectrum, and that Roberto D'Aubuisson, "the outspoken conservative," is a fascist linked to death squads, accurately described by former U.S. Ambassador Robert White as a "pathological killer."

I was less surprised than many by the behavior of the media. When I was active in the Overseas Press Club of America in the 1950s and 1960s, I learned by daily contact that those who moved into key positions in the media were those who identified emotionally with big business and presented its viewpoint in their writing. I later helped my friend, sociologist John Pollock, in his important study of the social and educational background of U.S. foreign correspon-

dents, a study that confirms the conclusions I had reached
by personal observation. I should add that the entire blame
is not to be laid on the foreign correspondents. Not a few of
those I have met in Central America since 1980 have told me
that what appears in print is often radically different from
what they wrote. In addition, those on assignment know
from experience what to send and what to ignore. I was in
El Salvador in November 1984 when a Lutheran minister
was seized one evening by a death squad and his tortured
and mutilated body was found the next day. An ABC team
went to San Miguel to make a filmed report. Asked on their
return to San Salvador if it would be on U.S. national news
that evening, one of them laughed. "We won't even send it,"
he said. "A dead Salvadoran is not news. It would have to be
an American priest or minister. We file it here, just in case
some later development might make it newsworthy. We
have a big library."

Given the U.S. Administration's pretense that the government it supports in El Salvador does not violate human
rights, the policy of denying political asylum to the hundreds
of thousands of refugees who have fled to the United States
is logical. Since 1980 I have devoted much of my effort to
working for these refugees. I have visited survivors of the
Río Sumpul massacre, where a combined operation of the
Salvadoran and Honduran armies killed six hundred de-
fenseless people of all ages, an action that Washington cooperated with the parties directly responsible to hide for
months. The survivors lived in constant fear of new attacks,
as they hid in the Honduran mountains overlooking the
river, kept alive by the Honduran peasants who had scarcely
enough to feed themselves. Traveling with Father "Beto"
Gallagher, the priest from Santa Rosa de Copán whose perti-
nacity finally broke the wall of silence, I have climbed the
sheer hillsides—at times on hands and knees—to record the
accounts of massacres provided by the survivors.

Yvonne Dilling spent eighteen months with Salvadoran
refugees in Honduras and was eyewitness to many atrocities. I have known Yvonne, who is a volunteer missionary of
the Church of the Brethren, for many years, both of us asso-

ciated with an ecumenical commune called Tabor House. Yvonne's diary, *In Search of Refuge*, describes her experience in Honduras. I wrote an appendix that puts it in the broader context of contemporary Central America. Her most excruciating moment was on the Rio Lempa. It was 19 March 1981, and little more than a month after her arrival in Honduras. Let me quote briefly.

"I have no idea how many children I carried across on my back. Some were so small that we tied them onto me. Others were old enough to hang on, but most of them were terrified, crying, gripping like steel. I tried carrying a girl about twelve years old, and I barely made it across; I couldn't hold my own head up, swimming under water the last part of the way because she weighed too much. . . . No matter how long we swam, the Salvadoran side remained packed. There were probably a thousand still in that small area, trying to hide in the foliage, frantic that they would be killed. . . .The helicopter first swooped down low on the Salvadoran side and started machine-gunning the shoreline. Then it went off down the river, gained height, turned around, swooped down, and fired on the Honduran side. . . .The soldier in the helicopter was incredibly intent on killing people. Over and over again he laid a path of machine-gun fire only a foot away from the people in the water. Once he swooped so low that he almost touched the tree tops above us. One little boy was killed. I saw him jump into the water with an arc of bullets in his back. He was flailing his arms, still trying to swim while all across his back there was streaming blood. Then the water carried him downstream."*

Yvonne is particularly convincing in her blow-by-blow documentation of something well known from other sources but insistently denied by all the parties to the intrigue. Washington is perfectly aware that the Salvadoran guerillas have the support of the overwhelming majority of the peasants and that the Salvadoran peasants in turn support their Honduran neighbors. If the armed minority in El Salvador backed by the United States is to win, it is essential to close

---

*Yvonne Dilling, *In Search of Refuge*. Scottdale, Pa.: Herald Press, 1984, p. 39 ff. (Quotation below at p. 261.)

off the boundary with Honduras and break the lines of com-
munication between the two countries. The first phase was
the movement of refugees near the border to the camps of
La Virtud and Mesa Grande, carried out in 1982. Yvonne details the open collaboration of the Salvadoran and Honduran
armies, and also of ORDEN, in pressuring the refugees to
move. This included the assassination of various social workers. As for the unfortunate refugees, they were treated
worse than animals.

What comes out clearly is that Washington orchestrates
the entire tragedy, seeking to reduce the number of refugees for publicity reasons and to exercise total control over
them. Even the various representatives of the UN High
Commissioner for Refugees (UNHCR) are shamefully sub-
servient. Yvonne sums the situation up very well:

"On March 28, Eugene Douglas, U.S. White House Adviser on Refugees, came, bringing with him several State
Department Latin American officials. I've always heard
about the 'Ugly American'; now I've seen one in action. Douglas and company arrived in a military helicopter, spoke to
UNHCR officials, and refused to talk to refugees or to other
international staff. At La Virtud he acted like the imperial
commander, saying he would make sure the relocation was
completed quickly. At one point, when people attempted to
speak to him about the repression, he brushed them aside,
saying he had not come to hear sad stories, but rather to
'kick UNHCR's ass into gear.' "

As I write, the unfortunate refugees, those who have not
fled the camps or been killed, are being moved still further
from the border to provide a wider free-fire zone.

I have also helped two other Tabor House members, Sister Betty Campbell and Father Peter Hinde, to prepare for
publication their account of their experiences with refugees,
an experience that embraces El Salvador, Honduras, Guatemala, Nicaragua, Costa Rica, Mexico and the United States.
Both Peter and Betty spent more than three months inside
El Salvador in the winter of 1981-82. Among other things,
Peter worked with the Human Rights Commission and had
access to much first-hand information on disappearances,

torture, and assassinations. Betty, a nurse who is author of a first-aid guide in Quechua based on her experience on Peru's altiplano, went through the Salvadoran countryside teaching women how to care for victims of aerial bombing and napalm burns. They confirmed what I had learned from other sources about the genocidal practices made possible by the U.S. training and supplying of Central American armed forces.

By the middle of 1981, it had become clear to many working with the Central American refugees both in Arizona and in other parts of the United States that the Administration was determined to deny their rights under international and domestic law. To work within the guidelines established by the Immigration and Naturalization Service, as the Task Force for Central America of the Tucson Ecumenical Council and others had been doing since 1980, was not saving them from expulsion to what for many meant torture and death. Months of discussion led to the decision to notify the Attorney General that on 24 March 1982, the second anniversary of the assassination of Archbishop Oscar Romero, several churches were reviving the age-old concept of sanctuary and committing themselves to protect and care for Central Americans who had fled the terror in their homelands.

"We take this action," the letter read in part, "because we believe the current policy and practice of the U.S. government with regard to Central American refugees to be illegal and immoral. We believe our government is in violation of the 1980 Refugee Act and international law by continuing to arrest, detain, and forcibly return refugees to the terror, persecution, and murder in El Salvador and Guatemala.

"We believe that justice and mercy require that people of conscience actively assert our God-given right to aid anyone fleeing from persecution and murder. The current Administration of the United States law prohibits us from sheltering these refugees from Central America. Therefore we believe that administration of the law is immoral as well as illegal."

The church communities who acted on 24 March 1982

were Southside Presbyterian in Tucson, the University Lutheran Chapel in Berkeley, California, First Unitarian in
Los Angeles, Luther Place Memorial in Washington, D.C.,
and the Community Bible Church, Lawrence, Long Island,
N.Y.

The Administration spokesmen officially adopted the position that these gestures from obscure, publicity-seeking
little groups did not deserve notice. They would go the way
of other fads. If they really believed this, they were deeply
mistaken. Almost overnight, these initiatives captured the
imagination of people all across the United States. They
were obviously striking a chord in the folk memory of a people whose ancestors had found sanctuary in the North
American continent from religious and political persecutions
in Europe and who had engraved their gratitude and cove-
nant on the Statue of Liberty: "Give me your tired, your
poor, your huddled masses yearning to be free."

I have recorded the details of this Great Awakening of the
1980s in *Sanctuary: A Resource Guide**. Suffice it to say
here that by April 1985 declared sanctuaries included thirty-
six Catholic, thirty-six Friends, twenty-eight Unitarian,
twenty-two Presbyterian, thirteen United Church of Christ,
eight Lutheran, eight Methodist, seven Brethren, seven
Mennonite, seven Baptist, five Episcopal, two Disciples of
Christ, eight Jewish, twenty other Protestant, ten universities, four city councils, and a seminary. A year later, the
total exceeded three hundred, including sixteen cities and
the State of New Mexico. Supporting these hundreds of
declared sanctuaries are thousands of faith communities
whose participation has led them to a deeper commitment to
do justice and struggle for justice. Enriched by the witness
of refugees who, coming from a situation of hopelessness,
retain a spirited, vital flame of faith and hope, they are acquiring a new vision of their role in life. Central America is
no longer a name without a face. Rather they know that its
tragedy is ultimately the tragedy of the United States.

As yet we do not have the massive battle casualties that
the U.S. forces suffered in Vietnam and Cambodia. The
deaths that have occurred in the undeclared war on Nicara-

*Gary MacEoin, ed. San Francisco: Harper & Row, 1985.

gua and the camouflaged support of Salvadoran state terrorism are classified secrets. But the enormous U.S. military
build-up in Honduras and the unending naval maneuvers in
the Caribbean have their own dynamism. So far, the Administration has succeeded in hoodwinking the vast majority of
citizens as to its intentions and bellicose activities in Central
America. Unless we wake up, we are going to find ourselves in a quagmire deeper than Vietnam. At a minimum,
millions of innocent people will die. We have no guarantee
that conflict will not escalate into the doomsday holocaust.

As a journalist, I can only deplore the shameful failure of
the communications media. With the fidelity of Pavlov's
dog, they have salivated to the Administration's bellringing.
Surveys of coverage of Central America since 1980 have established that seventy to eighty percent of all "news" origi-
nated in the propaganda machine of the White House, the
State Department, the Pentagon, the U.S. Mission to the
United Nations, or U.S. embassies in the region. Distortions
were swallowed unquestioned, even when the facts were
easily recoverable from the computer banks of newspapers
or news agencies. No whisper of protest is heard when the
pathological killer who masterminded the assassination of
Archbishop Romero is feted in Washington. Who called for
the resignation of the Administration spokespersons who in-
sinuated that the four U.S. religious women raped and killed
in El Salvador got what was coming to them? Censorship in
Nicaragua gets more headlines than the killing of a score of
journalists and the violent suppression of all opposition
media in El Salvador. House arrest of a priest captured with
a carload of explosives in Nicaragua is front-page news, but
the mutilation and killing of a Lutheran minister in El Salvador does not merit a paragraph on an inside page.

Adapting the appeal made to the U.S. president by Archbishop Romero a few days before his assassination, I ask my
fellow journalists, I implore them in the name of God, in the
name of the people of Central America: tell the truth about
Central America, throw no more fuel on the fires of hatred
and distortion, ensure that peace has a chance before destruction becomes inevitable.

The Road to Utopia

It has been a long pilgrimage in both space and time—even longer and more complicated within the confines of my own mind. I have been told that people's most vivid memories tend to be of unpleasant experiences. I do have bitter memories, as of the uncouth priest who when I was about nine years old bullied me into saying I had damaged some property I had never even touched. But most of my childhood memories are happy. I can still see the salmon jumping at the weir as they fought their way upstream to spawn, and the excitement of gaffing one. I relive the freedom of shedding shoes in spring, wading in the river and snaring eels with a running noose woven from hairs pulled from a horse's tail, or with agile fingers catching a small trout as it hid under a rock. I recall the annual excitement of the village fair, savor the live cockles and periwinkles washed down with lemonade. I gambol with the new-born lambs in spring, smell the new mown hay on long, lazy summer evenings.

My entire life I see in such a perspective. It has had its bitter moments, and I have not forgotten them. But they are in a perspective in which the positive and worthwhile dominate. I have experienced many reinterpretations of reality, shed progressively beliefs and viewpoints that I came to believe mistaken. But I am not bitter about the process. I could not have reached the present point on the road without traveling the miles and leagues that separate me from my starting point. The way to truth and liberation is dialectic, the solution to each contradiction leading to a new contradiction on a higher plane. It is a process that never ends; or when it ends, so does life as we know it. And so I am grateful to all the people and experiences that taught me whatever I know. If I no longer agree with many who shared with me their understanding of the human purpose, I realize that the partial truths each conveyed played a part in enabling me to explore further horizons.

Arnold Toynbee's seminal concept in *A Study of History*, namely, that the well-being of a civilization depends upon its ability to respond successfully to challenges human and environmental, has always impressed me. I would apply the same concept to the individual. We thrive and grow under challenges with which we can cope. We are destroyed by those that overwhelm us. Obviously, the level of acceptable challenge varies greatly from individual to individual. I see myself as fortunate in my ability to rebound from adversity and build on it. The critical moment for me was when at age twenty-five the door was shut without explanation on what had been my ambition and life objective. I know more than a few people who were so overwhelmed by precisely this challenge that they never regained control of their lives.

I do not pretend to know why I was able to respond successfully. All I can say is that I was determined to prove to myself and others that, in spite of what had happened, I was somebody. But what did it mean to be somebody? Within the framework of my experience and self-understanding, it meant acquiring a status that would allow me to make my own decisions, so that I would never again find my destiny determined by the arbitrary decision of another. It was an ambitious project, a first step in which was to secure the pieces of paper in the form of academic degrees that in the society in which I lived were major measures of one's worth. With that base, I could climb the capitalist ladder to a height at which I could count on at least relative independence.

Interestingly enough, this vision of a career devoted exclusively to economic and material advancement was per-

fectly compatible with the moral and ethical values I had up
to then absorbed. Not only the Roman Catholic religion,
about whose tenets I had learned considerably more than
most of its adherents, but—as I would in due course discover—the major parallel Protestant institutions had become the legitimators and the beneficiaries of the status
quo. They had allowed themselves to be replaced by something reverently called Science as the directive force of society, content to be allowed to function in an irrelevant area
known as spiritual—irrelevant because society ruled by Science had decided that only the material mattered. This pri-
vatization of religion was additionally fostered by Kantian
influences in theology that tended to see the self as related
to God in Kierkegaardian isolation, all sense of social meaning and social identity lost. Although the traditional formula
of avoiding evil and doing good survived, in practice religion
concerned itself with legalistic definitions of what constituted evil to be avoided, with primary emphasis on sexual
mores, an area of unconcern for society, and secondary emphasis on roles of positive support for society, such as employee diligence and observance of contractual obligations.

Given this context, I had no difficulty in relegating the religion that up to that time had been central to my concerns
and activities to the irrelevant niche in which it belonged in
society, devoting my energies to the practical task of getting
ahead in the world. It was a world in which I did not take
very long to find myself comfortable. Injustices did exist
and they were too obvious to be overlooked. But I was so
conditioned that I was unable to consider seriously and objectively any solution other than those proposed by the so-
called ordinary magisterium of the church. That restricted
me to such anachronisms as the medieval guilds dear to
Chesterton, to the corporate state briefly embraced by Pope
Pius XI, or the more general thesis of the papal social encyc-
licals, namely, that by sweet reason we could persuade the
captains of industry, commerce, and banking that it was in
their interest to give a better break to those who have their
labor to sell. Such rationalizations or sophistries satisfied me
for a time. Social injustice was not of my making, and there

was effectively nothing I could do about it. That was the job
of those with wealth and power, and we ordinary people
could only wait, hope, and pray for the moment when they
would be converted and hear the inspired calls of our religious leaders.

I could not, however, continue to relegate myself to the
role of impotent spectator when I had climbed into the ranks
of the middle-level actors in the global drama as newspaper
editor, as executive of the Caribbean Commission, as a
member of the powerful communications monopoly, combining journalism, public relations, and advertising, that me-
diates Latin American reality to the U.S. public and U.S.
reality to Latin America. It was a question many of us asked
ourselves, one that we often discussed at length in luxury
hotels and elegant night clubs in Caracas, Bogotá, Mexico
City, Havana, or New York, at congresses of the Inter-
American Press Association, or at conventions hosted by
machinery, fertilizer, and drug companies at Miami Beach.

For the journalists there was an elegant out. We did not
make decisions. We simply reported the facts. We were consequently engaged in an objectively neutral service ideologically, a service that was equally beneficial to all parties in
the process of development and modernization that we all
accepted as inevitable and also desirable. The sellers and
promoters of goods and services had equally clear consciences. Even those whose stock in trade consisted of comic
strips, pantihose, or under-arm deodorants in countries
where the masses lacked potable water, nutritious food, or
the rudiments of hygiene, were convinced that they were
not only satisfying needs but were transferring skills that
would gradually enable the countries in which they worked
to enter the promised land of the American Way of Life. In
these self-serving convictions we were all confirmed in the
early 1960s by the Alliance for Progress with its promises of
a quick fix that would create human living levels for all the
peoples of the hemisphere.

Most of my colleagues moved to vice-presidencies and gra-
cious retirement without ever questioning these assumptions. The slums that engulfed the great cities of Latin

America in their lifetimes never impinged on their consciousness, still less could they imagine that the growing poverty of the masses of Latin Americans and their prosperity were the obverse and reverse faces of the same coin. In this, they are—sociologically speaking—typical. Thousands commute daily from their Westchester homes on the Grand Central that takes them over Harlem to offices in midtown and downtown Manhattan without ever in their lives walking the pot-holed streets and smelling the uncollected garbage of New York's most celebrated slum. The vast majority of the affluent whites in U.S. cities live close to people of other races without once having entered one of their homes and without having a single one of them as a friend; and also without ever having questioned the assumption that their own better homes and lifestyles result from greater commitment and intelligence in a contest in which all engage on equal terms. In all these instances we are looking at the same phenomenon that turned Koreans and Vietnamese into "gooks." A dominant group has succeeded for its own purposes in reifying a dominated group, in converting them from humans into things.

I never quite succeeded in dehumanizing the poor. I had myself come from a culture of poverty. When I moved to the West Indies, I was appalled by levels of poverty beyond anything I had previously imagined. On the Latin American mainland I found similar and at times worse conditions. For some years I was able to protect myself emotionally by my self-identification as a journalist, an observer whose duty it was to see and observe, not to become involved. But as I saw how facts were interpreted and often perverted by the journalists in the field, and even more by their employers, always in the interests of the advertisers and governments whose support was essential to their success, I gradually realized that journalism was as much a part of the business world as selling machinery or bubble gum. I was a link in an integrated system.

The gradual change that occurred in my evaluation of the impact of the rich countries on Latin America was not, however, primarily a cerebral operation. The basic element, I believe, is that I never succeeded in reifying the poor. From my earliest experiences, I knew poor people as persons and as friends. Wherever I traveled, I did not limit my movements to tourist hotels, night clubs, and casinos. I sought out urban slum dwellers and rural hovels as well. My work with the Colombian Coffee Federation gave me a unique opportunity to penetrate rural living in the Andes. It was Federation policy to stress that much of Colombian coffee was grown by poor peasants, so that any increase in the price of coffee in the supermarket translated automatically into better prices and higher living standards for the peasants. This line was sedulously promoted in advertising and public relations campaigns in the United States, the principal market for Colombian coffee. To develop it, I had to familiarize myself at first hand with the entire structure of the coffee industry in Colombia.

It is true that in the 1950s peasants farming a few acres produced a very large part of Colombia's coffee (this is less true in the 1980s, the absorption of small holdings by big land owners and the conversion of their owners into landless laborers having intensified in Colombia in the interval, as generally in Latin America). They lived in hovels in abject poverty, with minimal health facilities and little prospect of the children getting more than one or two years of primary schooling. Parents and children alike were engaged in an endless round of activities related not only to the coffee production but to the growing of plantains, corn, and other food on their rocky hillside farm. Observing them confirmed for me a seldom recognized truth that had come to my conscious awareness in a slum in Panama City, that the poorer one is, the harder one works, and the less one achieves. Or to synthesize ancient wisdom formulated in the Bible: the poor rise early, but though they work to sundown, their children go hungry.

Contrary to the Federation's publicity contentions, an increase in the sale price of coffee in the United States was not translated into comparable benefits for these small producers. The laws of supply and demand did not reach to them. The economy within which they functioned involved a com-

plicated network of relationshiops, dominated by debt that
tied each to one middleman who fixed the price at which he
bought and fixed the price at which he sold the salt, sugar,
and other basic commodities the peasant needed to survive.
Ultimately, all the profit beyond what was needed to ensure
the survival of the system remained with the small wealthy
group who manipulated the economic and political system. I
remember spending several hours one day with such a peasant family, then driving to the nearby city of Pereira to be
entertained at the most palatial club I have ever entered,
and I have been in the best of New York, London, Paris, and
Rome. It was built and is maintained on coffee. I am told
there are two more splendid clubs in Goiania in the Brazilian
backlands, but I cannot vouch for this, having only driven
past them in a jeep. Understandably, the peasants there are
even poorer than those of the Colombian Andes.

Generalized thought develops out of specific human experiences, and this experience illustrates what gradually
emerged for me as a determinant characteristic of the economic system that decided the distribution of benefits between the participants in the world economy: its hypocrisy.
The United States trumpeted its altruistic aid to the poor
countries and assured them that they had only to grant full
freedom of operation within their boundaries to the global
corporations that would bring them capital, know-how, and
wellbeing. The other industrial powers echoed the promise.
All of them proclaimed that the most needy were the primary objects of their beneficence and assured them that in a
little time the wealth and good life would trickle down to
them.

The reality contradicts all of these claims. Even in the initial allocation of—for example—rural credit under USAID
programs, practically all of the credit went to big farmers
who had the collateral to borrow from commercial banks,
while the peasants with no other source of funds seldom got
even five or ten per cent of the aid. Each year, the rich countries withdrew in profits at least three times what they provided in credits. They quickly acquired control of the most
dynamic sectors of the economy of the poor countries, while

saddling them with astronomic debts aggravated by ever higher interest rates each time the debt had to be renegotiated because there was no money to repay it. The poverty of the masses was consequently not an accident or a misfortune. It was the logical result of the policies established by the external overlords, especially the international bankers who control credit, and the local oligarchs who benefit from executing these policies. As long as such policies persist, the existing evils can only be aggravated. The enormous gap between rich and poor countries, and between rich and poor in the poor countries (also in the rich countries) will grow progressively wider, ensuring an absolute as well as a relative decline each year in the food, clothing, shelter, health, education, and dignity of the Latin American masses.

Swedish political economist Gunnar Myrdal has said that the best way to help poor countries is to abstain from organizing corruption among them. "The multinational corporations and both public and private organizations in the rich countries," he has written, "are all guilty of contributing to corruption among the leaders of the poor countries. Widespread fraud characterizes the relations between them: bribes, false or misleading statements, and shady deals in finance and trade."* Sociologist and Catholic theologian José Comblin agrees: "The churches in rich nations should convince Christians that the best thing to help the poor is to stop robbing them, to respect their own identity and destiny. . . .For this, Christians need a conversion, an attitude of atonement and retreat from domination. It calls for inner change, for a different mentality."*

It would have been more difficult, and perhaps impossible, for me to face up to and accept such radical re-evaluations of my world were it not for the no less radical reformulation of my religious beliefs provided by Vatican Council II earlier in the 1960s. In spite of ambiguities and Byzantine language in the Council documents, two of them in particular—that on the church and that on the church in the Mod-

---

*Quoted by José Comblin in *LADOC*. Washington, D.C.: U.S. Catholic Conference, #64. May–June 1976, p. 23.

Ibid, p. 25.

ern World—added up for me to a new Weltanschauung. They present the church less as a hierarchy, in which a few are privileged to dictate and the many are limited to obeying, than as a collegial entity in which the voice of the people is once again the voice of God. Not less important, they accept the Teilhardian concept of a continuing creation in which all of us have the specifically human task of helping to move the world toward the perfection that is the goal of the evolutionary process. In addition, they reformulate the concept of good and evil. The test of our love of God is less the effort we make to avoid acts forbidden by him than our positive commitment to serve him in our neighbor. Finally, they relativize the Roman Catholic church both in terms of its authority and ability to judge human events, and in terms of its possession of the means of salvation. The autonomy of the world is proclaimed. The function of other Christian denominations, of Judaism, and of other religions as channels of grace, is recognized.

By the late 1960s, the exhaustion of the potential of the capitalist system had become clear to me. As Pope Pius XI had said, paraphrasing Karl Marx, it was intrinsically evil because based on greed and selfishness. There remained, nevertheless, a serious problem: the longtime stress of Christian leaders on reconciliation, their insistence that the rich and powerful can be persuaded that their self-interest counsels a more equitable sharing of the gross national product. The Latin American bishops at Medellín in 1968 had fallen into this trap. After a logical and forthright repudiation of capitalism, they assured us that "the social teachings of the popes" point the only way to the new just social order.

My repeated on-the-spot observation of the development of the Doctrine of National Security in one Latin American country after another, starting with Brazil in 1964, gradually convinced me that every attempt to alter the socioeconomic system even slightly in favor of the dispossessed would be met with the level of force, of institutionalized violence, needed to thwart it. This experience confirmed the lesson of all history, namely, that privilege only yields to superior power. The rich will continue to use religion, as they have always used it, to provide an ideological rationalization for genocidal oppression of the masses as a permanent feature of the system.

What has happened in Latin America in the past twenty years becomes intelligible only within the framework of the Doctrine of National Security as an ideology embraced with religious fervor by the military elites of the entire continent, including the United States which has played a leading role in disseminating it. It rests on three principles: that the state is absolute and the individual is nothing; that every state is involved in permanent warfare, its present form being "communism" versus the "free world"; and that the "free world" can survive only if totally controlled by the armed forces which constitute its natural leadership in the struggle against subversion.

The first two of these principles derive directly from the ideology of Nazi Germany, an ironic reminder that the loser in an armed conflict often proves in the light of history to have been the real winner. The primacy of the armed forces—subordinated to the Leader and the Party in Nazism—is in part a self-interested rationalization but also in large part their selection by the United States for the dominant role. Nelson Rockefeller's report, on which President Nixon based his Latin American policy in 1969, publicly acknowledged that role by describing the Latin American military establishment as "a major force for constructive social change in the American republics."

Also, unlike Nazism, the Doctrine of National Security is not directed against minorities represented as undesirable. Rather, its purpose is to reify as a preliminary to despoiling the majority of the citizens in each country. Its primary purpose is economic. It permits the distortion of the national economy in the interests of transnational business, ensuring that the external overlords are the principal beneficiaries, with enough left over to maintain the lifestyle and status of the local oligarchs and the armed forces. This is called "free enterprise" and any who challenges is automatically a communist, a subversive, and an enemy to be eliminated.

An Open Letter to North American Christians signed by

a number of religious leaders of Latin America summed up the situation as it had developed by 1977. "Friends and Fellow Christians, it is time that you realize that our continent is becoming one gigantic prison, and in some regions one vast cemetery.... We—with the exception of Cuba—are trapped in the same system. We all move within one economic-political-military complex in which one finds committed fabulous interests of financial groups that dominate the life of your country and the creole oligarchies of our Latin American nations. Both groups, more allied today than ever, have held back time after time the great transformations that our people need and desperately demand."

The following years brought further escalation of oppression. The U.S.-trained and equipped armed forces of Brazil, Argentina, and Chile, with the open cooperation of paramilitary forces at the service of the local oligarchies, maintained some semblance of order without justice through assassinations, "disappearances," institutionalized torture, and mass exile of dissidents. But as one area was "pacified," the "permanent warfare" proclaimed by the doctrine of National Security simply moved elsewhere. The ousting of the Somoza dictatorship in Nicaragua in 1979 set off a chain process in Central America, a region in which U.S. hegemony had never before been seriously threatened.

Here, more clearly than ever before, the usually well hidden levers of hemispheric economic and political power were revealed. The heterogeneous coalition that had ousted Somoza had made the usual promises of social change once it had come to power. Many elements in the coalition had no such intention. All they wanted was to substitute themselves as the rulers, while continuing the inequitable distribution of the national product. When, however, it soon became clear that the most powerful elements in the coalition, the Sandinistas who had borne the brunt of the fighting and in consequence enjoyed the support of the triumphant people's army were seriously committed to radical social change, a commitment in which they had the support of significant elements of the Catholic and Protestant churches, the power brokers in Washington took fright.

There was in fact good reason for Washington's concern. The so-called domino theory does indeed function provided the conditions are right. And the conditions were right everywhere in Central America, particularly in El Salvador and Guatemala, where the exploitation of the masses by a privileged minority was similar to that of Somoza in Nicaragua. The success of the people of Nicaragua understandably raised the hopes and expectations of their neighbors, leaving Washington with uncomfortable options.

The logical and just option was unthinkable. It would mean that the United States and the associated rich countries of Western Europe, plus Japan, South Africa, and Australasia, would have to accept a new world order in which each worker's rewards would be based on his or her skills and contribution to the general welfare. By that measure, the coffee farmer of Central America, Colombia, or Kenya would earn far more per hour than the worker on an automobile production line in Detroit. The United States, with five percent of the world population would no longer be able to consume thirty to forty percent of the world's annual production of goods and services.

The alternative was to misrepresent the causes of unrest in Central America, as they had earlier been misrepresented in Brazil, Argentina, Chile, and elsewhere. For this purpose, the second principle of the Doctrine of National Security was ready-made. Every state is involved in permanent warfare, its present form being "communism" versus the "free world." So Washington quickly patched together a scenario in which the cause of all unrest and demand for social change in Central America resulted from communism, a tool devised, owned, and manipulated by the Soviet Union to conquer the world. To promote its purposes, the Soviet Union used Cuba and Nicaragua, already controlled by its minions, as its Trojan Horses to infiltrate the rest of the region.

The third principle of the Doctrine of National Security next came into play to prevent discussion or reasoned questioning of the Washington scenario. By definition, ultimate wisdom resides in the armed forces. They alone are safe from infiltration and immune to the communist virus. Even the churches, long the bastions of the status quo against the godless communists, could no longer be trusted. When Archbishop Romero of San Salvador said the people would not settle for less than justice, he was dismissed as a communist dupe. When the bishops of the United States and the leaders of the major Protestant churches insisted with rare unanimity that U.S. weapons were the last thing Central Americans need, they were told they should stick to their services and leave practical decisions to the military who understand such matters. It complicated things when France, Mexico, Denmark, Sweden, Holland, Belgium, Norway, Greece, and Ireland established full diplomatic relations with the Nicaraguan government and recognized the popular opposition in El Salvador. But by this time a fourth principle emerged in the Doctrine of National Security. In the same way as Moscow had long insisted that it alone can interpret officially and inerrantly the Marxist teachings, so Washington now arrogates to itself a similar infallibility.

Where does all this leave me? For one thing, while I believe violence is evil, I am convinced that there are situations in which it is to be encouraged. I no longer accept the view long proclaimed by the church that in life we are always faced with a choice between good and evil. In the real world, the choice is often between two or more evils, and the challenge is to select the lesser or least of the alternative evils. The issue came up in a dramatic form while I was interviewing Archbishop Romero on Canadian television about a year before his assassination. When I raised the question of his attitude to violence, he responded emphatically that the Christian is absolutely opposed to violence.

"Bishop," I said to him, "I'd like to ask you the question an Indian in the Guatemalan highlands posed a missionary friend of mine. 'Father,' the Indian asked, 'what would the Good Samaritan have done if his donkey had run faster?'"

We discussed the various options: the possibility that he might have reined in his animal and waited on the other side of the road until the robbers had finished beating the poor man and taken off with their spoils; or, alternatively, that he would have waded into the fight and tried to beat the robbers off with his whip. We finally reached agreement that there are circumstances in which it is not only the right but the duty of the Christian to use counterviolence against unjust violence.

Another friend subsequently added a further dimension to the parable. "Let us suppose," she said, "that the Good Samaritan passed the same way every week and nearly every time he found someone who had been beaten up and robbed. Would he fulfil his Christian duty simply by binding up the wounds of each and taking them to hospital at his expense? Rather, would he not have to recognize that he was dealing, not with casual violence, but with institutionalized violence, and—while helping the victims—concentrate his major effort on finding and eliminating the source?"

Who is to judge what means are appropriate and acceptable in the struggle to build a better world? I got what I consider a wholly satisfactory answer some years ago in strange circumstances. I was spending some days dialoguing informally with students of the University of Antioquia in Medellín, Colombia. One issue I was investigating was the growth of pacifist movements in Latin America, and I was excited when I learned that a small pacifist group did in fact exist at the university. "How is your movement progressing," I asked the leaders when I met them. "It's not," they said. "Why not," I asked. "When we began," I was told, "we went to explain our ideas about nonviolence to people in the slums that are all around us here in Medellin, and we got what we read as a very favorable reaction. But as the dialogue developed, something more basic became clear to us. We are not wealthy, but as university students we belong to a privileged class, the class that for centuries has prostitued the teachings of Christ to deceive the peasants into accepting the unjust social system as the design of God. We have lost all right to tell them what means are legitimate, and what are not, now that the situation has changed and they have committed themselves to assert their basic rights. Only they can make that determination."

I think that is true of all of us who are the inheritors of the benefits of that worldwide unjust system. We cannot be the impartial decision makers, the honest brokers, no matter how noble our intentions. History has marginalized us.

In other words, we are—like it or not—members of a class that has historically dominated and exploited the working class. I do not find the discussion of whether class conflict is or is not inevitable or inherent in the human condition very helpful. What I do know is that class conflict is an obvious fact, and that the capitalist system did not invent it. The existence of classes and of class exploitation is recorded in all known societies. It is a leitmotif of the entire Jewish Testament. The Greeks concurred. "Every city," said Plato, "is two cities, a city of the many poor and a city of the few rich; and these two cities are always at war." But if we compare capitalistic society with the feudalism and mercantilism that preceded it, we find that capitalism intensified enormously the conflict between the classes even in its most constructive and fruitful phases. Today in its rot and decline, the process is accelerated, as the capital requirements of ever changing technology cut progressively deeper into the worker's share of world production.

It must by now be clear that I share the widely held and growing belief that capitalism is approaching its end and that, if the world survives its death throes, socialism will replace it as the next system of social and economic organization. It is a prospect I welcome. Just as capitalism represented a great advance over previous systems and a necessary step in the humanization of the world, so I believe socialism can maintain capitalism's advances while adding a significantly more equitable distribution of the benefits of production and giving workers meaning as producers, that is, as creators, to replace their subhuman role as consumers in our society.

This does not, of course, mean that I endorse everything done by the many countries that today describe themselves as socialist or in the process of building socialism. The Soviet Union, in particular, I see as having radically distorted the principles on which it claims to rest, both in its treatment of its own people and in its cold-blooded and imperialistic control of subjugated nations within its political borders and its nominally independent satellites. But neither do I ignore the remarkable advances made by the Soviet Union in the material living conditions and the educational levels of the masses. And while I lack adequate information to make a firm judgment on China, it seems definite that it has progressed even more rapidly in these respects. To speak of the comparison I am most competent to make, I point to the progress Cuba has made since 1959 in providing food, clothing, shelter, education, health, and dignity for all its citizens, at a time when every other country of Latin America has seen a steady deterioration in all these indices. As for the state of religion, I am satisfied that it is at least as good today in Cuba—which is not saying much—as it was under capitalism. What impresses me more is that my Catholic friends both in Cuba and in Poland can imagine no circumstances in which they would choose to return to the pre-socialist regimes in their countries. The Poles would obviously get rid of Russian domination if they could—the Cubans find it less irksome—but they would want to retain a basically socialist society, a socialism with a human face as Western Europe's Eurocommunists say.

Nor am I surprised that the many disparate experiments in socialism that already exist around the world all fall short of theoretical perfection. For one thing, the created reality by definition must always fall short of theoretical perfection. The most we can hope for is a closer approach to an ideal that can never be fully realized. But, in addition, I see the many socialist experiments within the framework of evolution, a process in which a million abortive experiments precede the quantum jump that marks the establishment of a higher life form. I believe that process applies to society as it does to the forms of vegetable and animal life. How long will it take? It takes a long time.